A Cord of Three Strands

A Cord of Three Strands

LINDA RANEY WRIGHT

Fleming H. Revell Company
Old Tappan, New Jersey

Quotation from RAISING CHILDREN, by Linda Raney Wright © 1975, used by permission of Tyndale House Publishers.
Quotation from "Paul, Women, and the Church," by Dr. Walter Kaiser, used by permission from *Worldwide Challenge* magazine, September, 1976. Copyright © Campus Crusade for Christ, Inc., 1976. All rights reserved.
Quotation from "Women Elders: Sinners or Servants?" by Richard and Catherine Kroeger used by permission of the Council on Women and the Church, Room 1151, 475 Riverside Drive, New York City, New York, 10115. © 1981.
Quotation from "The 'Head' of the Epistles," by Berkeley and Alvera Michelsen, February 20, 1981. Used by permission of *Christianity Today,* © 1981.
Quotation from *STAYING ON TOP WHEN THINGS GO WRONG* © 1980, 1983 by Linda Raney Wright. All rights reserved. Used by Permission Tyndale House Publishers, Inc.

Unless otherwise identified, Scripture quotations are from the New American Standard Bible, © The Lockman Foundation 1960, 1962, 1963, 1968, 1971, 1972, 1973, 1975, 1977.

Scripture quotations identified KJV are from the King James Version of the Bible.

Scripture quotations identified JERUSALEM are excerpts from *The Jerusalem Bible*, copyright © 1966 by Darton, Longman & Todd, Ltd. and Doubleday and Company, Inc. Used by permission of the publisher.

Scripture quotations identified NIV taken from the HOLY BIBLE: NEW INTERNATIONAL VERSION. Copyright © 1973, 1978 by the International Bible Society. Used by permission of Zondervan Bible Publishers.

Verses marked TLB are taken from *The Living Bible,* Copyright © 1971 by Tyndale House Publishers, Wheaton, Ill. Used by permission.

The Scripture quotations contained herein identified RSV are from the Revised Standard Version of the Bible, Copyrighted © 1946, 1952, 1971, by the Division of Christian Education of the National Council of the Churches of Christ in the United States of America, and are used by permission. All rights reserved.

Library of Congress Cataloging-in-Publication Data

Wright, Linda Raney.
A cord of three strands.

Bibliography: p.
1. Marriage—Religious aspects—Christianity.
2. Women in Christianity.   I. Title.   II. Title:
Cord of 3 strands.
BV835.W746   1987   248.8'4   86-28032
ISBN 0-8007-1523-3

Copyright © 1987 by Linda Raney Wright
Published by the Fleming H. Revell Company
Old Tappan, New Jersey 07675
Printed in the United States of America

TO my teammate, Rusty Wright
and to
five strong women in my life
Laura Elizabeth Raney
Dorothy Clark
Barbara Fain
Joyce Hopping
Kathleen Santucci

Acknowledgments

I am deeply indebted to many individuals who have assisted with this manuscript. Since this has been an eleven-year effort there are many who must go unnamed due to space.

For help in research and editing I wish to heartily thank Rusty Wright, Berkeley and Alvera Mickelsen, Evelyn Bence and Carol Barrington. Each has spent a great deal of hours on this manuscript. Without their contribution this book would not be possible.

Thank you to the exceptional crew at Revell who have worked so carefully on each detail of this manuscript.

There have been others who have given many hours carefully reading, editing, and making suggestions at various stages. Thank you Anne Iverson, Barbara Fain, Kathleen and

Hugo Santucci, Judy Douglass, Dorothy Clark, Beverly and Dave Garrett, Ann Bowman, Betty Taflinger, Carolyn Buhl, Dave Orris, Sharon Hemker, Barbara Pines, Pat Gundry, Mary Graham, Shirlee Fragel, Patty Burgin, Nancy Berry and Linda Silas.

Many theologians were also of great assistance in thinking through scholarly issues. I am indebted to Dwight Hervey Small, Dr. Walter Kaiser, Dr. Walter Liefeld, Dr. Catherine Kroeger, Dr. Timothy Weber, and Dr. Gilbert Bilezikian.

A book of this kind needs endless typing. Since I have not had a word processor, this has left much work for such hearty souls as Carol Puckett, Beverly Garrett and the word processing crew at 27th street complex.

Finally, but by no means last, I wish to publicly acknowledge our great Lord and God who has led me at every turn in the production of this manuscript. The contribution this book will make to His purposes are His doing; the errors, my own. For those of you who prayed, and specifically our seventy prayer warriors who carry the ministry of Rusty and Linda Wright before the throne of God, rich blessings on you.

ACKNOWLEDGMENTS

Contents

Part II: Called to Service   141

Introduction

In the late 1960s and early 1970s, as the divorce rate among Christians skyrocketed and as disillusioned wives left the home to find work, greater fulfillment, and intrigue, concerned Christians began to look for a solution. The church could have entertained a number of options at that time: It could have examined the root problems of dissatisfaction in marriage and their solutions; it might have seen each marriage as unique unto itself and dealt with each accordingly; it might have assessed total needs and considerations before drawing a conclusion; it might have encouraged communication between husbands and wives; or it might have observed what was happening between secular couples to determine whether Christian couples could learn anything constructive. While many churches chose to do some of these things, others chose instead to tell women that, to preserve order, they must adhere to a male hierarchy.

Some churches gave a similar message to men. Instead of encouraging them to greater responsibility and participation, they were given an extreme "one rule fits all" dictum: "You must not just participate; you must lead. You must not just be responsible; you must be the authority." Many churches could not see that this plan did not provide for lasting ways of relating and fulfillment. But more important, many failed to take a hard look at Scripture and determine if this view was really biblical.

One friend asked, "Since many past missionary biographies do present partnership marriage, and since Christian marriage books of the last generation rarely refer to a man being over his wife, when did this current teaching begin?"

When I was in Bible school, twenty years ago, I was taught the triangle concept. The triangle looked like this:

Woman   Man

Our lesson on marriage was this: As the man and woman grow closer to the Lord, they will grow closer to each other. During that time the favorite book about marriage was by Dwight Hervey Small, *Design for Christian Marriage*, in which hierarchy was not mentioned.

Within five years, perspective had changed dramatically. Now the relationships were portrayed like this:

God
↓
Man
↓
Woman
↓
Children

One couple's story illustrates the second model:

Billy and Caren went to a marriage seminar only after years of marital conflict. Twice they had been separated, but reunited "for the children's sake." At the marriage seminar they learned that the reason their marriage was not running smoothly was because Billy was not leading as he should and Caren was not submitting.

"Since the marriage conference was kind of a last resort," shares Billy, "we decided to try their advice. We were really surprised and pleased to find that as I became more in charge and Caren submitted to my authority, things really did run more smoothly. Even the kids settled down as they observed lessened conflict.

"For a while things continued smoothly. Only now and then did I have to remind Caren to submit to me. Actually I felt she took to that role quite well, and it made me think this kind of teaching was correct.

"When we hit a crisis, however, Caren became her old self. She didn't like a decision I had made, and my attempts to remind her that God was working through me to make the decisions in our family met with volatile reactions. When the pastor intervened and reminded Caren that her wifely role was to follow my decision, it helped for only a few days. Then Caren abruptly left. I looked upon her as a rebellious wife and a poor example of a Christian.

"At this time I had no conscience problems, believing I was biblically justified in my responses. Several other members of our church, including women, supported my judgment. I was convinced that I was right. Yet I had lost Caren!

"When she did not return, I slowly began to doubt my position in the matter.

"Finally, I talked with an elder in our church. Surprisingly, he did not agree with the teaching we had received.

" 'But it seemed so simple, so right,' I told him. 'If we could just continue with my being in charge and Caren submitting, it would end a lot of our heated discussions.'

" 'Certainly,' he replied, 'It simplifies life in one sense, because there's no contest of wills. But seen in another vein, it is bound to boomerang eventually, because there is no serious attempt to let both husband and wife function as full people. In reality, you were treating your wife as one of your children.' "

Billy did not get Caren back. "Even after hearing of my plans to change, she could not bring herself to return. She had no emotional energy left to make another attempt."

Billy and Caren's story is more bleak than most hierarchical marriages, but in the pages of this book I'd like to present a better way—a way firmly based on Scripture, a way that allows both men and women to become individuals whom God can use to their maximum potential.

I believe that the Scriptures are God's Word, inspired, infallible, and inerrant. God gave us the Bible to help us learn how to live.

However, there are many obstacles to obtaining a biblical view on any subject: A few include tradition, prejudice, and popular secular teaching. In addition many current translations of the Bible don't help the problem of good interpretation. Translations are meant to interpret a Greek, Hebrew, or Aramaic word or phrase into the best understanding of a contemporary language (such as English). Yet the average Bible reader may be astounded to find how imprecise many translations are, and in fact, how biased a translation may be on certain subjects.

There is a distinct difference between a literal translation and a personal interpretation or application added into a translation.

In *Christianity Today*, Berkeley and Alvera Mickelsen wrote:

> If we really believe in the absolute authority of the Word of God, we dare not add to or subtract from what the text says. If the text itself is ambiguous—the meaning is not clear or is open to several possible interpretations—conscientious translators must leave the material ambiguous and open to several possible interpretations. If they "clear up" the difficult section by choosing which interpretation they like best and incorporate that into their translation, are they not claiming for themselves the divine inspiration that belongs only to the Word of God as it was originally "God breathed" by the Holy Spirit? If the Holy Spirit inspired words or thoughts that are ambiguous or open to several interpretations, should we attempt to "improve" or "clear up" what the Holy Spirit chose to do?[1]

The editor's note in the *Christianity Today* article quoted above says there is a great deal of interpretation, application, and even bias in translations. Consider just a few examples: Concerning some areas this book will address, the King James Version of the Bible refers to Aquila and Priscilla—in spite of the fact that, in the Greek text, Priscilla is clearly named first (this Greek order implies Priscilla's prominence) [Acts 18:26]. In 1 Timothy 2:11, the King James Version translates *hesuchia*, "let the woman learn in *silence*," but when referring to men (2 Thessalonians 3:12) it renders the same word, "with *quietness* they work, and eat" (*italics mine*). Psalms 68:11 in King James reads, "The Lord gave the word: great was the company of those that published it." Yet the original reads, "Great was the company of women who publish the Word of the Lord."

"On the other hand, the King James Version correctly notes the feminine *Junia* in Romans 16:7, in contrast with most contemporary translations, which, with little or no justification, transform, *mirabile dictu*, the feminine *Junia*, into the male *Junias* to avoid the unthinkable—a woman among the apostles!"[2]

The question of what is a right interpretation of a passage hinges on many things. There are many aspects of sound biblical interpretation, and a primary principle is that any position should be reasoned from the whole to the particular. That is, we must note what the overview of Scripture teaches on a subject. (When studying a subject in depth, I make it a practice to start in Genesis and read all the way to Revelation, observing every mention of the subject. On the subject of marriage and women I highly recommend this to every reader.)

In Ecclesiastes 4:9–12 (*italics added*) Solomon writes:

Two are better than one because they have a good return for their labor. For if either of them falls, the one will lift up his companion. But woe to the one who falls when there is not another to lift him up. Furthermore, if two lie down together they keep warm, but how can one be warm alone? And if one can overpower him who is alone, two can resist him. *A cord of three strands is not quickly torn apart.*

Mutuality, unity, comradeship, partnership, and teamwork are all important elements in relationships, marriage, work, and ministry. But there something much higher is the underlying thesis of this book.

For, if two are better than one—what must three be? Man, woman, and God, an unbeatable combination!

Tradition has left its own kind of bias. It subtly implies that what some feel is a dominant *practice* on the issue of men and women, in marriage and ministry, is of necessity *the* scriptural view. Actually a great deal of important research on the subject I will be addressing has not been advanced until the twentieth century; much of it coming in the last ten to fifteen years. In the process not only have biases been discovered in translations but biblical dictionaries, lexicons and commentaries as well. This needn't be looked upon as a plot, but we must realize that renewed interest on the subject has provoked honest men and women to look harder.

Among those who lead the way on this important issue and have given their endorsement to this book (though not necessarily agreeing with every detail) are such outstanding Christians and biblical scholars as: Dr. Kenneth Kantzer, dean emeritus, Trinity Evangelical Divinity School, former editor, *Christianity Today*; Dr. David Scholar, dean of the seminary and Julius R. Mantey professor of New Testament, Northern Baptist Theological Seminary; Dr. Walter Liefeld, professor of New Testament, Trinity Evangelical Divinity School; Dr. Timothy Weber, associate professor of church history, Denver Seminary; Dr. Robert E. Webber, professor of theology, Wheaton

College and Wheaton Graduate School; Dr. Gilbert Bilezikian, professor of biblical studies, Wheaton College; Dr. Ronald B. Allen, professor of Hebrew Scripture and chairman of division of biblical studies, Western Conservative Baptist Seminary; Dr. Willard M. Swartley, director, institute of Mennonite studies, Associated Mennonite Biblical Seminaries; Dr. Samuel Southard, professor pastoral theology, Fuller Theological Seminary; Dr. Vernon C. Grounds, president emeritus, Denver Seminary, president, Evangelicals for Social Action; Dr. Berkeley and Alvera Mickelsen, professor emeritus of New Testament, Bethel Seminary and former journalism professor Bethel College (respectively); Dr. Philip Barton Payne, visiting professor of New Testament, Gordon-Conwell Theological Seminary; Dr. John Hannah, chairman and professor of historical theology, Dallas Theological Seminary; and Dwight Hervey Small, professor emeritus, marriage studies, Westmont College.

Of course many others have joined with these men in recent years, to expound their biblical convictions along the same lines. Many Christian counselors and pastors have joined with these men in recent years, to expound their biblical convictions along the same lines. Many Christian counselors and pastors will concur with the thinking in this manuscript, after years of finding their offices filled with confused Christians trying to sort out popular Christian teaching from genuine faith and practice.

*   *   *   *

INTRODUCTION

PART I

CALLED
TO
UNITY

ONE

Authority
in
Marriage

Ed and Betty were a perfectly suited couple. Pragmatic Ed and carefree Betty became Christians several years after they were married. Sometime later the Holy Spirit began impressing Ed that he should direct his life into greater Christian ministry.

He says, "I had told myself that I would minister more actively when I retired, but one day I knew that I could no longer deny God's inner direction."

But what about Betty?

She remembers her reaction to Ed's conviction: "The thought of moving into another sphere of life, where finances were limited, where a secure home and surroundings were not guaranteed, scared me."

When she expressed her reservations, Ed assured her that he would not make the move unless Betty was 100 percent with him, and in turn Betty felt challenged to pray, "Lord, make me willing to do Your will."

Ed adds, "The job change wasn't the most serious issue here. In all our church activity, no one had ever taught Betty or me to obey the leading of the Holy Spirit or to search the Scriptures on our own for answers. Rather, we were spoon-fed from our pastor. We depended on his counsel because we believed that was what we, as good Christians, were supposed to do. As a result, Betty and I became faithful church members, devoted to our family, but we weren't self-sustaining in the Word of God or in tune with the Spirit of God.

"Years after giving my life to Christ," continues Ed, "I met some dedicated Christians who served God with contagious exuberance. From them I learned that God could empower and lead me. I became so enthusiastic that I wanted to teach others how they, too, could be led by God. I continued to seek God's leading, and Betty prayed that God would help her to be as eager as I was. Eventually Betty and I each reevaluated what was most important to us and finally agreed to make the change. I was glad that Betty had come to this decision independently of me, based on her own personal interaction with the Lord. It confirmed that God had indeed led me."

What caused Ed and Betty to leave comfortable jobs and security to launch out into the unknown? The leading of the Holy Spirit.

Now, a number of years later, Ed and Betty are employees of a worldwide Christian organization. Betty remarks, "When we stopped listening to other people and decided that both of us should seek God and His personal leading, life really began for us. Knowing that we are where God wants us and knowing that our lives are directly involved in reaching the lost and building up new Christians has so encouraged and rewarded us that our life now is no comparison to our life before."

"The great lesson here," explains Ed, "is that husband and wife should both seek and follow the leading of the Holy Spirit and respect that leading in each other's life."

But how does this work?

Authority is a word loaded with emotion and easily misun-

CALLED TO UNITY

derstood. But one Gospel story gives some interesting insight into the meaning of the word:

> And a certain centurion's slave, who was highly regarded by him, was sick and about to die. And when he heard about Jesus, he sent some Jewish elders asking Him to come and save the life of his slave. . . . Now Jesus started on His way with them; and when He was already not far from the house, the centurion sent friends, saying to Him, "Lord, do not trouble Yourself further, for I am not fit for You to come under my roof; for this reason I did not even consider myself worthy to come to You, but just say the word, and my servant will be healed. For indeed, I am a man under authority, with soldiers under me; and I say to this one, 'Go!' and he goes; and to another, 'Come!' and he comes; and to my slave, 'Do this!' and he does it."
>
> Luke 7:2, 3, 6–10

Note that the centurion, who ruled 100 soldiers, said he was a man *under*, not *of* or *with* authority. Because the centurion had placed himself under the authority of Rome, Rome backed him up. Placing himself under Caesar's authority gave him authority. For whatever he did, Rome stood behind him.

Likewise, when we have submitted ourselves totally and completely to the lordship of Jesus Christ, we have become involved in His domain. That domain of angels and power works in our behalf. To have authority, men and women must be under God's authority, which is manifested in the Word of God and by the Holy Spirit, who empowers our walk (Galatians 5:16), prayer (Ephesians 6:18), strength (Ephesians 3:16), witness (1 Corinthians 2:4, 5), gifts (1 Corinthians 12:7–11), plus produces in us love, joy, peace, patience, kindness, goodness, faithfulness, gentleness, self-control (Galatians 5:22, 23).

How is authority manifested in the Word of God in marriage? My husband, Rusty, and I need to live each day under the authority of the Word of God, for we have discovered that under that authority we have authority. That authority is available to men *and* women who place themselves at God's disposal.

But what part does the Holy Spirit's authority play in marriage?

Often people finally give up trying to make their marriages work because they have reached a state of hopelessness: They fear they can't change; they fear their partners can't change; their marriages seem doomed because they lack mutual purpose. But the leading and power of the Holy Spirit can effect change.

God's help is available, but how do we practically apply that help to the complexities of love and marriage?

After I walked down the aisle and said, "I do," I was shocked at my reactions to the man I loved. My usual cool and calm approach to life dissolved. Generally, I don't take people's opinions or remarks so seriously that it disrupts my life. But with Rusty I wore my feelings on my sleeve.

It took a while for me to determine why I overreacted, and I got control of the situation as I yielded to the authority of God's Word. At first I acknowledged the problem to God and asked Him to give me insight. I prayed that prayer often, and He answered it.

As I began to understand the source of my overreaction (usually fear, guilt, or resentment), I asked God to deliver me from it. First, I asked God to fill me with the Holy Spirit, so I would experience His authority over these deep-seated reactions. Then I read specifically about these areas in the Bible and memorized a few verses that helped strengthen me.

As I helped Rusty understand what I had come to understand about myself, when he could see why I overreacted to him, his insight helped him watch his behavior toward me.

Rusty asked the Holy Spirit to fill him and help him be gentle and supportive of me. He memorized verses like Proverbs 10:19, "When there are many words, transgression is unavoidable . . . ," and for the most part, he has developed greater sensitivity. (I discuss the concept of how to change patterns of thinking and living in my book *Staying on Top When Things Go Wrong.*)

Rusty relates another incident, "When we married, I wasn't

very in touch with *my* feelings. So I was not capable of understanding Linda's feelings. After I got a good look at my insensitivity, I determined, with God's help and encouragement, to change.

"I have often prayed for understanding of where people are and why. I sometimes grill Linda to find out what's behind her decisions, how she sees others. The Holy Spirit has assisted me time and time again in urging me to observe and learn. When I become insensitive, I admit to God that I am wrong; as a result, I am again filled with His Spirit, who continues to help me develop in this area."

For Christians, the beautiful part of a marriage relationship is that we have a Helper, the Holy Spirit, to aid us in making the best decisions. Let's say there is a legitimate financial crisis in a family—not an imagined one, like "We can't afford a new TV," but a real one. The big question is whether or not the wife should work. If you ask one set of people, they will say, "Certainly. In fact, the woman may not be fulfilled unless she has a career." Another group would answer, "Certainly not. A wife or mother should never work."

But such broad, all-inclusive statements fail to acknowledge that the Holy Spirit speaks to individuals. When you throw out the "always" and "never" statements and the "marriage mold," you and God have to come up with an acceptable solution for your particular situation.

God knows each of us intimately. He knows what is best for us—what will hurt us and what will help us. As we seek Him He gives us the right solution, *if* we are not already hemmed in too tightly by the "experts." You see, in the Christian life, each person can be his or her own expert under the leadership and authority of the Lord. This doesn't mean that we don't seek counsel. Counsel is part of God's plan, but we are not bound to counsel, current popular thinking, preconceived ideas, or pat answers.

God promised the power of the Holy Spirit to enable Christians to live more effectively. The Holy Spirit enters a person the moment he or she believes in Christ, and He will never leave that person (Hebrews 13:5). However, *the Holy Spirit only empowers an individual as that person allows Him to.* God promises all the power and love resources we need, but our wills are the switches that allow the power to become operative.

Spiritual Blessing

When Rusty or I find ourselves becoming uptight, angry, or anxious, we try a simple exercise, sometimes called "spiritual breathing," that helps us return to a more positive mental attitude. Physical breathing has two main aspects: exhaling and inhaling. You exhale the bad air and inhale the good. Spiritual breathing works the same way.

Exhale: When we become aware of sin in our lives (that is, something that displeases God in our attitudes or actions), we simply admit (confess) to Him that we have sinned. *To confess* means "to say along with," to agree with God concerning our sin. We don't have to try to work up feelings of remorse or sorrow. We simply agree with God. A first-century Christian wrote, "If we confess our sins, He [God] is faithful and righteous to forgive us our sins and to cleanse us from all unrighteousness" (1 John 1:9). We are forgiven for all our sins the moment we receive Christ. But confession of sins, as we become aware of them, helps make this forgiveness real in our experience. Perhaps we can think of exhaling as "getting it off our chests," with God. We confess; He forgives and cleanses; then we can thank Him that we are forgiven and cleansed.

Inhale: Once we have confessed, we then ask God—in the Person of the Holy Spirit—to empower (or fill) our lives again. When the wind fills the sail of a boat, the moving air provides the power the boat needs to move along the water. In a similar way, the Holy Spirit will fill (empower) our lives, if we let Him. He will produce the "fruit of the Spirit" (that is, the behavior that results from being filled with the Spirit), which is "love, joy, peace, patience, kindness, goodness, faithfulness, gentleness, self-control" (Galatians 5:22, 23).

CALLED TO UNITY

God *commands* Christians to be filled with the Spirit: "And do not get drunk with wine, for that is dissipation [waste], but be filled with the Spirit" (Ephesians 5:18). He also *promises* that if we ask Him something that is His will, He will answer: "And this is the confidence which we have before Him, that, if we ask anything according to His will, He hears us. And if we know that He hears us . . . we know that we have the requests which we have asked from Him" (1 John 5:14, 15).

We know that God wants us to be filled with the Spirit. So if we ask Him to fill us, He will. This is inhaling: asking God to fill us with the Holy Spirit and believing (based on His promise) that He has done it.

After hearing about spiritual breathing, one man said, "My problem is that I'm afraid I'll be panting like a cat on a hot tin roof!" Certainly every Christian frequently needs to breathe spiritually. However, as one grows in faith, he or she will find his or her attitudes and perspectives will also grow. We do not become sinless, but we do sin less and less.

We should also be cautious about looking for immediate changes in *feelings* when breathing spiritually. Most often the change is one of attitude. Rusty and I find that as a problem comes in our relationship, we first have to be sure our relationship with God is right, by breathing spiritually (confessing and appropriating the filling of the Spirit). Then we have help as we confront difficult points of discord. (For more information on the Spirit-filled life, we recommend the Transferable Concept series of booklets by Bill Bright, which are produced by Here's Life Publishers, Arrowhead Springs, San Bernardino, California 92414).

There is hope for any marriage under the authority of God's Spirit. Maybe you are just starting out. Or maybe you have stacked up a series of disappointments and discouragements through the years. Regardless, there is hope for unity and for ministry.

If you are a Christian availing yourself of the power of the Word of God and the Holy Spirit, God can bring about positive and permanent change for the better.

TWO

Marriage
Is a
Relationship

During our engagement, Rusty and I began to hash through some of the teaching we had heard. "You know," I said to Rusty one evening, "I heard one woman teach that when something is bothering me or I want something very much, I shouldn't bother you about it. I should talk only to God. What do you think of that?"

"Don't you go sneaking to God behind my back." Rusty laughed. "If you've got something on your mind, I want to know about it." Rusty wasn't arguing against my personal involvement with God; he was joking about being maneuvered. But more seriously Rusty wanted a relationship between two whole people who could interact honestly and openly, because we were humans and Christians, not because we acted out roles or rules.

There are several different ideas about roles and rules in

marriage. One group asserts that a man and woman should practice hierarchical roles—the man in charge, the woman following. Another group argues for equal roles. A third group argues for no roles at all (each should do his or her own thing).

There is also divergent thinking regarding roles in Christianity. Within the church, *role* comes to mean a certain mode of operation. The members of one group may define their Christian role legalistically, that is, they keep certain fixed standards. Another group may define their Christian role emotionally, that is, they need to be on a constant high. Other Christians define their role evangelistically, that is, they see themselves as being called to witness. Still other Christians define their role self-centeredly—a mixture of Christian and worldly thinking as it suits them. But with all the rhetoric about roles, definitions, pat answers, and principles, we often forget that Christianity is a *relationship, not a role*. And every relationship between God and His children, though governed by the Word of God, is unique.

Some Christians don't talk to God the same way you do. Others don't have the same needs and temptations as you. That's because you are an individual. God may have to push you to get you started, while someone else may need to wait on the Lord. You may be a great visionary. Someone else may be a great plodder. The list goes on and on. The differences in individuals suggest that each person has a different and unique relationship with God, through Christ. As Christians, our maturity, personality, temperament, abilities, background, and so forth, all suggest that God deals with us uniquely.

The same often overlooked principle exists in Christian marriage. We hear someone teach that marriage partners should use more discipline on their kids, not practice birth control, have family devotions every morning at breakfast, have sex twice a week, attend church services Sundays and Wednesdays, teach their children at home instead of sending them to school, let the man make the decisions, and so forth. Then we practice this teaching, without question, as if it were mandatory, when, in fact, that role may not fit our situation at all.

A basic reason we are vulnerable to this one-rule-fits-all thinking is that we have put too much stock in our teachers and not enough in the Teacher.

We are also vulnerable because we are caught in a dilemma between wanting security and wanting freedom. Most humans resist change and don't like having to adjust daily to variables. We would like to structure our lives and those about us to precipitate as little surprise as possible. Yet on the other side of the coin, to the degree we tightly legislate our lives into predetermined stereotypes and close ourselves off to change, we limit what God would have us be.

Several years ago I met Connie. She ran life not by the Bible, but by the book—books with simple answers to everything and stereotyped rules that could be followed with as little thought as possible. One of those stereotyped rules was that she did whatever her husband told her (or so it appeared). While outwardly she catered to his desires (and he was a good and kind man), she had her own schizophrenic way of maintaining individuality. She got fat.

"Sometime into our marriage, I realized what I was doing," shares Connie. "I liked the rules for the security they gave me; I didn't have to think much. But I hated the rules for the lack of freedom I had. At the one extreme, I told myself that Carl would be my leader. At the other, I told myself that no one was going to tell me what to do. Eating became my rebellion against my love-hate relationship with the stereotyped rules. Eventually I realized I had neither real security nor freedom."

Another reason we have been vulnerable to the one-rule-fits-all mentality is that we have segregated and defined "men" and "women" too dramatically. Within the Christian community many have purposely centered on the "differences" between men and women, rather than on their commonalities. Whether from a fear that Christians may embrace homosexuality, or for some other reason, we have come up with varied opinions on what men are supposed to be and what women are supposed to be. But are these universal or even biblical distinctions? The fact is, some women think more like their men friends than their women friends. Some men's temperaments are more like their women friends' temperaments than those of their men friends. Background, personality, insight, and maturity may be more closely related to some members of the other sex than to some of the same sex. (Note: I said *other sex*, not *opposite sex*, an unbiblical term that tends to drive men and women apart. The Bible's position is that men and women are complements, not opposites.)

In our society generalizations abound concerning men and women. Yet every time someone says that women are more sensitive than men, can you not think of a marriage where the man is more sensitive than the woman? When you hear that men handle pressure better than women, do you ever think of the tens of thousands of single-parent women who hold down jobs and run households at the same time? Whenever someone states that it is natural for men to lead and unnatural for women, do you think of some of the gifted women leaders in the world? Or when women are reported to be the worst gossips, do you ever consider what passes for communication in a men's locker room?

I will not make attempts to define *men* and *women*, because the Bible does not go to extremes to do so and because information available through social studies or personal observation may not be the final word. Finally, I'd fear that, given a limited definition (whatever that might be), some may feel compelled to make up new rules for *everybody* to live by. We've had enough of that.

But there is a much more important consideration here. What is each man and woman supposed to be? Who determines what that is—society, the Christian community, or God Himself?

Only men and women who totally surrender their lives into the hands of God will ever express their true femininity or masculinity as He designed it to be. Within the boundaries of being led by God through the Word and the Spirit, femininity may include great strength, faith, perseverance, fortitude, unconquerableness, and steadfastness. Such was the femininity of Mary

Slessor who, in the late 1800s, single-handedly (with the Lord's enabling power) reached the deep interior of the African continent with the message of Jesus Christ. Fearlessly facing death, starvation, illness, she saw no need for artificial roles to duplicate. Barefooted and in the least flattering clothing, but with a heart of love, she settled disputes between natives, rescued children from death, took long treks inland to reach the forgotten with the Gospel, and healed whomever she could help. She duplicated her Savior, and her femininity emerged naturally and uniquely, without apology.

Likewise, men who surrender their total beings to Jesus Christ need not fear how they portray themselves to others. A gentle spirit they need not cloak; a forbearing attitude they need not disguise. Releasing a worldly view of masculinity, they can "become all things to all people" as Paul did, without needing to fear stepping outside of a role.

God has built us so that we needn't conform to an image or a role. We need to lay our lives down, and He will raise them up as full persons, apart from stereotypes and roles.

But there's more to be said on this issue. "Be imitators of me," Paul said, "just as I also am of Christ" (1 Corinthians 11:1). This command was given to all Christians, men and women alike. When we think about the life of Jesus and the many commands for us to be "Christlike," the subject of Jesus' manhood rarely, if ever, occurs to us. Why? Because the Bible doesn't make an issue of Jesus' masculine traits as opposed to His personal traits.

For example, was Jesus' anger at the temple a masculine trait? Was His frailty in Gethsemane a masculine or feminine trait? Neither? Was Jesus' generosity or compassion or courage or faith masculine? Feminine?

The Wrong Question

So what is the point? Throw out all the rules? Switch roles? No. The point is that we have been asking the wrong questions.

We have been asking:

CALLED TO UNITY

What is the role of the man in marriage or ministry?
What is the role of the woman in marriage or ministry?
What are the differences between men and women?
Who is ultimately responsible for the home?
Who should make the final decision?

Instead, we should be asking:

How can I be the best possible Christian in my marriage?
How can my spouse and I use all that we are to reach the world for Christ?
What does love motivate us to do in this situation?
What is God leading us to do?

In light of the individual background, temperament, intelligence, training, personality, needs, likes, and dislikes of each partner, how should we arrange our marriage for mutual growth and satisfaction and Christian outreach?

But is this approach really biblical? God *has* left us plenty of guidelines to work with *each* individual situation. The Bible in its entirety is broad enough to encompass many Christian life-styles, as illustrated by Janice and Tom:

"I didn't want to get married," says Janice, "because I had felt like a full person under God as a single woman. God had been 'over' me—my one and final life authority. Since God knew and understood me intimately, this was great. He knew what was best for me. But also He worked from within me to give me motivation and strength for what I did. When I learned that Tom was supposed to be the 'authority' in my life, I hated the idea."

"I never liked the idea that I was Janice's authority," shares Tom. "It put a lot of stress on me to be right all the time. I had thought that one of the advantages of marriage was that two could jointly share the stresses, struggles, and decisions of life. After marriage, I came to believe that I carried the responsibility for the relationship and answered to God for its success or failure. I was overwhelmed. Instead of finding someone to halve my burdens, my burdens were doubled."

"Something else I discovered," continues Janice, "was that since I believed that God led through Tom, and his was the final authority, getting my needs met depended on Tom. So I pressured him. After all, if he didn't cooperate or agree, either by listening to me or to God on behalf of me, I had no alternative for getting my needs and desires met."

Fortunately, Janice and Tom were confronted early in their marriage with some excellent teaching.

"Basically, what we learned," says Tom, "was that marriage was a relationship, not a role. We each were to be the best Christians we could be, both answering to God, both being led by God, both making decisions and taking responsibility for our own spiritual growth and walk with God. Instead of following rules of marriage, we practiced being committed Christians in each other's presence."

"The heart of the whole transformation," Janice added, "was how we viewed one another. We stopped seeing each other as people with certain roles to perform. We stopped categorizing what husbands are supposed to be and what wives are supposed to be. We stopped putting expectations on each other as to what we were supposed to be according to the marriage books and seminars. Instead we got back to scriptural basics."

"It is a relief to have a teammate," says Tom. "With Janice's help, I am under less pressure and a better person."

"I'm out to change my world now," shares Janice. "Before it required little or no courage to let Tom run things. But now I see that I'm responsible for myself, to follow God and be His instrument."

Team Marriage Is God's Support System

"You would think," continues Tom, "that our recent thinking would increase conflict and differences. But we've learned that the Holy Spirit doesn't work against Himself. If He leads Jan to do something, He often gives me peace about it and maybe insight to help her. Janice gives me the same support. If not, we work through the problem and usually grow some in the process. Thank God we no longer have the pressure of living out roles. As marriage partners, we just try to be the very best Christians we can."

How does this work out practically in terms of Christian living in marriage? Every Christian who desires a mature Christian marriage must become a mature Christian. There are no shortcuts. There have only appeared to be some shortcuts, in the form of rules and roles.

What is really required is that every believer know (*thoroughly* know) the Word of God for *his or her own self.* And we need to specifically understand biblical teaching on marriage and ministry.

But what is that teaching?

THREE

Created
for
What?

Lisa and Bill were sweethearts in high school. Both were heavily involved in Christian activities. Their future seemed secure as they headed off to Bible school. Bill studied and became a pastor. They had three children, one right after another, and Lisa had her hands full with household responsibilities.

"Christianity was a very serious matter to us," shares Lisa, "but somewhere down the line we got off the track."

Their sojourn away from God began under some popular Christian teaching on marriage and ministry. The teaching included the perspective that men should be the final authorities in the home and the church.

"We tried," states Lisa. "And we really thought we were being the best Christians we could be. But I found the teaching more and more difficult to live with. There was plenty of structure in the teaching, but not much teaching on relationships, understanding the uniqueness of your partner, inner fulfillment, the leading of the Holy Spirit, and the love and grace of God. Slowly I began to rebel. Most of my friends thought I was a poor Christian. Actually, I was dying inside and didn't know how to get help. I tried diligently to be what others wanted so as not to give offense and to obey my husband and church leaders, for this was supposed to be the will of God. But did they really know what was best for me?

"Almost ten years down the road, the light finally dawned. I wondered, *Is it God I can't come to terms with, or is it the teaching we are under?*

"Slowly and painfully Bill and I began to pull ourselves out of our carefully structured teaching and to look again at Scripture. Through verbally confronting God and asking Him to teach me His will, I arrived at a better understanding of God's love and purpose for my life. One truth, presented in two different verses, helped in our new and diligent study of Scripture. One was Jesus' principle, 'If you abide in My word, then you are truly disciples of Mine; and you shall know the truth, and the truth shall make you free' (John 8:31, 32). The other was Paul's teaching, '. . . Where the Spirit of the Lord is, there is liberty' (2 Corinthians 3:17). Never again would we let someone else's teaching put us in such bondage. If we were getting the truth under the leading of the Spirit, it would be genuinely freeing and liberating. The Holy Spirit would be our Teacher as we carefully and daily searched the Word of God. As we listened to the teaching of others, we would practice '. . . examining the Scriptures daily, to see whether these things were so' " (Acts 17:11).

Today, Lisa and Bill's personal lives and marriage are full of enthusiasm and a blessing to those around them. One of the reasons is that they came to appreciate God's basis for the Christian church and the beauty of Christian marriage.

When Rusty and I married, we had both asked God for a partner in marriage and ministry. We desired that each would respect the other; honor Jesus Christ in the other; acknowledge the leading of the Holy Spirit in the other's life; support the gifts of the other; give love, joy, and forgiveness to the other; and honor and worship the Lord as "a fellow heir."

When the trials have come and when we have had to make the major and minor decisions of life, we have had a basis for knowing God's will and following it—together. Whether we are planning worldwide evangelistic strategy, covering prayer needs, helping others, or handling finances, we seek to implement what we early on determined to be the framework of a successful marriage—teamwork under the leadership of the Holy Spirit.

We view our marriage as a triangle. God is at the top corner and Linda and Rusty are at the bottom two. We find that, as we grow closer to God, we also grow closer to each other. Of course, there are rough spots along the way, but the fact that we're each following the same Leader makes those rough spots easier to handle.

Does Jesus make a couple's life better? We're convinced that He does. Two marriage partners who have growing relationships with Christ will grow closer to each other: spirit to spirit, mind to mind, body to body. Their love, commitment, and communication will become increasingly dynamic. As one California woman put it, "Twenty-two years as a wife (and the last eight and a half years as a Christian) enables me to agree with you one hundred percent!"

I believe a team marriage and ministry is what God created Rusty and me for—and for other Christians as well. But to understand why I believe this, we will have to begin in Genesis. In the creation account we can appreciate the identity, authority, and responsibility that God gave to both men and women. Then we will look at the New Testament to determine the identity, authority, and responsibility of men and women as they are re-created in Christ.

In God's Image

In eternity past, God conceived a great plan that culminated in a planet we call Earth. Upon that planet He placed plants, animals, sea creatures, birds, and one more creation—humans.

These humans were created as lower than His other creation, angels. But, through faith, they have the distinction of becoming higher than the angels—heirs of God and joint heirs of Jesus Christ (Hebrews 1, 2; Romans 8:17). How did this all begin?

"And God created man in His own image, in the image of God He created him; male and female He created them" (Genesis 1:27). To some, this reads that man is created in God's image and that later woman is created in man's image, but the passage actually reads that God created man (the word used in Hebrew is generic) in His own image (*see also* Genesis 1:26; 5:2). The essence of God's image was expressed in the male and the female.

What does it mean to be created in God's image, and why is this important to marriage and ministry? Like God, we possess the ability to think, reason, and make decisions. Like God, we have a conscience, self-consciousness, and we feel emotion. Both in doctrine and illustration it is evident throughout Scripture that *both* men and women possess these faculties. For example, both Sarah and Abraham (Genesis 11:27–25:12) have intelligence (mentality), for they both think and reason; they both are able to make decisions (volition); both possess standards by which they make those decisions (conscience); both are aware of their own existence (self-consciousness); and both experience pain and pleasure (emotion). All humans (both men and women) were designed to function in God's image with these (and possibly other) attributes.

Identity in Christ

Just as it is important to see how man and woman were *created* initially, so it is important to see how they were *recreated* in Christ. Both men and women (through the cross) possess the image or identity of being "in Christ."

Exactly what is the identity of those who, in humility, have invited Jesus Christ to be their Savior? Is there a biblical distinction (presented in Scripture) between the man and the woman who has become a "new creation" in Christ?

According to the New Testament, at "new birth" *both* men and women become:

Children of God (John 1:12)
Completely forgiven (Colossians 1:14)
Heirs of God and joint heirs of Christ (Romans 8:17)
Priests before God (Hebrews 10:10–14)
Kings before God (2 Peter 1:11)
Sanctified and set apart for God (1 Corinthians 1:2, 30)
Sharers of Christ's destiny (Ephesians 1:5)
Clothed in God's righteousness (2 Corinthians 5:21)
Possessors of eternal life (1 John 5:11, 12)
Reconciled to God (2 Corinthians 5:18; Ephesians 2:16; Colossians 1:20, 21)
Regenerated to spiritual life (John 3:10–18)
Sealed and eternally secured by the Holy Spirit (Ephesians 1:13)
Indwelt by Christ (Colossians 3:16)

At creation, men and women are both made in God's image, so at their new creation, when they place their trust in Christ, *both* men and women receive their new image (or identity) as outlined above. Thus we begin to lay proper foundations for who men and women really are. I am not saying there are no *differences* between men and women. But isn't it interesting that, from the initial account in Genesis, "made in God's image," to the identity of each believer "in Christ" in the New Testament documents, the thread between men and women is distinctly one of commonality, not difference? Of course this is not a firm conclusion about New Testament personhood or marriage, nor is it intended to be. We are simply laying foundational truth upon which to evaluate other Scriptures.

Blessed a Little More?

What else does the initial biblical account teach concerning men and women?

Genesis 1:28 says, "And God blessed them . . ."—both Adam and Eve. This statement seems clear, yet some men and women betray their suspicions that God blessed one sex more than the other. Recently I was visiting in a home and heard a couple's conversation.

"I need an afternoon free so I can relax and feed myself mentally and spiritually," announced the wife. "We need a baby-sitter."

"We can't afford it," replied the husband.

"But we *can* afford your new golf clubs and your monthly fishing trips," she returned.

"That's different," he explained. "I work hard all week and need time off."

"Why is it that *your* needs are so deserving, but *mine* are not?" she retorted.

"Don't raise your voice to me."

"All right," she tried another tack. "I guess I'll just continue tired and spent, if I can't get a break in my schedule."

"That's more like it," he resumed. "You'll do fine. And we'll save more money."

I sat there, painfully uneasy. I was totally embarrassed for the woman—embarrassed that a mere comment of her need was not regarded with as much respect as one might give a fellow employee, embarrassed because her husband seemed proud of dominating her and watching her timidly respond to him, but more embarrassed because he did not seem to realize that God blessed his wife and that in His eyes they were equally important.

Are the man and woman both blessed by God at re-creation, when men and women receive Christ as Savior? Yes.

"Blessed be the God and Father of our Lord Jesus Christ, who has blessed *us* [all believers] with every spiritual blessing in the heavenly places in Christ" (Ephesians 1:3, *italics added*).

Recipients of Authority and Responsibility

Genesis 1:28 continues by saying, ". . . and God said to them, 'Be fruitful and multiply, and fill the earth, and subdue it. . . .' " God gave this injunction to both the man and the woman. Even in a test-tube society it is essential for both a man and woman to participate in the propagation of humanity, but subduing the earth? Was this to be done only by the one partner? No. God felt it expedient to place this task in the hands of both the man and the woman. In so doing, He gave them both responsibility and authority.

Let's take a look at these two words, *responsibility* and *authority*. *Webster's Seventh Edition Dictionary* defines *responsibility* as: 1. The quality or state of being responsible, as (a) moral, legal, or mental accountability, (b) reliability, trustworthiness. 2. Something for which one is responsible, burden.

Webster's defines *authority* as: power to influence or command thought, opinion, or behavior; persons in command.

Were responsibility, accountability, and burden given to man and woman? Were power and influence to command thought, opinion, or behavior granted in the garden? Yes. Authority and responsibility, power and accountability, were given to the man and woman alike. (Note: The man is not given authority over the woman, or the woman over the man.)

Recently Rusty and I attended a meeting where the speaker argued, not for the difference in worth of a man and woman, but for a difference in position. Using Genesis as his text, he pointed out that Adam was created first and therefore was given authority over the woman. If this were true, we asked him later, why aren't the animals over Adam, for they were created before the man? Or why didn't God always choose the "firstborn" to be the leader? (*See* Jacob and Esau [Genesis 25:22–24] or David [1 Samuel 16:1–13]. The principle of the firstborn as related in Exodus 13 deals with setting apart the firstborn male for service or holiness. It was to commemorate the slaying of the firstborn in Egypt on Israel's night of deliverance.) The speaker then quoted a controversial New Testament passage as his proof text. That text (1 Timothy 2) is dealt with elsewhere in this book.

Another argument, along the same line, says that since woman was taken from man (Genesis 2:22), man is over woman. Paul answers this thesis quite directly in 1 Corinthians 11:11, 12: "However, in the Lord, neither is woman independent of man, nor is man independent of woman. For as the woman originates from the man, so also the man has his birth through the woman; and all things originate from God."

Still other people argue that Adam had authority over Eve because he named her (Genesis 2:23). Yet Eve named her children (Genesis 4:25). Did Eve have more authority than Adam over Seth because she named him? The Scripture never implies that the act of naming includes the assumption of God-given authority.

The above arguments proposing that God gave man authority over woman at creation because he came first, Eve was taken from Adam, or Adam named Eve, are speculations unsubstantiated by Scripture itself. If speculation is our criterion for truth, then we could just as easily turn the tables and say, "Because the woman was created last and is the pinnacle of creation, she should have authority over the man." Or, "Because the woman can bear children and a man cannot, God has favored her, and she should be in charge." We might even claim, "Because a woman is more beautiful. . . ."

"But all creation speaks of a hierarchical order," one man wrote. He went on to say that the animal kingdom clearly demonstrates that the male of the species dominates the female. Although this is often the case, in terms of leading the herd, ruling the roost, providing food, or raising the young there is variance in gender responsibilities within the animal kingdom. Even if generalities may be made about the animal kingdom, God doesn't seem to have made such comparisons.

In the angelic kingdom there is obviously no gender. Therefore on what basis is one angel in a higher position than another? Abilities, faithfulness, God's divine choice may be some of the answers, but God did not need to establish "gender" in order to establish order and efficiency among the angels.

Authority and Responsibility of a Christian

What of the "new creation"? Are authority and responsibility given to both men and women who have experienced the "second birth"? Keeping in mind the *identity* of the "new creation in Christ," let's look first at the *responsibility* of *every* believer.

In Christ, men and women are to be:

Imitators of Christ (Ephesians 5:1)
Ambassadors for Christ (2 Corinthians 5:20; 1 Peter 3:15, 16)
Fulfillers of the Great Commission (Matthew 28:18–20; 2 Timothy 2:1, 2)
Lights of the world (Matthew 5:14)
Salt of the earth (Matthew 5:13)
Warriors in the battle against Satan (2 Corinthians 10:3–6)
Prayer intercessors (Ephesians 6:18)
Users of their gifts (1 Corinthians 12; Romans 12; Ephesians 4)
Students of the Scriptures (2 Timothy 2:15)
Followers of the Scriptures (2 Timothy 3:16, 17)

But what of authority? All ultimate authority is given to the Lord Jesus Christ, but each Christian acting in *His name* and on the basis of *His Word* utilizes that authority.

In Acts 1:7, 8 Luke states Jesus' last words while on earth:

It is not for you to know times or epochs which the Father has fixed by His own authority; but you shall receive power when the Holy Spirit has come upon you; and you shall be My witnesses both in Jerusalem, and in all Judea and Samaria, and even to the remotest part of the earth.

Acts 1:14 indicates that both men and women received the promised Holy Spirit, and in light of this authority, all believers (men and women) are to reign as *kings* and *priests* upon the earth (1 Peter 2:5–9).

God gives responsibility to every believer, coupled with appropriate authority and power to carry out the task; and responsibility, biblically defined, includes a conscious concern for others (1 Corinthians 13; 1 Peter 5:1–5).

　　　　　　　　　　　CALLED TO UNITY

Who Is Her Leader?

One example to consider from the Old Testament is the Proverbs 31 woman. There are many noteworthy things about her. For one thing, she exercises a great deal of responsibility. While her husband serves as a "judge" deciding matters of importance for the city,[1] this woman is involved in business, takes charge of her own earnings, and is active in welfare, administration, farming, sewing, and so forth. But does she possess authority? Yes, over her own life and household. She makes her own decisions about buying, selling, planting, and so on. Does she have authority over her husband? The passage does not say. Neither does it say that her husband has authority over her. Is she required, in this essay, to seek his permission or even his advice? No. It does say, "The heart of her husband trusts in her . . ." (v. 11). And it does say she fears and reverences the Lord (v. 30).

Does this passage suggest any hierarchical order in the household—that the man is in charge and delegates responsibilities to the wife? Does it indicate that he is in business, while she stays in the home? Does it *define* different positions for each of them? No.

Teamwork

After saying that God blessed Adam and Eve and told them to multiply and subdue the earth, Genesis 1:28 continues: ". . . and rule over the fish of the sea and over the birds of the sky, and over every living thing that moves on the earth." Not only do men and women have responsibility and authority over the earth, but they are to rule over "every living thing." Teamwork is the obvious intent of this creation account.

There is no suggestion in this verse or others that the husband is in charge of the home, that he delegates the responsibility of dealing with nature or children or anything to his wife, or that the wife is in charge and leads the home on her own. They were *both* put in charge. One of the Ten Com-

CREATED FOR WHAT? 43

mandments says, "Honor your father and your mother" (Exodus 20:12). Ephesians 6:1 strengthens this command: "Children obey your *parents* [*goneus* in the Greek]. . . ." (See also Colossians 3:20; 1 Timothy 5:4; Deuteronomy 6:4–7; 21:18, 19). Are both to have the responsibility of teaching their children?

Proverbs 1:8 states the case succinctly. "Hear my son, your *father's instruction* and do not forsake your *mother's teaching*" (*italics added*). Ephesians 6:4 states, "And, fathers, do not provoke your children to anger; but bring them up in the discipline and instruction of the Lord." Some actually have interpreted this verse to mean that *only* men are to instruct and discipline children. But does giving an *extra* reminder to one party undermine or eliminate the admonition to another party who has been given the same command? Not at all. It most likely indicates that this party needs an extra reminder. The apostle Paul is saying in Ephesians 6:4 "Do not provoke . . . *but* . . . discipline and instruct." When men (or women, or Jews, or Gentiles, or any group) are singled out in any passage, it does not follow that all others are excluded. A look at the whole of Scripture will tell us if this is the case. In the whole of Scripture both men and women are given authority and responsibility over the home.

All We Need

Genesis 1:29 continues, "Then God said, 'Behold, I have given you every plant yielding seed that is on the surface of all the earth, and every tree which has fruit yielding seed; it shall be food for you. . . .'"

The provision of God is the same for the man and woman, and there is a similarity between the physical provision in the creation account and the spiritual, physical, and emotional provision given to the new creation.

Provisions for the saints include:

Wisdom (James 1:5)
Financial help (Luke 6:38)

Food (Matthew 6:31–34)
Guidance (Proverbs 3:5, 6)
Words for witnessing (Matthew 10:18, 19)
Sound mind (2 Timothy 1:7)
Comfort (2 Corinthians 1:4)
Encouragement (Romans 15:5)

The provision at creation and at re-creation are the same for both men and women.

Very Good

"And God saw all that He had made, and behold, it was very good ..." (Genesis 1:31). The Hebrew word *tob*, translated here as "good," also means "pleasant" or "agreeable." What God saw was good: a man and woman both made in His image, both given the same blessing, responsibility, authority, and both equally provided for.

What God sees in the new creation (the Christian) is also good and acceptable: both men and women identified "in Christ," given the same spiritual blessing, responsibilities, authority, provision, and given the title "beloved children." God has given men and women the righteousness of Christ Himself and the status of "children of God." Therefore the saints (men and women) are as agreeable, pleasant, and "good" in God's sight as is His Son Jesus Christ. Whereas at creation we were made a little lower than the angels, now "in Christ" both men and women are higher than the angels themselves (Hebrews 1, 2).

But there is more. . . .

FOUR

As God Created...

When I was about nine years old, my mom was busy washing dishes and I was sweeping the kitchen with our large broom. It must have been a pretty satisfying day, because I remember suddenly remarking to Mom, "When I grow up, I want to be a mom just like you and have a little helper just like me." I was so proud to be Mom's helper. Let's take a moment to examine how the concept of "helper" affects this issue of team marriage.

Created as Helpers

Look at Genesis 2:18, first in the King James Version, then in the New American Standard Version.

"And the Lord God said, 'It is not good that the man should be alone; I will make him an help meet for him' " (KJV). "Then the Lord God said, 'It is not good for the man to be alone; I will make him a helper suitable for him.' "

It is difficult for me to read the term *help meet* without thinking of Mama's little helper. *Helper* is one of those words that, whether or not we think about it, tends to be loaded with visual meaning. Let's face it, our common English term *helper* often implies to us "assistant," "vice-president," and the like. But the word *helper* as we often envision it is inadequate, even misleading, for this verse. Let's take another look at Genesis 2:18: "Then the Lord God said, 'It is not good for the man to be alone; I will make him a helper suitable for him."

The term "help meet" or "suitable helper" combines two Hebrew words, *ezer* and *neged*. The word *ezer*, translated "help," "helper," or "helpers," is used twenty-one times in the Old Testament.

In the great majority of these verses, *ezer* is used to describe God as the "helper" of humans. For instance it is used in Psalms 70:5: ". . . Thou art my help and my deliverer. . . ." Now, if we really want to make a case of this word, we might conclude that a woman is superior to man, as God is superior to humans. In fact, the Old Testament usage of this word suggests that more than it suggests equality. But I am not arguing for superiority of either sex, because the word *neged* puts the word *ezer* in a clearer perspective.

Neged is a Hebrew preposition, but when you translate it as an English preposition, the word becomes obscure. According to Brown, Driver, and Briggs, it should be translated, "according to what is in front of, equal, corresponding to."[1]

Dr. R. David Freedman, a specialist in Semitic languages, wrote that the most accurate translation is "a power (or strength) equal to him."[2] Eve was an equal and adequate strength, an equal and adequate partner for Adam. That is precisely why Adam exclaimed, "At last, bone of my bone, and flesh of my flesh" (*see* Genesis 2:23).

What parallel do we find in the New Testament account? Are we teammates in the Christian life even as Adam and Eve were suitable partners?

Paul gives us a glimpse of New Testament teamwork when he addresses the Philippians (1:27): ". . . So that whether I come and see you or remain absent, I may hear of you that you are standing firm in one spirit, with one mind striving together for the faith of the gospel." Two believers joined together in marriage are joined together in an even stronger bond—as brother and sister in Jesus Christ. The bond of human marriage is "till death us do part." The bond of brother and sister in the Lord Jesus Christ is eternal. As Adam and Eve were fitting or equal partners for the task set before them, even so "in Christ" marriage partners are laborers together for the sake of the Gospel.

One of the most enjoyable books I have read is the biography of Francis and Edith Schaeffer. In *The Tapestry* Edith writes a living account of team marriage and team ministry. She describes their partner relationship,

> The scope of going through life shoulder to shoulder in work, home, and vacation, includes a variety of changing "roles" if you want to use that word which I don't like. So I did dressmaking, and I designed, made and sold leather belts and buttons. . . . Fran shared in a weekly thorough house cleaning in which we polished everything, washed windows, shook out our little rag rugs, washed and waxed floors, and so on. . . . A homey feeling.[3]

When she describes the first time she met Francis, she writes,

> Our conversation was about serious things of Christianity— not just its defenses, but the wonder of all we believe. However, we had met on the battlefield and now forty-nine years later we are still fighting together on two sides of the room, so to speak, but on the same side of the issues in a diversity of places and in the midst of an ongoing history.[4]

Edith felt that her greatest contribution was assisting Francis in his work, but many people will remember her for her separate contribution, her books. Even though Francis and Edith have their names on different books, have spoken to different crowds, and counseled different individuals, the core of their ministry is the product of their unique relationship, each participating in each other's life through prayer, discussion, shared burdens, and following God's leading—together and separately. They were indeed equal and suitable partners. But more than that, they were "colaborers" for the sake of the Gospel.

Cleave

The next reference to God's creation of a man and a woman is in Genesis 2:24. "For this cause a man shall leave his father and his mother, and shall cleave to his wife...." This word *cleave* or its derivative is used some forty times in the Old Testament, including Psalms 102:5 (KJV) "... My bones cleave to my skin" and Joshua 23:8 (KJV): "But cleave unto the Lord...." Basically, the Hebrew word means to "cling, keep close," whether physically, in a personal relationship, or spiritually, in fellowship with God. And the verb is almost always used for a weaker person cleaving to a stronger. For example, it is used of Israel cleaving to God, but not the other way around.

This command, to cleave, was given to the man, not the woman, and the phrase is probably paralleled best in Ephesians 5:25: "Husbands, love your wives, just as Christ also loved the church and gave Himself up for her."

Does leaving and cleaving indicate that the man has authority over the wife? No. However it does indicate responsibility and dependency.

A Complete Union

The end of Genesis 2:24 reads, "... and they shall become one flesh." This phrase, "one flesh," means far more than physical union. It is complete union—emotional, mental, and physical—and this is consistent with everything God has said about man and woman so far.

Not very long ago, I was discussing this issue with some

friends. One woman argued that every situation calls for a leader and a follower. She quoted one Christian teacher, "Someone always has to go first through a revolving door."

I responded, "But does it always have to be the same person?"

Then she stated her case again, "One person must always be in charge."

I reworded my same response, "Do you mean the same person, in every situation must be in charge?" That conversation went round and round, but it brought to my mind numerous exceptions to the premise that one person must always be in charge: business partners, boards of directors, roommates, siblings, stockholders, democracies. Our own democracy illustrates this point. Our system of checks and balances is designed to prevent one person from ever assuming final authority in our country.

The New Testament church was to be governed by a conglomerate of elders (1 Peter 5:1, 2). Those strong in certain gifts were to lead others with those gifts (as the *team* of Priscilla and Aquila). Those gifted in Bible teaching (men or women) were to lead those weaker in the faith (as the *team* of Paul and Barnabas). Those good at administering or serving were to govern others in administering or serving (Acts 6, where a *team* of seven men was chosen to administer and serve tables). And Jesus sent the disciples out "two and two," never indicating that one had authority over the other (Luke 10:1). But consider also that prayer power and authority were heightened not by one person having the final word on what was to be prayed, but by two or more coming to "agreement" about prayer (Matthew 18:19). Some commentators believe that this passage in Matthew's Gospel relates to church discipline. If so, it merely serves to strengthen the case for team leadership. In fact, in the larger passage surrounding this verse (vv. 15–20), Jesus indicates that the power and authority of witnesses as well as the power to loose and bind on earth and heaven are facilitated by "agreement of two or more." The word *agree* is from the same root word as the word *agreement* in 1 Corinthians 7:5, which is an example of how decision making is to be done in marriage. The emphasis in these passages is on maturity in leadership. The Bible doesn't insist on single-person leadership. Harmonious leadership and authority by two or more is common in the Word of God.

In Genesis 1 and 2 we see that God developed Adam and Eve as a mutual union, not an organization, a political hierarchy, or a parent-child relationship. God gave *both* man and woman the same likeness, the same blessing, responsibility, authority, provision, partnership; and then He made them "one flesh"—a union! Yet does any gender-deferred order exist in marriage? Perhaps. But before we can understand what men and women are in marriage, it is essential to understand them as individuals.

The Creator's Opinion

What did Jesus say about leadership in marriage? Did He say who was to be in charge? Did He support or contradict the creation account?

Jesus said absolutely nothing on this important issue of leadership. On the contrary, He quoted Genesis 2:24, "For this cause a man shall leave his father and mother, and shall cleave to his wife; and the two shall become one flesh" (Matthew 19:5), and he indirectly questioned the double standard the Jews had devised concerning adultery (stoning only the woman, not the man) (John 8:1–11). But Jesus never taught or implied or reasoned from the position that one person or one sex should be in charge in marriage.

Why is the concept of "union" so difficult for some? I got a glimpse of the reason recently when a friend's husband called. "My wife," he began, "is making a lot of changes. After twelve years of marriage, she is telling me that she wants her own identity and that I'm standing in the way. I want Anne to be a full person, but I also want her to depend on me. That's a man's need, you know, for a woman to depend on him."

"Well," I replied, "what do you mean 'depend on you'?"

"Well," he answered, "I'd like to feel that I'm in charge. And I think I'm losing that responsibility."

"How does that make you feel?"

"It's making me feel very insecure and afraid that I might lose her altogether."

"Have you ever been loved by someone you did not control?" I asked.

He paused. "My parents," he offered.

"Could part of your fear, even a substantial part, be that you fear losing love and companionship if you cannot control Anne?"

"I see what you're getting at. Yes, maybe that is what I fear. But don't you think that God made men to be in charge, to have a certain amount of control over their wives?"

"Do you think control is needed to have a fulfilling marriage?" I returned.

"Well, isn't Rusty in control of your home?"

"No."

"Well, how do you keep order?"

"We both seek God's will and try to please Him and each other."

"Does that give you order?"

"Yes, far better order, plus security, balance, and two healthy, productive individuals, each striving to be all that God designed him or her to be."

"But, my wife isn't much of a Christian."

"What do you mean?"

"You see, she doesn't follow God the way you do."

"Maybe that's because she has been too busy following you," I suggested.

Our conversation ended with his saying that he would think about what I said.

Whom to Follow?

In my midtwenties I made a critical decision. Simultaneously I was hearing two different messages in the Christian community and had to decide which one I was going to follow. On the one hand, I was told to become all *God* wanted me to become: develop my gifts, be filled with the Holy Spirit and led by Him, study and obey the Bible, share my faith, develop godly strength and character, learn to make biblical decisions, excel in leadership.

The other message, taught right alongside the first, said a Christian woman should prepare for marriage, which included being ready to fit into her husband's plan, not threaten him by being a more mature Christian than he, not make more money or be more established in gifts and abilities than he, let him be the spiritual leader in the relationship.

This is exactly the dilemma we must consider.

As we have already seen, at creation and re-creation, God has laid down certain fixed principles.

Both men and women are:

At Creation	At Re-creation (New Birth)
Made in God's image	"In Christ"
Blessed by God	Given every spiritual blessing in the heavenly places
Responsible to populate and subdue earth	Responsible to populate heaven, build up the body of Christ, and glorify God
To rule every living creature	To reign as kings and priests before God
Given physical provision	Provided every need
Pronounced "good"	Beloved children
Fitting and equal partners	Colaborers
One flesh	One spirit

It is His preeminent plan and purpose that Christians operate as outlined in the right-hand column. *Any teaching on marriage or ministry that violates, diminishes, suppresses, impedes, or is inconsistent with each individual's (husband's or wife's) identity, blessing, responsibility, authority, laboring, or union needs to be reex-*

amined. Any teaching on marriage or ministry that does not encourage the above needs to be reexamined. Christian marriage is the union of *two individual believers.*

"Lord," I finally prayed, after hearing the two contradictory teachings on what I was to be as a Christian and as a woman, "it looks as if I have one of two choices. I can either be what a man is supposed to need, so that I will be appealing to men, *or* I can become all that *You* want me to be, develop all *You* made me to be, and trust *You* for a man who loves me as *You* designed me to be. Lord, I choose to follow You."

Now, years later, I have no doubt that I made the right decision.

Soon after we married, someone asked Rusty, "Do you ever feel threatened or intimidated because of Linda's writing or other gifts?"

"I did briefly when we first met."

"What did you do about it?"

"I recognized I had a problem and confessed it to God as *sin.* Then I asked God to give me the security I needed to see and respond to Linda primarily as His person, not mine."

Today, when I speak, sing, or have a big success, Rusty's face lights up. He takes an interest in my involvements and rejoices in my accomplishments *just as I do in his.*

At one of my first public performances, I was singing for a large gathering of Christians. Rusty was with me and had been helping me set up my equipment. When I was introduced, my sound system failed. I traded mikes and chatted with the audience while awaiting a solution. Finally Rusty discovered that the plug was not firmly in the socket. At last, my singing got under way.

After the performance I met Rusty out in the hall. He looked worn out, even frazzled. I asked him what was the matter.

"I felt like a mother whose kid was giving her first recital," he sighed.

My productivity and victories and my husband's resulting pride in me come because I made a choice to be what *God* wanted me to be. I feel the same pride about Rusty. He is an accomplished writer and speaker with a significant impact for Christ. I participate in his ministry by writing and critiquing his speeches, praying for him, and helping him think through important decisions. How glorious to serve God, rather than men!

What a delight to be a fitting and equal partner, to see my husband leave father and mother and cleave to me, and to be part of a union. All this accomplished without either of us being the boss or final decision maker.

"All right," you may say, "maybe in light of the creation passage this would work. But what about the Fall? Women have been cursed. They must be ruled over."

FIVE

Overcoming

Can sin and its consequences be called good? Should sin and its consequences be perpetuated? *Or* are sin and its consequences to be overcome through Christ?

Consider this story: A Christian couple have a teenage son, Pete. Shortly after his sixteenth birthday, his dad and mom give him a car. They also provide him with sufficient money to maintain it, while he finishes school. But he is clearly told that the gas money he receives from his parents is for school events only.

More than once Pete runs out of gas, requiring his mom or dad to come and get him. In spite of repeated admonitions, Pete fails to act responsibly. Further, he consistently chooses to spend his gas money on other pursuits.

Finally, his father and mother sit down with him.

"Son, you have been consistently negligent in maintaining your car. You have been using money we gave you for purposes other than we agreed. All our words haven't seemed to help you remember to do what's right, so we're not giving you any more money for your car."

No car allowance is a painful way for Pete to remember to be responsible. But Pete finds a part-time job and is soon driving his car again. He even further redeems the situation by earning extra money for his other interests.

Perpetuated Sin?

When faced with his options, Pete had another choice, though not a very desirable one. He might have thought, *Well, because I disobeyed, I shouldn't drive the car. After all, losing my allowance from Mom and Dad was the result of my own sin. Because I have no money for gas, I can see that God doesn't want me to drive a car.* That perspective would have paralleled my initial questions: Are sin and its consequences good things to be perpetuated? The alternative Pete actually chose reflected an affirmative answer to my second question. Are sin and its consequences to be redeemed and overcome?

Adam and Eve faced this dilemma. They disobeyed God (Genesis 3:1–6) and certain consequences fell to both the man and the woman. The primary consequence was that sin entered the human race. Only a few of its many consequences are stated in God's words to Eve in Genesis 3:16: " '. . . I will greatly multiply your pain in childbirth, In pain you shall bring forth children; Yet your desire shall be for your husband, And he shall rule over you.' "

We have seen God's basic design and intent for the man and the woman as to creation. Now it seems that all is lost. After the "Fall" (a term referring to men and women losing fellowship with God), it seems that the union is broken, that one sex is in charge, while the other sex follows.

But let's consider further.

First note that God addressed the woman in Genesis 3:16, not the man. No responsibility or authority was given by God to the man in regard to his wife. God did not address the man and say, "From now on you are my chosen leader." This is a *very* important point. The man was not given authority over the woman.

Second, the woman is told, "Your desire shall be for your husband, And he shall rule over you." What did this mean?

Old Testament scholar Dr. Katherine Bushnell pursued the Septuagint, Peshitta, Samaritan, Pentateuch, Old Latin, Sahidic, Bahine, and Aetheopic versions and concluded that a more accurate translation for the word "desire" is "turning." Dr. Bushnell's rendering of the verse is "Thou art turning away! [from God] to thy husband, and he will rule over thee."[1] This principle can be seen in many areas of our spiritual lives. As one turns from God, he or she is ruled by the world, the flesh, and the devil. (*Note:* Some versions, such as the Jerusalem Bible, translate "he shall rule over you" as "he will lord it over you"—a system Jesus denounces in Matthew 20:20–28.)

One teacher suggests that Genesis 3:16 reads, "The woman would try to conquer the man but that he would (and even must) rule her." He goes on to point out that a man should never let a woman conquer him. This teacher fails to assess that if one part of this *consequence* is "trying to conquer," then another *consequence* is "ruling." In other words, the wife trying to conquer isn't the problem, and the husband successfully ruling isn't the solution. Both are the result or consequence of sin entering the world.

There is another interpretation of this verse. The word *desire* may be seen as a proper longing. (The same Hebrew word is used in the Song of Solomon 7:10 when the Shulammite says of the man "his desire is for me.") The desire may be for the oneness they experienced in the Garden before sin entered, but man, in "dominating" that desire, would thwart God's original purpose.

No matter how one chooses to define a woman's desire, a man ruling his wife is a *consequence* of sin.

But an even greater consequence of sin occurred in the Garden. Before Adam and Eve partook of the fruit, God warned them, "But from the tree of the knowledge of good and evil you shall not eat, for in the day that you eat from it you shall surely die" (Genesis 2:17). What kind of death was God speaking about? A spiritual death. As a result of dying spiritually, Adam and Eve would eventually die physically. Later, Paul announces that this dilemma is faced by all (Romans 5:12). But do we remain "dead in our sins"?

Both the Hebrew construction and the usage in both Genesis 2:17 and 3:17–19 indicate a predictive sense.

Consider other predictive verses: ". . . And all liars, their part will be in the lake that burns with fire . . ." (Revelation 21:8). ". . . For all those who take up the sword shall perish by the sword" (Matthew 26:52). ". . . Visiting the iniquity of the fathers on the children . . ." (Exodus 20:5). "The wages of sin is death . . ." (Romans 6:23).

Are sin and its consequences to be perpetuated at all cost, or are sin and its consequences to be redeemed and overcome? The Genesis 3 passage is saying how the world because of sin *will* go, not how it *must* go. The "curse" is best understood as a *prediction*, not a *decree*. Some teach that Genesis 3:16 means that the husband must rule the wife because God decreed that this must be. One man remarked to a friend of mine, "How dare you challenge the curse?"

"Oh, you like the curse?" she responded.

"Well, it doesn't make any difference whether or not I like the curse. God made the curse to be followed, and men are to rule women."

"I think you like the curse," she replied. "I'm not sure what to say about a person who likes to see sin and its consequences perpetuated. Besides, I don't see you perpetuating the problems presented to Adam in the Garden. You use fertilizer, weed killers, and other things to help stop the growth of thorns and thistles. Isn't that trying to negate the curse?"

Some, seeing the curse as a decree, teach that God will bring judgment upon the woman who is not under her husband's authority, as Jeannie and Mark illustrate.

When they first met, Jeannie and Mark imagined an exciting

future together. "We didn't understand why other couples fought so much," said Mark. "We were so compatible that we envisioned great happiness and Christian service."

But soon after they married, Jeannie and Mark realized they were not so compatible after all, especially when it came to money. After Jeannie had temporarily lost control of her checkbook, Mark told her she could no longer be trusted with her name on the checking account.

"I treated her like a child," says Mark, "but I felt justified. After all, she was under my umbrella of authority and protection, and I had to determine what was best."

But Jeannie, who had been under the same teaching, could not handle the humiliation and stress of having no money of her own. Whenever she needed something, she had to beg and justify her requests. Finally, she told Mark that she was going to get a part-time job so she could have some spending money. "No," refused Mark, "and, remember, if you get outside my authority, God will judge you."

"I was scared to death," says Jeannie. "The mere mention of a part-time job had made me paranoid. When I got in the car to go shopping, I thought for sure I would have an accident. After all, if Mark did not approve, God did not approve."

After a disagreement, another woman, Margaret, was told by her husband, "You must cease all of your Christian activities. You have rebelled against me, and you are no longer qualified to serve God."

A Christian man said to his wife, "You'll just have to adjust to my schedule. God has put me in charge of things, and I am choosing to work long hours." This man averaged about three hours a week with his family.

A fourth husband who regularly slept with another woman told his wife, "You will just have to learn to accept the fact that I'm a two-woman man."

These illustrations are not uncommon. Yet they are sometimes approved, even in the church, because people believe that God decreed that man *should* rule the woman. What these illustrations really point to are the results of sin: men who, because of sin, rule their wives. Was man given this kind of authority over woman? God never decreed or predicted anything different *to the man* about his role in marriage after the Fall. The creation plan was not done away with; its basic design and intent were not challenged after the Fall. The original plan stands firm, but sin mars it.

Sin can often be very subtle.

"I believe we have a partnership marriage," one man shared with me. Yet when I was alone with his wife, she confided that she had to beg him for every penny she received. Obviously he dominated the purse strings.

"We believe in teamwork," a woman shared, yet she had been holding something over her husband's head for years, threatening to expose him if she didn't get her way.

Though some of these illustrations may be extreme, the basic attitudes I want to challenge are sometimes quiet but piercing, respectable but crippling. They can often be polite but deadly or cloaked in Scripture but demeaning. Some of these sins abiding in Christian homes may be as harmful as the carefully plotted deeds of the unrighteous.

Nevertheless the need to control or rule another and the helpless state of being controlled can be overcome.

After God announced the consequences of sin entering the human race, He did an amazing thing. In Genesis 3:7–11 the man and the woman realized that they were naked and became ashamed, and 3:21 states, "And the Lord God made garments of skin for Adam and his wife, and clothed them."

God Himself made provision for their sin. In this case, He took care of their physical need, but later He also took care of the psychological and spiritual consequences. We look back at the cross of Christ, and in faith, have deliverance. Adam and Eve looked forward to the cross for deliverance, as decreed in Genesis 3:15, when God addressed Satan, the serpent, who tempted Eve: "And I will put enmity Between you and the woman, And between your seed and her seed; He shall bruise you on the head, And you shall bruise him on the heel." Satan had struck an awful blow, but it compared to an injury on the heel. How much more serious, even fatal, would be the blow to the head of Satan that Jesus struck by His death and resurrection.

The Overcomer

When Christ died on the cross, He bore the sins of the world. And because He rose from the dead, we can live victoriously even in the midst of a fallen world. Yes, sin and its consequences are still around, but, in Christ, there is the means of overcoming, if we trust and look to Him.

Let's be more specific. Paul writes in Galatians 3:28: ". . . [In Christ] there is neither male nor female. . . ." This verse is an announcement to all of full restoration to both men and women. Both have a higher calling than that to which sin or society relegates them.

A woman with whom I am closely associated came to Christ later in life. All her married life, she had been at the bidding of a very insecure and dominant husband. Her husband did not make her a victim; she was vulnerable and insecure because of her great need for love and approval, which was not yet being met in Jesus Christ. One Sunday morning this woman placed her life in God's hands. At forty-five years of age she sensed, for the first time, that she was deeply loved and forgiven. A miraculous thing began to happen. She began to gain self-respect, something she had never sought. From this love and better opinion of herself, she began to view what was happening in her marriage differently. She began to develop inner strength and didn't need to be a victim any longer.

One day she clearly told her husband that she would no longer stand for his treating her badly. Of course, that was not the end of it. But from that very day, a new relationship grew. Her husband could not mistreat her and get away with it. As a result, he began to view her differently. Over a period of time, he began to respect her, because she respected herself. Now, more than twenty-five years later, their marriage has become more mutual and fulfilling. One of the best results has been the mellowing of her husband's character. His dominance, challenged time and time again, has lessened, and he has come to see his own insecurities and to grow out of many of them. Their children, who had many times been ostracized by such a domineering father, became reconciled as he also began to see them differently.

The results of sin entering the world have affected *every* man, woman, and child. But Jesus Christ has redeemed us and provides victorious power to overcome our sinfulness and the often painful results of the sins of others. He makes a difference in the lives of those who seek and follow Him. A positive difference!

We've seen the dilemma the Fall has presented and the need for redemption to overcome vulnerability and dominance. But what about Ephesians 5? Doesn't that present a different view from the Genesis account's?

SIX

Head and
Submit:
Definitions,
Please

As we've already noted Christian marriage consists of *two individual* Christians. Each individual brings into the marriage his or her own identity "in Christ" with equal blessings, responsibilities, authority, provision, and Spirit. In marriage these unique individuals are united into a special partnership.

Each one, who is led of God individually, is now part of a union, seeking God's leading both *individually* and *corporately.* As marriage partners they strive for harmonious living, greater service, and glorifying God as a team. For "two *are* better than one" and a *"cord of three strands is not quickly torn apart"* (Ecclesiastes 4:9, 12, *italics added*).

But the Epistle to the Ephesians raises some questions about what we've established so far. Before you read this chapter any further, I suggest you read the entire Book of Ephesians for yourself.

The first chapter of Ephesians discusses what it means to be "in Christ" and all that is now available to us as children of God. Paul expands on this in chapter 2 and then shares the mystery of "Christ in us" in chapter 3.

In chapter 4 Paul switches to the practical dimensions of our being "in Christ" and Christ being "in us." Much of his advice deals with Christians working together as a body. Note 4:3: "Being diligent to preserve the unity of the Spirit in the bond of peace," and 4:4–6: "There is one body and one Spirit, just as also you were called in one hope of your calling; one Lord, one faith, one baptism, one God and Father of all who is over all and through all and in all."

A real emphasis in Ephesians 4:1–6 is *unity*. Paul follows up with a list of various gifts and sums up the passage by stating that gifts are distributed for the following reasons: "For the equipping of the saints for the work of service, to the building up of the body of Christ; until we all attain to the unity of the faith, and of the knowledge of the Son of God, to a mature man, to the measure of the stature which belongs to the fulness of Christ" (vv. 12, 13), and, "But speaking the truth in love, we are to grow up in all aspects into Him, who is the head, even Christ, from whom the whole body, being fitted and held together by that which every joint supplies, according to the proper working of each individual part, causes the growth of the body for the building up of itself in love" (vv. 15, 16).

Jesus Is the Head

Note who is called "head" in this context, and note what it means. Jesus is called the head of men and women in the church. As the head supplies the body, the body will grow.

Head presents a lot of problems for people in the English-speaking world, for the word means different things to us from what it did to the Greeks. And for that reason there has been a great deal of discussion over the word *head* in recent years. (The Evangelical Theological Society focused on the meaning of this word at their annual meeting, in November

1986.) One of the most influential writings on the subject is by Berkeley Mickelsen, professor emeritus of New Testament, at Bethel Seminary, and his wife, Alvera, past professor of journalism at Bethel College.

In an insightful article in *Christianity Today* they analyze the meaning of this Greek word, *kephale*, rendered "head" in Ephesians 4:15 and 5:23. Drawing on secular research that reveals what *kephale* would have meant to the first-century Greek reader, the Mickelsens then apply their findings to Paul's Epistles. Consider their concluding paragraphs:

> If Paul had been thinking about authority, or leader, there were easily understood Greek words he could have used, and which he did use in other places. He used *exousia* (authority) in Romans 13:1–2; and *archon* (meaning leader, ruler or commander) in Romans 13:3.
>
> The passages where Paul used *kephale* in a figurative way make better sense and present a more exalted, completed view of Christ when *kephale* is read with recognized Greek meanings that would have been familiar to his original readers. Among these meanings are: exalted originator and completor; source, base, derivation; enabler (one who brings to completion); source of life; top or crown.
>
> Can we legitimately read an English or Hebrew meaning into the word *head* in the New Testament, when both context and secular Greek literature of New Testament times seem to indicate that "superior rank" or "authority over" were not meanings the apostle Paul had in mind? Has our misunderstanding of some of these passages been used to support the concept of male dominance that has ruled most pagan and secular societies since the beginning of recorded history? Has this misunderstanding also robbed us of the richer, more exalted picture of Christ that Paul was trying to give us?[1]

The Greeks did not have access to modern scientific data that indicates that the brain controls the body. In fact, such an idea was largely foreign to their thinking. While Plato believed the head was the "root" of the body, Aristotle believed the heart to be the ruler, Epicurus the chest, and the Stoics were divided.[2] Most believed that the controller of the body was the heart, from which will and emotion came (*see* Romans 10:9, 10). The basic meaning of *head* was "extremity." All other meanings were derived from that.

In the context of Ephesians, Jesus is referred to as the source of life as top or crown or as the enabler and completer of the body of Christ. Of course Jesus is also the authority of the church, but that is established in other passages. In Ephesians 1:20-23 Christ is described as the "top" or "crown" and in Ephesians 4:15 He is the "source of life."

(*Note:* The full text of the Mickelsens' article appears in the Appendix. Before you proceed reading this chapter, turn to page 241 and read their work, as a thorough understanding of the word *kephale* is necessary.)

Because we Christians are part of a body (the church) supplied by Jesus Christ, the head, Paul admonishes us to not live as non-Christians. We needn't walk in darkness (Ephesians 4:17-24).

Then he continues: "Therefore, laying aside falsehood, speak truth, each one of you, with his neighbor, for we are members of one another" (4:25). Practical application follows, and chapter 14 closes with "And be kind to one another, tender-hearted, forgiving each other, just as God in Christ also has forgiven you" (v. 32).

Chapter 5 of Ephesians opens with the admonition to be imitators of God and illustrates some specifics of what that may entail (vv. 1-5). Then follows the command to walk in the light, not the darkness (vv. 6-14), and to walk wisely, not foolishly (vv. 15-17).

Submitting One to Another

Verses 18-21 continue: "And do not get drunk with wine, for that is dissipation, but be filled with the Spirit, speaking to one another in psalms and hymns and spiritual songs, singing and making melody with your heart to the Lord; always giving thanks for all things in the name of our Lord Jesus Christ to God, even the Father; and be subject to one another in the fear of Christ." (This last phrase is a participle, not an imperative.

It would be better translated *"subjecting yourselves* to one another in reverence for Christ.") The main verb in verse 18 "be *filled* with the Spirit" presents an imperative command. Then verses 19–21 tell us how this is manifest in a list of five participles: in speaking, in singing songs, in singing psalms, in giving thanks, and in subjecting ourselves to one another. The use of the participle *subjecting* indicates voluntarily yielding of ourselves *in reverence for Christ.*

What does "subjecting yourselves to one another" mean? To understand, let's look at how this word *subject* or *submit* is used aside from the Ephesians 5 and marriage passages.

Submission is one of the many beautiful teachings of the Christian life, and it is the foundation of this entire passage on marriage. Let's take a closer look at this principle.

Consider a conversation between the twelve disciples and Jesus:

> And there arose also a dispute among them as to which one of them was regarded to be greatest. And He said to them, "The kings of the Gentiles lord it over them; and those who have authority over them are called 'Benefactors.' But not so with you, but let him who is the greatest among you become as the youngest, and the leader as the servant. For who is greater, the one who reclines at table, or the one who serves? Is it not the one who reclines at table? But I am among you as the one who serves.
>
> Luke 22:24–27

The message is rephrased when the mother of James and John came to Jesus and asked that her sons sit on His right and on His left, when He came into His kingdom. Jesus answered: *"You know that the rulers of the Gentiles lord it over them, and their great men exercise authority over them. It is not so among you, but whoever wishes to become great among you shall be your servant;* and whoever wishes to be first among you shall be your slave; just as the Son of Man did not come to be served, but to serve, and to give His life a ransom for many" (Matthew 20:25–28, *italics added*).

Jesus points out that wanting to be the ruler, in charge, at the top, or the boss is not a proper attitude. What attitude of servanthood was Jesus referring to?

> Have this attitude in yourselves which was also in Christ Jesus, who, although He existed in the form of God, did not regard equality with God a thing to be grasped, but emptied Himself, taking the form of a bond servant, and being made in the likeness of men. And being found in appearance as a man, He humbled Himself by becoming obedient to the point of death, even death on a cross.
>
> Philippians 2:5–8

Most people see *ruling* as greatness. As a result of the Fall the world sees exercising authority over another as something to be coveted. Many, in fact, have a need to be in charge. The desire to be in control often speaks of insecurity, fear, low self-esteem, or pride. Jesus made it clear that being in charge is not to be our goal in the kingdom of God: *Serving* one another is to be our goal.

What else does the Scripture tell us about the mode of relating in the church of Jesus Christ?

> At that time the disciples came to Jesus, saying, "Who then is greatest in the kingdom of heaven?" And He called a child to Himself and stood him in their midst, and said, "Truly I say to you, unless you are converted and become like children, you shall not enter the kingdom of heaven. Whoever then humbles himself as this child, he is the greatest in the kingdom of heaven."
>
> Matthew 18:1–4

Again Paul writes, "You, my brothers, were called to be free. But do not use your freedom to indulge the sinful nature; rather, serve one another in love" (Galatians 5:13 NIV).

Paul's *emphases* are, as Jesus':

> Serve one another (Galatians 5:13)
> Encourage one another (1 Thessalonians 5:11)

Pray for one another (Colossians 1:9)
Build up one another (1 Thessalonians 5:11)
Honor one another (Romans 13:7)
Prefer one another (Romans 12:10)
Submit to one another (Ephesians 5:21)

At first glance, a Christian must wonder how in the world he or she can be subject to or submissive to all other Christians. The root meaning of the word *subject* or *submit* (*hypotasso*) is "to order," "to arrange," or "to put in place." In Pauline writings it occurs twenty-three times as a verb and eight times in noun forms. In all uses between humans it is voluntary. That is, nowhere is one believer or king or Christian leader directed to subject someone else to himself or herself. That prerogative is left to God (1 Corinthians 15:24–28; Romans 8:20; Philippians 3:21; Ephesians 1:21, 22). This word has also been used to refer to the ordering of a military column, but in the context of our discussion, whether submitting to one another or wives to husbands, this is not an appropriate rendition. Submission is an attitude recognizing the true place of whomever we are told to submit to. It is important, as with any interpretation of Scripture, that we view a word in context.

Even though we may feel more gifted than a fellow believer, or more mature, we must recognize that person's "place" as being "in Christ." It is his or her position "in Christ" to which we must submit. As we live with humility we will see others as more important than ourselves (Philippians 2:5–8). Further, *submit* is an attitude, as opposed to an action. *Obey* is an action word, but must never be confused with *submit*, which is an attitude of preference. Submission is one of the most beautiful elements of the Christian life. To submit ourselves to one another is a needed emphasis in this generation.

Within the context of our being united in Christ and Christ indwelling all of us, we are told that Christ is the head (enabler, completer, source) of the body of believers. We are instructed to submit to or be subject to or prefer or serve one another in order that the body may work properly.

Ephesians 5:21 is followed by a frequently misunderstood

CALLED TO UNITY

teaching about marriage. Some Christian teachers purport to separate the command "be subject one to another" from the marriage passage. As one man suggested to me: "Ephesians 5:21 is for all believers. It is not intended to apply to Christian marriage."

"Not so," I replied. "It is directly connected to marriage and is even more specifically seen as one of three themes of Christian marriage: being filled with the Spirit, praising and thanking God, and being subject to one another. The Greek links this section together. We dare not divide it."

How do we know this? In some translations, verses 21 and 22 are separated by a paragraph break. The Greek language would never allow for such division. In fact, the words *be subject* are not in the best original Greek versions of verse 22. It merely says "wives to husbands" and includes no verb at all. The translators include "be subject" because they believe the phrase is closely linked to the previous verse. In most Greek texts, verse 22 appears as a new sentence, but "being subject" in verse 21 is the verb that governs it. We might better translate it:

> And being subject to one another in reverence of Christ. Wives, to your own husbands, as to the Lord. For the husband is the head [enabler or completer] of the wife, as Christ also is the head [enabler or completer] of the church, He Himself being the Savior of the body. But as the church is subject to Christ, so also the wives to their husbands in everything.
> Ephesians 5:22-24

Evelyn Christiansen, noted Christian teacher and author, writes:

> In Ephesians 5:22 we always refer to women being submissive to their husbands, but the verse preceding it is grammatically part of the verse to wives. The preceding verse reads, "Submit to one another." For some reason we've got those verses separated. In fact, we even put Bible headings between those verses. And grammatically we can't divide the two. The

husband should submit to the wife and the wife to the husband.[3]

When one man challenged me, saying that submission meant a woman should do what her husband said, I asked him if "submitting to one another" (v. 21) meant he took orders from other Christians. As he demurred, I pointed out that verses 21 and 22 use the same Greek verb: If he expected his wife to obey him on that basis, he in turn had to obey other believers.

What does "Wives, . . . to your own husbands, as to the Lord" mean? I have heard women say that it means the wife is to submit to her husband just the same way she submits to the Lord. But look again. As in verse 21, where it says we are to subject ourselves to one another in reverence to Christ, so wives are to husbands with the *attitude* of serving God. A similar phrase is used in Colossians 3:23: "Whatever you do, do your work heartily, as for the Lord. . . ." Does this mean that your boss is the Lord or like the Lord? No. It means that our mind-set is always to present an attitude as to the Lord.

What does it mean to be subject to your husband as to Christ *in everything*? Well, just that. As the husband is told to submit to his wife so she is told to submit to her husband with the same attitude that she serves Christ.

Head: In Word Usage and Context

The same word for *head* (referring to Jesus) in Ephesians 4:15, 16 is used in chapter 5, referring to the husband. In chapter 5 neither the *word usage* nor *context* indicates that authority is implied. If Paul had wanted a word for "authority," he could have used one from the Greek (*exousia* or *archon*); then, by altering the context, he could have said: "The husband is the authority of the wife just as Christ is the authority of the church. (He Himself being the leader of the church.) Husbands lead or rule your wives just as Christ leads or rules the church and instructs her what to do, that she might be obedient to Him and follow His decisions."

Or Paul could have written about another aspect of Christ: "The husband is the mediator of the wife as Christ is the mediator of the church. . . ."

Or Paul could have referred to yet another aspect of Christ: "The husband is the judge of the wife as Christ is the judge of the church. . . ."

But instead the passage says: "For the husband is the head [enabler or completer] of the wife, as Christ also is the head [enabler or completer] of the church, He Himself being the Savior of the body. . . . Husbands, love your wives, just as Christ also loved the church and gave Himself up for her."

Not an Unlimited Analogy

Read the passage again and note that it does not say that the man is to the wife *just* as Christ is to the church. There are a great many analogies and comparisons in Scripture. Always they are to be limited to their use in context. For example, Isaiah 40:31 says that those who wait on the Lord will, like eagles, mount up with wings. But the context does not say we are like eagles in *other* ways or *all* ways. For instance, we do not peck our young to death if they fall out of the nest. So in Ephesians the husband is the enabler and completer of the wife as Christ is the enabler and completer of the church. He is not, as Christ is, the Authority, the Judge, the Creator, the Empowerer, the Forgiver, or the Mediator of the wife.

The husband is not just what Christ is to the church. The husband is the "head," *enabler* or *completer* of the wife as Christ is the *enabler* or *completer* of the church. The context rightly limits itself by the meaning of the word *head*. And it limits itself immediately afterward by the phrase "He Himself being the Savior of the body." This phrase is of the verse. It may be separated by a comma, but not by a period. It is, in fact, a clarification of what has just been said.

As Paul further clarifies what he means by "head," he uses the word *Savior*, which is *sōtēr* in Greek, from the root word *sōizō*, meaning "to make whole or complete, recover, save."

This word is used of the woman with the issue of blood. She said, "If I only touch his garment, I shall *get well* [*sōizō* literally "to be made whole or complete"]" (Matthew 9:21, *italics added*). So immediately after mentioning *head* (as enabler or completer), Paul uses another phrase "He, Himself being the savior of the body," to bring home the same point.

The Context Supports This Meaning of *Head*

Husbands, love your wives, just as Christ also loved the church and *gave Himself up for her;* that He might *sanctify her,* having *cleansed her by the washing of water with the word,* that He might *present to Himself the church in all her glory,* having no spot or wrinkle or any such thing; but that she should be holy and blameless. So husbands ought also to *love their own wives* as their own bodies. He who loves his own wife loves himself; for no one ever hated his own flesh, but *nourishes and cherishes it,* just as Christ also does the church, because we are members of His body.

Ephesians 5:25–30, italics added

(*Note:* Every italicized verb illustrates our established definition of *kephale* as "enabler" or "completer.")

The husband is the enabler or completer of the wife in the following ways:

Head (enabler or completer) of love—v. 25. (*Note:* He is to love her as his own body, vv. 28, 29).

Head (enabler or completer) of sacrifice—v. 25. (He is to sacrifice and subject himself to her to the point of dying for her.)

Head (enabler or completer) of ministering to her—vv. 26, 27.

Head (enabler or completer) of nourishing and cherishing—v. 29.

One way to understand *kephale* is to see how a stream is the enabler or completer of a river. As a stream pours itself into the river, the river grows and prospers. Just so, the husband is to pour his life into that of his wife, so she might become all she is designed to be. If the husband follows the example of Christ, he will encourage his wife to be greater than himself.

Jesus said, "... Greater works than these shall he do; because I go to the Father" (John 14:12).

Competition is removed from marriage when the attention or focus of the husband is on "what I can do to help my wife become all she was meant to be—all she is gifted for." When he asks, "How can I enable her to use her talents in a greater or more productive way?" he no more fears her becoming greater than he than a manager fears that the performer he represents will outshine him. With both husband and wife, the better one does, the better they both are doing their job. Contrary to the world's system, which says someone has to be boss, Jesus would encourage us all to minister to one another, including our spouses, that they may be more important, more usable, than we are.

What *Head* Does Not Mean

So far we see the husband as the enabler or completer. But none of the following statements or concepts have been alluded to:

The husband is to make the final decision
The husband is to rule the wife
The husband has the final responsibility
The husband is to delegate responsibility to the wife
The husband alone answers to God for the family
The husband decides how the wife will live
The husband makes the plans; the wife fits into them

All the above are human assumptions, rather than biblical statements. Maybe Paul could see the dangers of carrying the analogy of Christ and the church too far, for he continues: "For this *cause* a man shall leave his father and mother, and shall cleave to his wife; and the two shall become one flesh. This mystery is great; but I am speaking with reference to Christ and the church" (vv. 31, 32, *italics added*).

What did Paul mean? Here he's been talking about Christ and the church and husband and wife. Then after quoting the original Genesis account of the two becoming one flesh (indicating that the Fall had not altered God's original plan), he states that this is a mystery; and the mystery, he cautions us, really refers to Christ and the church.

I suspect Paul might have been giving balance to his presentation, for he continues, "Nevertheless [even though I am speaking of Christ and the church] let each individual among you also love his own wife even as himself; and let the wife see to it that she respect her husband" (v. 33). Paul's statement should encourage us to make sure we have seen this limited analogy within context.

Mutual Submission

The husband and wife are asked to submit to each other, as all members of Christ's body are to submit to one another. In fact, it is the theme and essence of this passage (Ephesians 5:21). By illustration, the husband is asked to submit to a greater degree, "give himself up for her." Although the wife is not asked to submit or sacrifice to the point of dying for her husband, teaching such as "Greater love has no one than this, that one lay down his life for his friends" (John 15:13) would lead me to believe that submitting to the point of death may be in line for all believers. Jesus is the example for all believers. Think how Jesus submitted to His disciples. He washed their feet. He cooked them breakfast. He died for them. He put their needs above His own, which is the full essence of the word *submit*. Love compelled Him to put their needs first, and love compels a husband and wife to put each other first.

Mutual submission launches this passage (v. 21) and is illustrated throughout. Yet some Christian men have trouble with the concept of submitting to their wives. Serving a wife and being the source of her becoming all God designed her to be comes harder than making decisions for her or running the show.

But every person who enters the kingdom of God needs a make-over. There is not a man or woman alive who, upon becoming a child of God, doesn't have a lot of kinks that need to be worked out. Rusty says, "When I entered the Christian life,

I had plenty of kinks. Still do. My needs to be respected, needed, loved, and approved were as great as anyone's, and it has taken a while to get me to a point where most of the time I love serving as much as being served. (I am still learning.) But I have found there is real freedom in not having to be 'in charge.' It has taken some doing to resist the desire—and at times the felt need—to be in control. But I am not to be in charge of Linda. I'm to be a servant to her."

The same is true of me. I am not to try to control Rusty, but to seek to honor and please him.

"But doesn't Colossians 3:18 command a wife to obey her husband?" a woman asked me.

"It appears so," I returned, "because some English translators use the word *obey* in the text. But the Greek word is the same as the one used in Ephesians 5:21, *hypotasso*, meaning to 'submit.'"

"Well, then," she replied, "since women are repeatedly told to submit, it must be something we are to do more than men."

But Paul mentioned submission in relation to women only in his letters to Ephesus and Colossae, cities in which women may have manipulated men in pagan temple worship. The women in those environments may have needed an extra reminder, but those passages in no way diminish the message to men to submit.

Another woman questioned, "Isn't it demeaning to say that a husband enables or completes a wife?"

In response, I recalled a scene from the Garden of Eden.

> Then the Lord God said, "It is not good for the man to be alone; I will make him a 'corresponding, equal fitting, strength and partner' for him. . . ." And the Lord God fashioned into a woman the rib which He had taken from the man, and brought her to the man. And the man said, "This is now bone of my bones, and flesh of my flesh. She shall be called Woman, because she was taken out of Man."
>
> *See* Genesis 2:18, 22, 23

Now hear Paul. "However, in the Lord, neither is woman independent of man, nor is man independent of woman. For as the woman originates from man, so also the man has his birth through the woman; and all things originate from God" (1 Corinthians 11:11, 12).

"Originator," "completer," "enabler," "source"? Do you see the completed circle? In Ephesians 5 the husband is the one who brings to completion. In Genesis the woman is taken from man and then completes him. In 1 Corinthians both are originators and enablers of one another.

Am I establishing exact parallels? No, I am not prepared to go that far. But the parallels nevertheless are here to consider.

At a recent men's retreat a pastor drew the following on the blackboard:

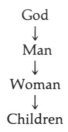

God
↓
Man
↓
Woman
↓
Children

"How many believe," he asked, "that this is God's order for the home?" Just about every hand in the room went up. "No," explained the pastor, "this is biblically incorrect. The diagram should look like this:

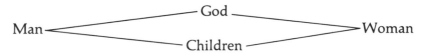

Man ———————————— God ———————————— Woman
——————— Children ———————

"God," he continued, "is the authority of both the man and woman, who in turn are to submit to each other."

One husband, Terry, shares: "When I first met Kathy, I knew very little about 'laying down my life' for her. But I knew a lot about my own needs. In my first years of marriage I really felt justified in telling Kathy that she was not submissive enough. Actually, I hated conflict and I felt that our marriage ran smoother when I was in charge.

CALLED TO UNITY

"Then, through the urging of my pastor, I began to search the Scriptures on marriage, and I was convicted. I realized that my main motivations were to keep the peace and control any attitude or discussion that threatened my own security. How far my motivations were from a sacrificial attitude! Yet I would tell Kathy that her attitude of wanting to have more was the reason for our increasing quarrels. I had the ability to beat her down with Scripture and ensure that she did not make waves.

"But since I really wanted to be God's man, I found a growing lack of peace within myself. Thank God, I faced it. But then I had another problem. Looking at my own selfishness, I became afraid that I could not change. After numerous attempts, I finally threw myself on the Lord. With His inner help, over a period of time I ceased trying to be in charge of Kathy and started, when arguments came, to ask myself several questions:

"Am I trying to control Kathy, or do I recognize God's control over her?

"Am I being honest about my real motivation?

"Is my attitude one of real love and sacrifice for Kathy, or am I just pretending to love her, while masking selfishness?

"Am I God's source of love, cherishing, ministering, and sacrifice to Kathy, in order that I may help her become all God designed her to be?"

Needless to say, with this new attitude, Terry and Kathy's marriage changed dramatically.

Let's hear Kathy's side.

"As I look back on our lives, I am amazed that I felt responsible for being a poor wife to Terry. I see now that I was rightfully challenging an unbiblical system. I had been taught to submit, but neither Terry nor I had ever come to grips with mutal submission. Terry made it clear that he was the leader, and I had no business challenging him. At times I felt suppressed and experienced loss of self-esteem. Other times I overreacted and challenged Terry on anything.

"Today I am different. I am learning to relax and pretty

much say whatever I think or feel without being afraid of a lecture or judgment. For the first time I am beginning to feel cherished and loved. I am beginning to act naturally and hear the Spirit of God. Terry has encouraged me to obey God and develop my gifts. Greater fulfillment has come through this, and I no longer feel that my ideas, gifts, or personal development are a threat to Terry."

"I can't believe the two of us lived in such bondage for so long," continues Terry. "One thing I should make clear. The change in our marriage is not a switch, on my part, from selfish authority to loving authority. Sacrificial giving means that *I don't have to have authority over Kathy.* I don't have to be 'in charge.' I just try to assume my God-given responsibility— ministering to Kathy. Then I let God and her work out her own life. Of course, I am always ready to assist, should she need my help; I am to love, nourish, minister, and enable and complete her as the Lord commanded me to do."

Divine Order?

Is there a divine order in marriage? Well, that depends on what you mean by order. Surely God has given specifics for every Christian as to how he or she is to live. Can those specifics be characterized as God's order? Possibly. When it comes to marriage, we find in Genesis and Ephesians 5 that responsibilities are defined: leave and cleave, unite, love, sacrifice, submit, and respect. But does that constitute an order? Is it like a company with a president and vice-president? Is one person put in charge? Not at creation. Not at the Fall. Not at re-creation. Not in Ephesians 5.

A friend of mine challenged me recently on this point by citing a working relationship he had been involved in.

"When I was in the air force, I was given an assignment of seeing a task completed. The only problem was that those I was told to supervise outranked me. I found myself in the difficult position of responsibility without authority. It was impossible for me to get the job done, until I told the officer above me. He solved the problem by letting the men know that whatever I did, I was acting in his name. Since he outranked them, I now had the authority I needed to get the job done. Isn't that the kind of authority God has given the husband over the wife?"

I saw things differently: "To be supported scripturally or to illustrate a Scripture, an analogy must fit at every key point. Your analogy is wrong in that God never put you in charge of your wife. You are not responsible to 'get the job done' in her life. The Bible says you are to love, nurture, sacrifice, and minister to her."

"But the Scriptures say I'm to present her spotless to God! Isn't that getting the job done?"

"The Scriptures state that the husband is to love and sacrifice. It is Christ who presents us all spotless before God.

"To put it another way, you weren't told to tell your wife what to do, make decisions for her, be the final word in order that she might be sanctified, washed, and presented. You were told to love and sacrifice and minister to her that Christ may fully accomplish that in her life. If you were to give me a work-related analogy to fit Ephesians 5, it would probably be that you were a maintenance worker on the project. As you participate you enabled the job to get done. Your authority was limited to getting your own task carried out. But you were not given authority over the project."

How does relationship with God affect relationship in marriage? Though helpful and needed information on communication, love, trust, and commitment in marriage has been readily available in the Christian community, an emphasis on arbitrary, man-made order, roles, and pat answers has often undermined the real fabric of marriage. *The real foundation of a Christian marriage is the relationship with God of both individuals. Both partners must be sold out to Jesus Christ and individually led by Him. This will enable both parties to submit to each other as well as encourage, serve, please, build, and love each other.*

But what if one of the parties isn't a Christian?

SEVEN

For the
Sake
of the
Gospel

One of the most effective couples in today's Christian world is Bill and Vonette Bright. Together Bill and Vonette have pioneered an evangelistic and discipling ministry, Campus Crusade for Christ, that is reaching to the far corners of the world. They have done it as a team, each playing a different role, yet sharing, in one accord, the goal of the fulfillment of the Great Commission in this generation.

Bill and Vonette travel extensively. In mideastern countries, where women do not have the freedom they have in the United States, Vonette has to be very careful. Normally a vivacious leader, she tones down her participation. The last thing the Brights would want to do is to put a stumbling block in the path of those who might come to know Christ.

This is the very issue Peter was addressing in 1 Peter

2:13-3:8. Before you go further in this chapter, please read the Book of 1 Peter.

For the Sake of the Gospel

One attitude we are asked to assume as Christians is the willingness to sacrifice in order to help others understand the Gospel. As Paul explains:

> Give no offense either to Jews or Greeks or to the church of God; just as I also please all men in all things, not seeking my own profit, but the profit of the many, that they may be saved.
> 1 Corinthians 10:32, 33

> For though I am free from all men, I have made myself a slave to all, that I might win the more. And to the Jews I became as a Jew, that I might win Jews; to those who are under the Law, as under the Law, though not being myself under the Law, that I might win those who are under the Law; to those who are without law, as without law, though not being without the law of God but under the law of Christ, that I might win those who are without law. To the weak I became weak, that I might win the weak; I have become all things to all men, that I may by all means save some. And I do all things for the sake of the gospel, that I may become a fellow-partaker of it.
> 1 Corinthians 9:19-23

The Epistle of Peter

The First Epistle of Peter is written to teach Christians appropriate conduct when trying to reach the lost. Peter addresses the alien Christians scattered throughout Pontus, Galatia, Cappadocia, Asia, and Bithynia. Peter reminds the believers of the great salvation that is bestowed upon them and urges a holy life-style in light of it. In 1:17, he states, "And if you address as Father the One who impartially judges according to each man's work, conduct yourselves in fear during the time of your stay upon earth."

Chapter 2 continues by admonishing the believers to *live* as Christians "for you once were not a people, but now you are the people of God; you had not received mercy, but now you have received mercy" (v. 10).

Peter goes on to exhort them on how to live in the presence of non-Christians: "Beloved, I urge you as aliens and strangers to abstain from fleshly lusts, which wage war against the soul. Keep your behavior excellent among the Gentiles, so that in the thing in which they slander you as evildoers, they may on account of your good deeds, as they observe them, glorify God in the day of visitation" (vv. 11, 12).

Then Peter gets more specific in verses 13–17:

> Submit yourselves for the Lord's sake to every human institution, whether to a king as the one in authority, or to governors as sent by him for the punishment of evildoers and the praise of those who do right. For such is the will of God that by doing right you may silence the ignorance of foolish men. Act as free men, and do not use your freedom as a covering for evil, but use it as bondslaves of God. Honor all men; love the brotherhood, fear God, honor the king.

Peter lays the foundation of "excellent behavior" before non-Christians. (*Gentiles*, according to most commentaries, refers to non-Christians. Certainly they include those who "slander [or malign]" the Christian to whom Peter is writing.) He then notes that our response to situations is observed by non-Christians and "foolish men." Peter urges us to act freely, but not so as to be stumbling blocks. As bondslaves of God we must keep in mind the mentality of non-Christians and not provide offense.

Peter continues:

> Servants, be submissive to your masters with all respect, not only to those who are good and gentle, but also to those who are unreasonable. For this finds favor, if for the sake of conscience toward God a man bears up under sorrows when suffering unjustly. For what credit is there if, when you sin and are

harshly treated, you endure it with patience? But if when you do what is right and suffer for it you patiently endure it, this finds favor with God. For you have been called for this purpose, since Christ also suffered for you, leaving you an example for you to follow in His steps, who committed no sin, nor was any deceit found in His mouth; and while being reviled, He did not revile in return; while suffering, He uttered no threats, but kept entrusting Himself to Him who judges righteously; and He Himself bore our sins in His body on the cross, that we might die to sin and live to righteousness; for by His wounds you were healed. For you were continually straying like sheep, but now you have returned to the Shepherd and Guardian of your souls.

Vv. 18–25

Peter has given us two examples of those who suffered for righteousness' sake: Slaves, who should bear up under suffering from non-Christian masters, and Jesus Christ, who suffered for us, are given as examples of how we should endure suffering in order to be a testimony to the non-Christian.

Then chapter 3 begins. Note that chapter and verse headings were added centuries after the Bible was written. There is nothing inspired about them. Chapter 3 follows the above verses and is part of the whole: "In the same way, you wives, be submissive to your own husbands so that even if any of them are disobedient to the word, they may be won without a word by the behavior of their wives, as they observe your chaste and respectful behavior" (3:1, 2).

Here, wives are cautioned to be submissive to their husbands, chaste and respectful, allowing their Christian behavior to "win" their non-Christian husbands.

Is This an Ideal Christian Marriage?

Is this a passage that describes how an ideal Christian marriage is to be run? Should we therefore teach it as a norm? In context (chapter 2 and *all* of chapter 3) the emphasis is on a

FOR THE SAKE OF THE GOSPEL   85 spiritually mixed marriage. (Note that "disobedient to the word," the phrase describing the husband in 1 Peter 3:1, clearly refers to a non-Christian in 1 Peter 2:7, 8.)

First Peter 3 explains how to respond under suffering in such a way that individuals may be won to Christ. It is an excellent verse for women (and men) with non-Christian spouses to consider. (*Note: The Living Bible* translation of 1 Peter 3:1, "Wives, fit in with your husbands' plans . . ." is an erroneous translation. Further, it is not a command to women in a Christian marriage.)

Understanding Peter's Admonition

Why did Peter give Christian wives such instruction? In the culture Peter is addressing, women had little position. They were to serve their husbands and could be divorced for the least offense. What was happening to these non-Christian husbands, when their wives exhibited their freedom in Christ or when they saw women in the Christian church whose husbands treated them as their "equal and fitting partner"? Perhaps they felt troubled that women were not acting according to tradition. Perhaps they feared that their own marriages might be in jeopardy. What was the non-Christian husband to think when suddenly his wife was filled with self-esteem and resented his treatment of her or constantly talked to him about Christ? Perhaps he would become jealous of her newfound faith or refuse to consider embracing it because of her less dependent behavior toward him. The salvation of the unbeliever is of paramount importance, Peter believes, and Christians should make a special effort to win their non-Christian spouses with good behavior rather than risk turning them away with preaching.

The passage continues, in verses 3–6:

And let not your adornment be external only—braiding the hair, and wearing gold jewelry, and putting on dresses; but let it be the hidden person of the heart, with the imperishable quality of a gentle and quiet spirit, which is precious in the sight of God. For in this way in former times the holy women also, who hoped in God, used to adorn themselves, being submissive to their own husbands. Thus Sarah obeyed [listened to] Abraham, calling him lord, and you have become her children if you do what is right without being frightened by any fear.

Women married to non-Christians should keep their emphasis on internal qualities and be attentive to their husbands so that the unbelieving spouse will not question the Gospel. "Be careful," says Peter, "that your newfound liberty doesn't scare your non-Christian husband off." (*Note:* The instruction to display "a gentle and quiet spirit" is not given by the Bible uniquely to women. Elsewhere, such as in the Beatitudes, all believers are admonished to be gentle and meek.)

In regards to Sarah obeying Abraham, Peter is illustrating the need for the Christian spouse to display gentle and quiet spirit. For example, if I am talking with someone about baking bread, I may refer to a friend who has strong hands. The conversation may be as follows, "To bake bread you must have strong hands for kneading the dough. Jane has strong hands." Now, did I say that Jane baked bread? No, I used Jane only to illustrate strong hands. In the same way, Peter tells Christian wives with non-Christian husbands to have a gracious spirit. Then he refers to Sarah's gracious spirit to illustrate graciousness. Just as referring to Jane illustrates someone who has strong hands, not one who bakes bread, so Peter refers to Sarah to illustrate graciousness, not a mixed marriage. Therefore, using Sarah and Abraham in this passage does not indicate that the passage is dealing with Christian marriages rather than mixed marriages.

The word *obeyed* can also be translated "listened to." In chapter 10 we will look closer at Sarah and Abraham and discover that in the sense of this passage Abraham also "obeyed" Sarah. By closely examining the life of Sarah and Abraham, we can better see what is being said here. The word *lord* is purposely not capitalized in the English here, as it is a word used to denote respect, not authority. It is a word similar to *sir* in the English language.

J. Vernon McGee says, "Now you may be thinking, doesn't

the Bible teach that a wife is to obey her husband? It does not. You cannot find that in the Word of God. Obedience has been imposed upon wives of Oriental and other pagan cultures, but it never has been true among Christians."[1]

Peter sums this section up by getting us back to our original thesis: ". . . And you have become her [Sarah's] children if you do what is right without being frightened by any fear." Even under unbearable circumstances, Peter reminds us to keep an eternal perspective—that the salvation of others is of prime importance. The Christian wife is to imitate Jesus, who submitted to suffering while entrusting Himself to His Father.

For the Sake of the Gospel

Before we continue with Peter, consider Peggy's story. When Peggy became a Christian she confronted her husband daily with the "good news." She was so captivated with Jesus Christ that she spent most of her time studying the Bible. Her conversations with her husband, which once reflected their mutual interests, became saturated with biblical information. The husband, who had always loved and respected his wife, became offended with her zealousness and lack of attention to him.

I watched this man for a year. My husband and I often shopped at the store he and his wife owned. Once a friendly salesman, he became embittered. I often became nervous when, as soon as I entered the store, the wife would take me to the side and begin overflowing with her latest insight. I was thrilled that she was growing as a Christian, but couldn't help but notice the disgust on her husband's face.

One morning, while her husband was standing less than five feet from us, she told me how her husband had nearly drowned the previous weekend. "It was God who saved him," she announced loudly. Her husband looked pitiful at this remark. Peggy was making it more and more difficult for him to consider the Gospel.

Finally she wised up. When I came in the shop one day and privately asked how her husband was, she remarked, "Much better. I've cut out some of my church activities and am doing more for him. I realized that because of my neglect of him and nagging, I have caused him not to want what I have."

In Peter's time some wives who suddenly began to operate as independent persons may have caused great offense. But today, in many homes, the reaction is often the opposite—as another couple's story illustrates.

Molly and Dave had a mutual marriage. They both worked and shared household chores. Their children helped around the house. Then Molly became a Christian. Her love for the Lord was great, and desire to please God consumed her.

In Molly's Bible class she began to hear about the "biblical" way of running the home. The husband was to be in charge of the home, and she was to take her orders from him. Furthermore, the wife shouldn't work but be at home with the kids.

Molly changed. She quit her job, which greatly diminished their income. She also began to center her life around her husband and children. When Dave talked to Molly, instead of a mutual interchange on views, wants, and desires, Molly started deferring to Dave. She no longer parlayed for her favorite restaurant (which used to amuse Dave), but sought to find out Dave's every wish and bring it about.

It was apparent that Dave missed the old Molly and wondered what had happened to her. Slowly his respect for Molly decreased, for she was no longer her own person who inspired and challenged him. In fact, she was more like one of the kids, whom he could tell what to do. Dave's attention wandered, and instead of becoming a Christian, he found another woman with whom he could share as an equal.

Dave and Molly's story is true and is being repeated often. Why? Because we have taken instruction (1 Peter 3:1) intended to *add* understanding to the Christian–non-Christian dilemma and suggested that it is describing an ideal Christian marriage.

The passage in 1 Peter continues: "You husbands, *likewise*, live with your wives in an understanding way, as with a weaker vessel, since she is a woman; and grant her honor as a fellow-heir of the grace of life, so that your prayers may not be hindered" (3:7, *italics added*).

The word *likewise* is again used, as in verse 1. We are still discussing the believer's testimony to the non-Christian. In this context, *woman* is referred to as the weaker vessel. The key word here may be *vessel*, that which houses the person. Most often this Greek word is used to mean the physical side of a person. Physical strength is one of the few differences in men and women that can be established satisfactorily. Some people, however, question if the woman is referred to as a weaker vessel because she is a non-Christian. (*Note:* This is *not* a command of God that women must be weaker.)

Peter's words to the husband are very strong here, "If a Christian husband does not treat his non-Christian wife as a fellow heir of the grace of life (salvation being open to all of us), his prayers (possibly for her salvation) will not be answered." Peter is telling the men that both men and women originate from God and are on equal footing in light of creation. For a man to have his prayers for his wife's salvation answered, he must condition his wife with a graceful attitude, just as the woman must condition her husband to respond to the message of Christ by a gentle and gracious spirit. A non-Christian wife who is treated as an equal by her Christian husband would probably find her husband's faith very attractive. Again, a submissive attitude is important for the Christian husband with the non-Christian wife and for the Christian wife with the non-Christian husband.

Finally, let's see how Peter summarizes this passage:

> To sum up, let all be harmonious, sympathetic, brotherly, kindhearted, and humble in spirit; not returning evil for evil, or insult for insult, but giving a blessing instead; for you were called for the very purpose that you might inherit a blessing. . . . But even if you should suffer for the sake of righteousness, you are blessed. And do not fear their intimidation, and do not be troubled, but sanctify Christ as Lord in your hearts, always being ready to make a defense to everyone who asks

you to give an account for the hope that is in you, yet with gentleness and reverence; and keep a good conscience so that in the thing in which you are slandered, those who revile your good behavior in Christ may be put to shame.

Vv. 3:8–9, 14–16

Peter reiterates that this message is appropriate for all believers. His commonsense approach to handling difficult situations with the non-Christian is good advice for today. Yet how blessed are those who are equally yoked together in Christ. They need not have the cautions given for a mixed marriage, but can come together in agreement, as the next chapter illustrates.

EIGHT

Symphonic Melody ... in Marriage?

Imagine a symphony orchestra tuning up: first, the lighter instruments, the violins, piccolos, flutes; and then the bass instruments, the tuba, French horn, trumpets, cymbals, and drums.

The conductor taps the wand. Instruments are raised. Then to our immense delight the melodious sounds fill the chamber. We are delighted as the tone and quality of each individual instrument blends in harmonic sound. In this chapter we want to discover the biblical basis of harmonious interaction in marriage.

One passage that deals directly with practical Christian marriage and that, incidentally, is often not addressed in marriage seminars and teaching in the Christian community, is 1 Corinthians 7. Please read that passage and then we'll take a look at what it teaches—and what it doesn't.

Just prior to this chapter, Paul has addressed the area of sexual intimacy, urging purity and advising all to "flee immorality . . ." (6:18). Then, in 7:1, 2, he writes, "Now concerning the things about which you wrote, it is good for a man not to touch a woman. But because of immoralities, let each man have his own wife, and let each woman have her own husband."

Immediately we sense commonality in Paul's argument. He could have said, "Let each man have his own wife," and left it at that, possibly implying ownership or priority. But he addressed both men and women.

Paul continues, "Let the husband fulfill his duty to his wife, and likewise also the wife to her husband" (v. 3). The word *duty* comes from the root word *debt*. Paul is citing intimate responsibilities that are due one another. "The wife does not have authority over her own body, but the husband does; and likewise also the husband does not have authority over his own body, but the wife does" (v. 4).

Nowhere in Scripture is authority mentioned in regard to marriage—except in 1 Corinthians 7. This Greek word, *exousiazo* is a derivative of *exousia* ("power to act, authority") and means "to exercise authority over." Clearly the man and woman are both given such authority. *What* are they given authority over? Each other's body.

Moses (Genesis 2:24), Jesus (Matthew 19:5), and Paul (Ephesians 5:31) have all related that "the two shall become one flesh." The physical union is a picture of the whole of the relationship, symbolizing oneness and unity. Here Paul states that at the core of the marriage, authority is given to both spouses.

This statement is similar to an Old Testament account. In the Song of Solomon both the bride and the bridegroom remark, "I am my beloved's and my beloved is mine" (6:3; 2:16). Possession of each other (Song of Solomon) and authority over each other (1 Corinthians 7) are both marks of functioning as a team in marriage.

Individual Responsibility

Much extrabiblical teaching is inconsistent with the teaching on commonality and team marriage presented in 1 Corinthians 7 (and other passages we've looked at). Some of this teaching is presented in such a way that the listener comes to think that it is derived straight from Scripture, even parallel with Scripture. One of those principles is: "The man is ultimately and singly responsible for the home *and* the one who answers to God for the success or failure of the home."

This teaching can be extremely misleading. Nowhere in Scripture is there any indication that *anyone* answers for another, but that every person will give an account to God for how he or she treats, teaches, or ministers to one another (Hebrews 13:17). A person does not give an account for how another person *responds* to him or her.

Early in our marriage, Rusty and I felt differently about how money was to be spent. Initially Rusty reasoned that if my value system was not the same as his, mine was amiss. But more important, he believed that he answered to God for what *I* did. "I'm an adult," I told him. "I answer to God for myself." We now function respecting each other's unique point of view. Together we have come up with a plan as to how we divide up our salary. Rusty, using his value system, spends his share of the money as he believes God would have him do. I spend my portion of the money the way I believe God is directing me. Each answers to God for his or her own actions, not for each other. "So then each one of us shall give account of *himself* to God" (Romans 14:12, *italics added*).

One afternoon I talked on the phone with a woman who insisted that the man was ultimately responsible and accountable to God for the home. After I pointed out that I could find no biblical justification for a statement like that, she responded, "If a husband is doing his job correctly, the wife will lovingly respond and the children will honor God."

"Whew," I said, "that's expecting a lot. Even though I would certainly agree with you that a Christlike husband and father makes it easier for everyone within the family to respond positively, I don't think you can say that the total *response* of the wife and children rests on his shoulders."

She wanted to hear more.

"Christ loves the entire church," I said.

She agreed.

"And He has perfectly loved, ministered to, and even died for her."

She again agreed.

"Well, if He is performing His job as perfect lover, provider, and Savior, why is so much of the church carnal and unresponsive to Him?"

She was alert and starting to get the point.

"Christ perfectly loves us," I continued, "yet He is not responsible for the responses of members of the church. A husband can be thoroughly Christlike, yet the wife and children must individually make and be accountable for their own response."

The story of Ananias and Sapphira vividly illustrates this principle of independent accountability (Acts 5:1-11), as does the marriage of Adam and Eve (Genesis 3:14-16) and Ahab and Jezebel (1 Kings 21:23-29).

Some marital teaching says the husband is to be *the* spiritual leader in the home. If the man does not want or have the discipline to establish and maintain spiritual devotions, then such teaching counsels that the wife should resign herself to the situation. But the Bible teaches that a woman is as responsible as the man to rear and teach her children (Proverbs 1:8; Deuteronomy 6:4-7; 4:10). If she abdicates this responsibility because of some unbiblical teaching, she and her family will undoubtedly pay the penalty for the error. No Scripture indicates that the man is responsible for *everything* spiritual in the home. The husband should be a spiritual leader in the home, and the wife should be a spiritual leader in the home. If the wife is more gifted at spiritual teaching and nurturing, then she must use her gifts. All will be blessed by it.

The May 1985 issue of *Christianity Today* reported a survey on marriage, conducted by Canada's *Faith Alive* magazine.

Couples who listed both husband and wife as "spiritual leaders" rated their marriages as happier than those where the husband or wife alone was the spiritual leader.

Except by Agreement

First Corinthians 7:5 continues, "Stop depriving one another, except by agreement for a time that you may devote yourselves to prayer. . . ." This is the only passage that deals directly with specific decision making in marriage, and here a decision is called for regarding abstaining from sexual intercourse for a time to devote oneself to prayer. How is that decision arrived at? By agreement.

Let's take a look at this word *agreement*. The Greek word is *symphonos*. Can you recognize its source? It is where we get our English word *symphony*, and it speaks of each partner "tuning in" (so to speak) in order to strike a chord of harmony and agreement.

Who is in charge in an orchestra? Does the tuba rule over the piccolo? If this were permitted, the tuba might drown out the smaller, softer instrument. Is the viola allowed to control the oboe? No. For harmony would never be the result. How then do we come by harmony in a world filled with discord? With the help of the conductor, of course.

Is God a God of order? Certainly. But in the biblical accounts order and harmony are synonymous. Why? Because the Conductor coordinates the whole. When He is in charge, and when each individual instrument (in this case the husband and the wife) lets Him lead, together they can work toward "agreement."

". . . For God is not a God of confusion but of peace . . ." (1 Corinthians 14:33).

Teamwork in Marriage

What else do we see in 1 Corinthians 7? After a short discourse (vv. 7–11) on the possibilities of remaining single and on the responsibilities of both husband and wife to remain together, Paul continues:

> ... If any brother [Christian] has a wife who is an unbeliever, and she consents to live with him, let him not send her away. And a woman who has an unbelieving husband, and he consents to live with her, let her not send her husband away. For the unbelieving husband is sanctified through his wife, and the unbelieving wife is sanctified through her believing husband; for otherwise your children are unclean, but now they are holy. Yet if the unbelieving one leaves, let him leave; the brother or the sister is not under bondage in such cases, but God has called us to peace. For how do you know, O wife, whether you will save your husband? Or how do you know, O husband, whether you will save your wife?
>
> Vv. 12–16

Unlike the double standard that prevailed in Judaism at the time of Christ, New Testament Scripture presents no unequal rights. In matters of separation, sanctifying, and salvation, what applies to one spouse applies to both spouses.

"Yes, but the husband is told to rule the household; the wife isn't. Ruling isn't teamwork." That's what a newlywed husband suggested to me.

"Let's take a look at that," I said. "What is your scriptural source? The husband turned to 1 Timothy 3, a passage dealing with the selection of elders and deacons. He pointed to verse 4, "He must be one who manages his own household well, keeping his children under control with all dignity." The young husband shared that some translators deem the word *manage* to be *rule.*

"There is question as to whether or not this passage is speaking of men only," I began. "But, even so, let me show you another passage." I turned to 1 Timothy 5:14 and read, "Therefore, I want younger widows to get married, bear children, keep house, and give the enemy no occasion for reproach."

"Where does it say anything about the woman ruling?" my friend asked.

"The verb *keep house, oikodespoteo,* occurs only once in the New Testament and means 'to rule over the household.' The noun form, *oikodespotes,* is used twelve times and clearly denotes 'the master of the house.' It is a much stronger word for 'rule' than the one found in 1 Timothy 3:4."

Again we see the coruling of men and women in the home as established in Genesis 1 and 2.

Another extrabiblical idea inconsistent with the concept of mutuality, commonality, and teamwork in marriage presented in 1 Corinthians 7 is the statement, "God created men with a need for respect, but women with a need for love."

I challenged a man concerning this statement one morning, and he replied, "Well, then how come the Bible never tells a man to respect his wife and never tells a woman to love her husband?"

But the Bible clearly tells *all* believers to respect all men and women and to "give honor to whom honor is due" (*see* Romans 13:7). Titus 2:3, 4 does specifically tell older women to teach younger women to love their husbands.

Another extrabiblical teaching which many Christians associate with Scripture is the man as initiator, the woman as responder. This statement may be derived from the Christ-and-church analogy, yet it seems to me that it may be stretching the point beyond the analogy.

Are men the only initiators? Of course not. A woman may be more adept at setting a romantic situation than a man. It is *her* plan and her efforts that form a quiet romantic evening. She may initiate fun times, devotions, spiritual projects, and so on. Sometimes the woman is the initiator, and the man is the responder. Initiation and response are not attitudes or actions that we have to limit to one sex or another because of some biblical restriction.

Another extrabiblical teaching regarding a man's responsibility for his home is that the husband is his wife's sole protector. Yes, the husband is to protect his wife, but the wife also protects her husband.

Rusty protects me in many ways, by seeing that the car is in good working order; by carrying the financial responsibility,

CALLED TO UNITY

to relieve me from stress; by protecting my reputation in alerting me to certain aspects of a situation, and so forth. But I protect him as well by seeing that he eats nutritiously, by warning him about possible problems in a decision he is about to make, by providing him with insights into others (so important in protecting his reputation and ministry), and so forth. Many men and women could give much longer lists as to the way they protect each other.

Are men the only providers in the home? "Yes," remarked a pastor friend, "that command is perfectly clear in 1 Timothy 5:8. 'But if any one does not provide for his own, and especially for those of his household, he has denied the faith, and is worse than an unbeliever.' "

"That verse," I returned, "is written concerning providing for *widows*. The insert of 'he' and 'his' is not in the Greek. However, I believe it applies to husbands as well."

Pleasing One Another

Continuing in 1 Corinthians 7, after some brief discussion on circumcision, slavery, and singleness, Paul discusses mutually "pleasing" each other.

> But I want you to be free from concern. One who is unmarried is concerned about the things of the Lord, how he may please the Lord; but one who is married is concerned about the things of the world, how he may please his wife, and his interests are divided. And the woman who is unmarried, and the virgin, is concerned about the things of the Lord, that she may be holy both in body and spirit; but one who is married is concerned about the things of the world, how she may please her husband.
>
> Vv. 32–34

Here Paul presents another aspect of mutuality. Marriage, he insists, will cost both man and woman a great deal. Both need to be ready to pay the price of pleasing each other, should they embark upon that relationship.

What other biblical teaching comes under the heading of commonality, mutuality, and teamwork in marriage? Many things: confessing our faults to each other; building up each other; encouraging each other; teaching each other; rebuking each other.

Rusty and I reserve the right not only to encourage each other, but to teach each other, build up each other, confront each other, and rebuke each other as needed. We point out inconsistencies, hypocrisies, contradictions, and unbiblical attitudes in each other, and we both profit accordingly.

For we are each individual Christians. We are each "in Christ," given blessings, responsibilities, authority, provisions, and are pronounced "beloved children."

Christian marriage incorporates *all* that we are as believers in Jesus Christ.

CALLED TO UNITY

NINE

Practical
Decision
Making
in Marriage

Recently a friend of mine returned from a week-long Christian seminar. Since she was a new Christian, I expected Evelyn to be overjoyed at the teaching she received. Instead she came home burdened. When asked what was bothering her, she related how overwhelmed she felt in light of what was expected of her as a Christian. "It's too much to ask any one person to be or do," she said. "The decisions I'm required to make concerning my life seem awesome."

Life is full of pressures, complexities, and decisions; and nowhere is grappling with decision making more pressing than in the day-to-day events of marriage and family. In the midst of these challenging situations, marital symphony, as suggested in 1 Corinthians 7, may be difficult to achieve. Some of the many considerations involved in marital decision making are: What needs are present? Who will the decision affect the most? Are there consequences to either spouse? What is the financial investment? What are the short- and the long-term implications for both partners? What is the cost in terms of time and energy? In view of the inherent difficulties in coming to agreement on such questions, it's no wonder that many have avoided the whole process by building unhealthy response patterns when confronted with the resolving of conflict or decison making.

Sidestepper

When faced with these problems in marriage, people react differently. One common response is to sidestep the real issue. Such was the case with Jill and Paul when their car broke down. The simple question seemed to be whether or not they should have the car repaired. Paul wanted a new car. Jill argued that they couldn't afford one. Paul then bought the car, arguing that he would find a way to meet the payments.

But what was really happening in this interchange? Jill and Paul were sidestepping the root issue. To Jill, buying a car meant that Paul's wish was more important than the new carpet in the living room, for which she had waited many years. The emotional issue, which they thoroughly avoided, was that Jill felt Paul always thought of his needs before hers. Sidestepping the root issues and not dealing with the emotions involved can produce underlying tension that will quickly sour a marriage.

One way to spot a person who sidesteps issues is to notice his or her verbal response to conflict. ("I don't want to argue about this," or, "Let's discuss this later.") In many marriages, women who prefer to "keep the peace" rather than work through conflict conveniently say, "Well, you're the one in charge; you make the decision." Although this avoids conflict *now*, the wife eventually feels resentful about unmet and unspoken needs, and the husband usually feels guilty about having an unfulfilled wife.

Competitor

Another way of dealing with decision making in marriage is to *compete*. Ron and Mary have a strong, respectful marriage. Recently they were listening to a married couple discuss an impasse they had reached on a decision. The discussion revolved around roles and who was in charge in marriage. Finally, Mary announced, "This discussion is really not about roles. It is about selfishness." She could see that the real problem was two people trying to force their own wills upon each other. In this case, the two competitors probably saw themselves as standing up for their own rights or positions.

Accommodate

Another way to deal with conflict is by *accommodating* others. Out of a deep desire to be loved, a person who falls into this trap of always accommodating will make almost any personal sacrifice to achieve the goal of acceptance.

In a marriage, because of fear of guilt or rejection, one partner may continually try to avoid displeasing the spouse. As a result, he or she becomes preoccupied with preventing negative situations. What the accommodator may not realize is that such actions ensure that his or her own needs will not be met and that anyone who, because of unresolved needs, is being led by others, will have a difficult time sorting out personal needs and God's leading in life.

Not uncommonly, Christian women mistake accommodation with biblical submission.

Compromise

Compromise is another way of dealing with decision making and is often a good short-term way of handling a situation. However, its effectiveness depends on the maturity of the two partners involved. For example, one partner wants to go to a French restaurant; the other wants to go to a Mexican restaurant. A good compromise is to go to a French restaurant this week and a Mexican restaurant next week. A bad compromise is to go to neither a French nor Mexican restaurant, but an Italian restaurant instead, a compromise with which neither is really happy.

Are you a sidestepper, competitor, accommodator, immature compromiser, or do you maturely assess Scripture, assume responsibility for your life, reason with your spouse (as appropriate), consult God, and think through the best decision? Do you and your spouse make final decisions in light of greater goals?

Who is to make the final decision in marriage? Does one person have to always give the final word? "Yes" is a simplistic answer to these questions—one that fails to take into account the whole of Scripture and the complexities of human nature.

Recently I was talking with a friend who believed in the husband and wife mutually submitting to each other, yet she also felt that the husband was the final decision maker in case of an impasse.

I was curious to hear more. "How does that work out practically?" I asked.

"Well, when we have hashed something over and still can't reach a conclusion, then I have to finally let Jim make the decision."

"How often does this happen?" I asked.

"Not very often."

"Well," I continued, "do you ever hash things out and finally Jim comes to accept your point of view?"

"Sure."

"Then is your decision the one that stands?"

"Yes."

"What do you call that?"

"I call that submitting to each other."

"Let me tell you what I'm hearing. When Jim bows to your decision, you call it 'submitting to each other.' But when you bow to Jim's decision, you call it 'Jim is the final authority.'"

"Hm," she replied, her eyes widening. "I never saw it that way."

Another woman expressed a different but very common attitude in such situations. "What I've come to learn about marriage," the speaker began, "is that it's important to let a man *think* he's the final decision maker. For example, one evening I approached Hank with the idea of going on vacation. He wasn't interested in going anywhere. I knew that he hated camping trips; so do I. Yet at length I tried to convince him that I wanted to go camping. Finally, my worried husband turned to me and said, 'Look, we both like the ocean. Why don't we go to the ocean for the weekend?' I said, okay, if that was the way he wanted it, we could compromise. We would take a vacation, which is what I wanted, but he could name the spot. All smiles, I acted like the perfect submissive wife. Yet going to the ocean is what I wanted in the first place."

How often on this subject of marriage do we put our energies into creating an appearance of what we think marriage ought to be, rather than each individual simply striving to be all God designed him or her to be? Why should we have to pretend we prefer camping when we really want to visit the shore?

Well, you say, this attitude illustrates a misuse of what God intended. No. I am saying that Scripture does not indicate that either spouse is the boss or final decision maker, but that both have authority. Further, I believe final decisions can be made by "agreement," with both partners learning to yield in case of an impasse.

Simplistic Answers Are Short-term Answers

Simplistic answers are often short-term answers for simplistic problems. Marriage is for the long haul and presents highly complex problems.

One simplistic answer regarding marriage is that male leadership will insure order, harmony, and happiness. The problems in marriage, many surmise, are the result of the wife's rebelliousness. When she starts submitting to the leadership of her husband, marriage problems will be solved. Yet one person in charge will not alter a complex and confused marriage. It may simplify it *for a time* (after all, one person making the decisions saves a lot of dialogue), but dialogue and struggle have an ultimate purpose for the Christian. Maturity is always bought with a price. To short-circuit this struggle by insisting upon one person having the final word will not guarantee fulfillment. We cannot force a simple decision-making process on marriage and expect it to make that relationship what God intended.

Bob King, who heads a Christian counseling center in San Diego, California, comments, "The concept of a strong one-person authority in marriage is a worldly substitute for the biblical concept of harmonious relationships."

So keeping in mind decision making by agreement, what are some considerations that should be made in terms of which partner makes the decision?

Who Is Affected the Most?

Which partner will the decision affect the most? Henry Brandt, a leading Christian psychologist, states that most wives should have the final home-buying decisions, because they usually predominate in running a home. Of course, if the husband works at home or actively shares in chores and housetime, then other considerations will be involved. In another instance, if the husband is the only one who will use the power lawn mower, than maybe a decision about that lies in his department.

If the decision will greatly affect both partners, then time and prayer should be applied until both can come to terms with the decision. Rosalind and Jonathan Goforth, missionaries with the China Inland Mission, labored faithfully during the early 1900s and saw many Chinese turn to the Lord—but not without sacrifice. Disease and hardship took the lives of several of their children. When Jonathan Goforth announced that he felt God was leading him to move inland to parts of China that had not been exposed to the Gospel, Rosalind was greatly troubled. If life was so physically hard in China proper, how much more difficult would it be inland, where there was no access to other missionaries, doctors, and transportation, where disease was rampant? Rosalind could not bring herself to go.

Patiently her husband prayed and waited. That year was a difficult one for Rosalind. Finally, she came to terms with moving. Surely it could not be worse for her inland. She submitted to God's leading in her own life and joyfully told her husband that she was ready to go. From that time forward, the Goforths lost no more children, and hardships were met with unusual provision from the Lord.

This couple had mutual respect for the leading of the Lord in each other's lives—and for good reason. Consider what might have happened if Jonathan Goforth had insisted on Rosalind's going to inland China before her inner conflict was resolved. Most probably, resentment and deeper turmoil would have erupted. It is wiser to wait for God to work and to respect *His* work in the lives of others—especially in our spouses.

Greatest Expertise

Who has the greatest expertise in the area of the decision? Why should one partner make the final decision in an area where the other has far more understanding of the problem? In our home, I decide many issues dealing with writing and speaking, since communication skills are my background, education, and profession. However, the longer we work together in this field, the more of an expert Rusty becomes. In recent years he has taught me a thing or two. On the other hand, Rusty shoulders our financial responsibilities. He has the better overview of the situation, and I respect his judgment and advice. I am happy to let him make many of those decisions without consulting me.

Fairness

Another consideration is fairness in decision making. Mrs. Norman Vincent Peale fell in love with a beautiful farm. It had a wonderful barn, which she adored, but it didn't have a view, something her husband greatly valued. They bought the home with the barn, but after a number of years, they moved, this time to a farm with a view. In the first case, Mrs. Peale was the final decision maker on what house to buy. In the second case, Norman had that opportunity. Neither need be resentful or feel abused. More important, it gave each the opportunity of giving to the other. Principle: If your spouse has let you decide your last vacation, why not offer to let him or her decide the next? The real essence of fairness in decision making is a matter of the heart, not a tit-for-tat mentality.

Need

Is one partner's need concerning a certain decision greater than the other's? This situation is most common. Harriet's childhood had left her somewhat scarred and in great need of love and a sense of belonging. Therefore, when her husband, Jack, wanted to change churches, Harriet lacked enthusiasm. Harriet had invested many years in developing friendships and felt accepted in this church. Jack, on the other hand, admired his pastor's character but felt he was somewhat boring as a speaker. In considering this decision, Jack wisely felt that his need not to be bored one hour every Sunday was not as great as his wife's need to belong.

A parallel consideration is this: To whom is the decision most important? Dorothy and Chuck were discussing what color to paint Chuck's office. Although Dorothy was adept at decorating, she overruled her own biases in color selection because Chuck would have to live with the decision. Recognizing Chuck's preference in the situation suggested good common sense in coming to an agreement.

Sometimes Rusty says to me, "It's not so important to me. You make the decision." And sometimes I say to him, "It's not so important to me. You decide." I sometimes say to Rusty, "I don't have the energy to think about it. Do whatever you want." Or Rusty may say, "I can't be bothered with this decision. You think about it and let me know what you decide."

Further Considerations

Can compromise be reached? Is more time needed so that greater evaluation may occur and one partner or the other can come to better terms with the situation? Has one spiritually mature partner been given some definite direction from the Lord about the matter?

Can there be advantages to a partner refusing to compromise? Yes, provided it is for the right reasons. When Billy and Ruth Graham were married, they experienced conflict over which denomination to join. Billy insisted Ruth become Baptist. Ruth refused, maintaining her Presbyterian preference. Years later, Billy commented on the importance of this decision. In *Billy Graham: The Authorized Biography*, by John Pollock, Billy says that Ruth's decision enabled him to keep a broader perspective of the Christian community, a necessary help in his evangelistic ministry.

In the decision-making processes of life we get to know God better. In the decisions of life, marriage partners must get to know each other more intimately, not only to discover each other's needs, but the whys behind those needs. This requires deep respect for each other's point of view, a willingness to deny self for the other, and deepening love and understanding.

But it also involves another basic ingredient: common sense.

Working Through Common Sense

The man who knows right from wrong and has good judgment and common sense is happier than the man who is immensely rich! For such wisdom is far more valuable than precious jewels. Nothing else compares with it.

Proverbs 3:13–15 TLB

Let's take a look at why common sense is important to a marriage. Biblical common sense includes three elements:

1. *Analyzing*—breaking down an issue and seeing its component parts.
2. *Sifting*—filtering the component parts through a biblical grid or perspective.
3. *Synthesizing*—putting the components back together so that the solution appropriately fits the problem.

It can be truly difficult to rise to the challenges of marriage. For one thing it may be hard to understand our partners' behavior. But it may be even more of a problem to *analyze* our own responses. For example: We know a certain response is appropriate to a situation, but we don't follow it; we are bothered by trivial comments and actions of our spouses; we want our partners to love us as we are, but we are afraid to be open and vulnerable.

Self-revelation may be extremely painful, but it is a basic element in successful marital negotiation. We need to investigate our own motivations and responses, despite the fears involved in confronting our possible failure at being all we are meant to be. We may not want to see *ourselves* clearly, and for that reason analysis may be threatening.

But we may also want to keep our illusions about our partners. For example, if we are romantics, we may want to believe that our spouses are ideal. With these built-in defenses, marital analysis becomes practically impossible. Pat answers are preferred by both partners, who so pointedly wish to avoid dealing with their own real selves or their partner's real self. For example, I personally know of a number of couples who boast of never having quarreled. Often their answer is to simply ward off any kind of direct confrontation to keep from breaking through their illusions of themselves and each other.

On the other hand, a guilty spouse may also want to see a partner in unreal terms, determining to exaggerate the faults of the partner, so as to lessen his or her own sense of guilt and need for change.

How we view our partners reflects our own needs and problems, but despite our fears of what we might uncover, we are called to obey the apostle Paul's command, "Let a man [and that word is generic] examine himself . . ." (1 Corinthians 11:28).

Personal analysis in marriage should be a regular part of life, but it is especially important when: we become aware of our own or our spouses' unhealthy patterns of thinking, speaking, or behavior; we discover thoughts or actions that are contrary to scriptural principles; we observe ourselves or our partners overreacting to situations.

Helen and Jake are a good example of the need for common sense in marriage. Jake wanted to see a movie each weekend, but Helen did not like the rough language or the explicit sex scenes. Every week they had a confrontation.

"I'm tired," said Jake. "I've worked hard all week, and I deserve some relaxation. I relax best in front of a movie."

"I just cannot handle the movies you want to see."

"All right," replied Jake, "you choose the movie."

"That's not much help," returned Helen. "We have only three choices, and they're all bad."

"You always criticize what I want to do. Isn't there anything I can do to please you?"

"It's just that I don't like the movies. When you get home from the movie and want to have sex with me, I never know if you want me or the naked woman at the movies."

"Oh, there you go again, exaggerating things," continued Jake. "You know it's you I want. But can I help it that I'm a man and that other women appeal to me?"

"I won't go with you, Jake. I don't feel right about it."

"You have to go with me, Helen. You are my wife, and this is what I want you to do."

Helen conceded.

Common sense just lost out in this conversation—first, because arbitrary and unbiblical rules (the man is in charge) were maintained at the expense of biblical action; second, because the real issues were not addressed.

PRACTICAL DECISION MAKING IN MARRIAGE   111

Let's hear from Helen as she worked through the situation. "In the periphery of my mind I always knew the way we handled this situation was inadequate, but I didn't know how to turn it around. My first step, however, after talking with my pastor, was to take responsibility for my own thinking and actions. If I got railroaded into doing something that I knew displeased the Lord Jesus Christ, I had to accept the fact that it was my *own* fault. I needed to confess the fact that I was easily intimidated by Jake and actually preferred capitulating in a situation to putting forth the effort necessary to know myself and the situation better. I lacked the courage to stand up for what was right.

"When I was finally honest with myself on this score, dealing with the immediate situation became easier."

Instead of asking questions like: "Who is in charge in marriage?" which reflect stereotypical (one-rule-fits-all) thinking, Helen wrote down the following questions (taken from *Staying On Top When Things Go Wrong*) to ask herself about her own and Jake's responses. (*Note:* Not all the following questions apply to every situation, but they are guidelines for analyses.)

> Under what conditions does this problem or pattern arise?
> What events might have triggered this event in our marriage?
> Am I upset with myself?
> Do I feel guilty for not being the Christian I should be, and am I consciously punishing myself by my response?
> Am I trying to control my spouse to get my own needs met?
> Has something in my past experience triggered my response to the situation?
> Was my response the result of boredom? Discouragement? Fear? Self-pity? Unbelief? Avoiding confrontation?
> What thoughts went through my mind prior to this response?
> Is there a root cause of sin behind my response? Resentment? Jealousy? Self-centeredness? Pride?
> Am I absorbed with the fear of losing love if I do not respond in a certain manner?
> In this situation do I care more about pleasing a person than serving Christ?

CALLED TO UNITY

Is there any pattern to my responses? Does the problem in our marriage occur at a similar time of day? Does a certain type of situation produce the problem?

(*Note:* These same questions can be asked about a spouse's response.)

Now let's take a closer look at how Helen used common sense—analyzing, sifting, and synthesizing—in the movie situation.

"I began by praying. But instead of praying, 'Lord, help me submit, and help Jake to be a better husband,' I asked God to show me why Jake insisted on going to the movies and to give me the courage to ask why I always agreed against my better judgment. Next, I saturated myself with Scripture, looking up verses and passages that applied to our situation. (I also asked God to teach me during my regular times of Bible reading.) In response to that prayer, God began to open my mind as I asked myself the list of questions.

"First, I thought through Jake's actions. Asking the list of questions, I confronted squarely and without excuses that my husband had a lust problem. This was exhibited not only by his choice of movies, but by his own admission. Second, I was able to determine that he wanted me to go with him because my presence made him less embarrassed than if he went alone. Further, when I shared in the deed, it seemed to lessen his own guilt. Third, the way Jake covered his guilt was to blame me for not caring about how hard he worked. I had to face the fact that this was a decoy.

"Next, in light of what I clearly saw, I asked myself why I let him include me in his deed. My prime problem was that I hated conflict. I had learned early in marriage that, if I did not go along with Jake, he brought it up to me time and time again, always accusing me of not being a submissive wife. I had learned to cower under this treatment. What was most difficult was facing up to the fact that my commitment to Christ left something to be desired. The truth was that I would rather have peace in my home (though not a godly peace) than pay a price to serve Christ. If it weren't for my pastor encouraging me in this direction, I believe I could have hidden behind some popular teaching, telling myself I was only submitting to my husband. My pastor had to help me see that what I was wanting to call submission was nothing more than lack of courage. Finally, after sifting or filtering the problem through the perspective of Scripture, I was able to synthesize the problem into an appropriate response.

"I told Jake that if he wanted to see the movies, it was between him and the Lord, but I would not participate in something I knew displeased God. Despite the pressure he put on me, I held my ground and clung to Christ to hold me steady."

Marriage is a relationship, not a role, a set of rules, a system, or a chain of command. It is two Christians operating fully as Christians. And it is a beautiful order, in which decisions can be brought about not by arbitrary rules, but by the Spirit of God, alive and functioning in each believer's life.

TEN

Biblical Marriages

"Sarah obeyed Abraham without question," the speaker began. "And she is our model of the total submission and obedience God asks of Christian wives."

I've often heard such statements, but do illustrations of marriages in Scripture really present such a case? Do they teach, for example, that God leads the woman through the man? Do they encourage one-sided obedience by the wife or say that the husband makes the final decisions? At the other end of the scale, do they favor self-assertiveness at the expense of the other partner?

Let's look at several biblical marriages: Abraham and Sarah, Manoah and his wife, Hannah and Elkanah, the Shunammite woman and her husband, Job and his wife, and Abigail and Nabal.

Paul says the Old Testament is given to us "for our instruction" (1 Corinthians 10:11). Although Israel functioned largely as a patriarchal society (as a result of the Fall), it doesn't seem that God related to married people in keeping with that system.

As we examine the particular Scriptures, keep in mind that every biblical character isn't exemplary. However, when narrative supports clear doctrinal teaching and/or gives indication that God initiated or approved an attitude or act, then we may have reason to apply those illustrations to our own experiences.

Let's begin with Sarah and Abraham. The greater part of their story is found in Genesis 11:26–23:19. It would be helpful if you would read the whole story, but I will zero in on specific scenes.

> And it came about when [Abram] came near to Egypt, that he said to Sarai his wife, "See now, I know that you are a beautiful woman; and it will come about when the Egyptians see you, that they will say, 'This is his wife'; and they will kill me, but they will let you live. Please say that you are my sister so that it may go well with me because of you, and that I may live on account of you."
>
> Genesis 12:11–13

Abram and Sarai (or Abraham and Sarah) seem to be a normal married couple. They have disagreements (Genesis 21:8–12), obstacles and dilemmas to face (Genesis 12:10–13; 20:1–18). In Genesis 12 we see them traveling to Egypt and preparing a deceptive story to tell the Pharaoh. How did this scheme come about? Abram doesn't command Sarai, but clearly reasons with her. In Hebrew the word translated "please" means "to beg, implore, beseech, or pray." It does not suggest a command, but rather a request. Yet I have heard this story used as an example of how Sarai obeyed Abram without question. If he saw himself as the final authority, Abram probably would have commanded Sarai in this instance, as he reasoned that her cooperation was essential to preserve his life.

Sarai agreed to his request, but to their detriment, for Abram's idea was an unreasonable one, which almost cost Pharaoh and his house their lives (Genesis 12:14-20). Abraham and Sarah tried the same scheme, with equally disastrous results, recorded in Genesis 20:1-18, and both passages suggest God clearly did not bless this decision.

Should Sarah have vetoed Abraham's scheme to lie about her marital status? Abraham's advice lacked discernment and common sense, and it might have been better if Sarah had suggested that they both ask God's direction in the matter rather than rely on their own devices.

Consider another interaction between Sarah and Abraham.

> Now Sarai, Abram's wife had borne him no children, and she had an Egyptian maid whose name was Hagar. So Sarai said to Abram, "Now behold, the Lord has prevented me from bearing children. Please go in to my maid; perhaps I shall obtain children through her." And Abram listened to ["hearkened" or "obeyed"] the voice of Sarai.
>
> Vv. 16:1, 2

We find here the same Hebrew use of the word *please* that Abraham used of Sarah in 12:13. And Abraham conceded to this request.

Is this then a proof text that a man should obey his wfe? No. In fact, Abraham shouldn't have listened to Sarah in this instance.

Sarah later regretted this pressure she put upon Abraham. "And Sarai said to Abram, 'May the wrong done me be upon you. I gave my maid into your arms; but when she saw that she had conceived, I was despised in her sight. May the Lord judge between you and me' " (16:5).

But does God lead through the woman?

Let's consider another illustration from the marriage of Abraham and Sarah in Genesis 21:10-12.

> She said to Abraham, "Drive out this maid and her son, for the son of this maid shall not be an heir with my son Isaac." And the matter distressed Abraham greatly because of his son.

But God said to Abraham, "Do not be distressed because of the lad and your maid; whatever Sarah tells you, listen to her, for through Isaac your descendants shall be named."

In this part of the narrative God sanctions the word of Sarah and admonishes Abraham to listen to his wife. (The RSV version says "do as she tells you.")

God can lead through either spouse. In the story of Abraham and Sarah, the real lesson is *not which sex makes the decision, but who is following God's counsel.*

An illustration concerning God's directing both the husband and wife happened several years ago to Elizabeth and Russell. Through the generosity of a relative, a houseful of furniture was to be given to them. Since they were renting a furnished cabin, they wondered what they would do with the furniture.

Elizabeth and Russell decided to buy a house. They found an ideal home at a great price, but, when some financial obstacles arose, Russell resisted the idea of buying. Yet Elizabeth was absolutely sure God wanted them to have that home. "Because of this certainty, I persisted in my arguments for the house," says Elizabeth. Russell continued to resist, but one by one, the financial obstacles were overcome; within two weeks of viewing the house, they signed for it. God had supernaturally intervened.

Had Elizabeth not been sensitive to God's leading and obedient to Him, they would have missed the house. Russell now says that he is glad Elizabeth persisted when he resisted, for he could not see what God had given them.

Elizabeth can say the same concerning Russell. "Several years ago I was involved in a job-related decision. Russell warned me about some impending problems, yet I didn't feel his concerns were relevant. Sometime later, he cautioned me again. I felt he was making too much of the issue. Finally he asked me if I would be willing to hear his arguments. I agreed, and he carefully articulated a thorough case. I could see how strategic his advice was and how greatly I might have jeopardized the situation, had I not heeded his advice."

CALLED TO UNITY

From God to Woman

Consider Manoah and his wife, whose story is found in Judges 13.

> And there was a certain man of Zorah, of the family of the Danites, whose name was Manoah; and his wife was barren and had borne no children. Then the angel of the Lord appeared to the woman and said to her, "Behold now, you are barren and have borne no children, but you shall conceive and give birth to a son. Now therefore, be careful not to drink wine or strong drink, nor eat any unclean thing. For behold, you shall conceive and give birth to a son, and no razor shall come upon his head, for the boy shall be a Nazirite to God from the womb; and he shall begin to deliver Israel from the hands of the Philistines." Then the woman came and told her husband. . . .
>
> Vv. 2–6

Manoah and his wife were childless. *The wife* receives the message from the angel of the Lord, not only that she will have a child but that he will be a very special man of God. She then shares the information with her husband, and he believes her. If the hierarchical system (God leads through the man) is correct, why didn't God make His will known to the man, or at least the man and the woman?

Note whom the angel came to the second time:

> Then Manoah entreated the Lord and said, "O Lord, please let the man of God whom Thou has sent come to us again that he may teach us what to do for the boy who is to be born." And God listened to the voice of Manoah; and the angel of God came again to the woman as she was sitting in the field, but Manoah her husband was not with her. So the woman ran quickly and told her husband, "Behold, the man who came the other day has appeared to me." Then Manoah arose and fol lowed his wife, and when he came to the man he said to him, "Are you the man who spoke to the woman?" And he said, "I am." And Manoah said, "Now when your words come to pass,

what shall be the boy's mode of life and his vocation?" So the angel of the Lord said to Manoah, "Let the woman pay attention to all that I said."

Vv. 8–13

The angel, in effect, says to Manoah, "I have already explained this to your wife."

"Then the woman gave birth to a son and named him Samson; and the child grew up and the Lord blessed him" (13:24).

Possibly Manoah's wife was more developed spiritually than her husband, allowing God more access to her life. If so, it may answer a lot of questions as to who might have the greater leadership in marriage. Could it be that it is the partner who walks more closely with God?

Decisions of Grave Importance

Consider the story of Hannah and Elkanah, presented in 1 Samuel 1. Elkanah had two wives. Peninnah had several children, but Hannah was barren. Peninnah chided Hannah, making her plight seem even more unbearable.

Hannah's predicament can be felt by all of us to one degree or another. For it seems that there is always some unfulfilled longing within us that tests our faith and casts us upon the Lord. As we often are blinded to the good hand of the Lord in the midst of unanswered prayer, so Hannah could not see that God was preparing her heart to offer back to Him a choice servant who would serve Israel wisely throughout his entire life.

Then Hannah rose after eating and drinking in Shiloh. Now Eli the priest was sitting on the seat by the doorpost of the temple of the Lord. And she, greatly distressed, prayed to the Lord and wept bitterly. And she made a vow and said, "O Lord of hosts, if Thou wilt indeed look on the affliction of Thy maidservant and remember me, and not forget Thy maidservant, but wilt give Thy maidservant a son, then I will give him to the Lord all the days of his life, and a razor shall never come on his head."

Now it came about, as she continued praying before the Lord, that Eli was watching her mouth. As for Hannah, she was speaking in her heart, only her lips were moving, but her voice was not heard. So Eli thought she was drunk. Then Eli said to her, "How long will you make yourself drunk? Put away your wine from you." But Hannah answered and said, "No, my lord, I am a woman oppressed in spirit; I have drunk neither wine nor strong drink, but I have poured out my soul before the Lord. Do not consider your maidservant as a worthless woman; for I have spoken until now out of my great concern and provocation." Then Eli answered and said, "Go in peace; and may the God of Israel grant your petition that you have asked of Him." And she said, "Let your maidservant find favor in your sight." So the woman went her way and ate, and her face was no longer sad.

Vv. 9–18

There are some interesting details to note in this woman's dialogue with God. First *she* made a vow directly to God. This vow was serious, involving both her and her husband, Elkanah, yet the Bible records no seeking of her husband's permission. (Of course, she could have talked it over with Elkanah.) This bold-faced commitment to give away her child was done outright, and God heard and answered her.

. . . And Elkanah had relations with Hannah his wife, and the Lord remembered her. And it came about in due time, after Hannah had conceived, that she gave birth to a son; and she named him Samuel, saying, "Because I have asked him of the Lord."

Then the man Elkanah went up with all his household to offer to the Lord the yearly sacrifice and pay his vow. But Hannah did not go up, for she said to her husband, "I will not go up until the child is weaned; then I will bring him, that he may appear before the Lord and stay there forever." And Elkanah her husband said to her, "Do what seems best to you. Remain until you have weaned him; only may the Lord confirm His word." So the woman remained and nursed her son until she weaned him. Now when she had weaned him, she took him up with her, with a three-year-old bull and one ephah of flour and a jug of wine, and brought him to the house of the Lord in Shiloh, although the child was young. Then they slaughtered the bull, and brought the boy to Eli. And she said, "Oh, my lord! As your soul lives, my lord, I am the woman who stood here beside you, praying to the Lord. For this boy I prayed, and the Lord has given me my petition which I asked of Him. So I have also dedicated him to the Lord; as long as he lives he is dedicated to the Lord." And he worshiped the Lord there.

Vv. 19-28

Hannah gives God her son, names him, and tells Elkanah she is not going with him. Then she dedicates her son.

Through the entire story we observe a married woman who is apparently making decisions in matters of grave importance, in matters that affect her husband as well. Was she breaking some kind of rule? Her husband does not appear to be displeased, and she evidently did not offend God in any way. "And the Lord visited Hannah; and she conceived and gave birth to three sons and two daughters. And the boy Samuel grew before the Lord" (2:21).

Who Took Charge?

The next married couple is related in 2 Kings 4:8-37 and known only as the Shunammite woman and her husband. She is introduced to us as a great or prominent woman.

> ... Elisha passed over to Shunem, where there was a prominent woman, and she persuaded him to eat food. And so it was, as often as he passed by, he turned in there to eat food. And she said to her husband, "Behold now, I perceive that this is a holy man of God passing by us continually. Please let us make a little walled upper chamber and let us set a bed for him there, and a table and a chair and a lampstand; and it shall be, when he comes to us, that he can turn in there."

Vv. 8-10

The woman here takes the initiative in preparing a place for Elisha.

> One day he came there and turned in to the upper chamber and rested. Then he said to Gehazi his servant, "Call this Shunammite." And when he had called her, she stood before him.
> And he said to him, "Say now to her, 'Behold, you have been careful for us with all this care; what can I do for you? Would you be spoken for to the king or to the captain of the army?' " And she answered, "I live among my own people."
> So he said, "What then is to be done for her?" And Gehazi answered, "Truly she has no son and her husband is old."
> And he said, "Call her." When he called her, she stood in the doorway.
> Then he said, "At this season next year you shall embrace a son." And she said, "No, my lord, O man of God, do not lie to your maidservant."
> And the woman conceived and bore a son that season the next year, as Elisha had said to her.
>
> Vv. 11-17

Elisha chooses to honor the woman, even though her husband may have contributed to the building of the chamber. When calamity strikes, it is the mother who takes charge:

> When the child was grown, the day came that he went out to his father to the reapers. And he said to his father, "My head, my head." And he said to his servant, "Carry him to his mother." When he had taken him and brought him to his mother, he sat on her lap until noon, and then died. And she went up and laid him on the bed of the man of God, and shut the door behind him, and went out. Then she called to her husband and said, "Please send me one of the servants and one of the donkeys, that I may run to the man of God and return."
> And he said, "Why will you go to him today? It is neither new moon nor Sabbath." And she said, "It will be well." Then she saddled a donkey and said to her servant, "Drive and go forward; do not slow down the pace for me unless I tell you." So she went and came to the man of God to Mount Carmel.

And it came about when the man of God saw her at a distance, that he said to Gehazi his servant, "Behold, yonder is the Shunammite. Please run now to meet her and say to her, 'Is it well with you? Is it well with your husband? Is it well with the child?' " And she answered, "It is well." When she came to the man of God to the hill, she caught hold of his feet. And Gehazi came near to push her away; but the man of God said, "Let her alone, for her soul is troubled within her; and the Lord has hid it from me and has not told me." Then she said, "Did I ask for a son from my lord? Did I not say, 'Do not deceive me?' " Then he said to Gehazi, "Gird up your loins and take my staff in your hand, and go your way; if you meet any man, do not salute him, and if anyone salutes you, do not answer him; and lay my staff on the lad's face." And the mother of the lad said, "As the Lord lives and as you yourself live, I will not leave you." And he rose and followed her. Then Gehazi passed on before them and laid the staff on the lad's face, but there was neither sound nor response. So he returned to meet him and told him, "The lad has not awakened." When Elisha came into the house, behold the lad was dead and laid on his bed.

So he entered and shut the door behind them both, and prayed to the Lord.

And he went up and lay on the child, and put his mouth on his mouth and his eyes on his eyes and his hands on his hands, and he stretched himself on him; and the flesh of the child became warm.

Then he returned and walked in the house once back and forth, and went up and stretched himself on him; and the lad sneezed seven times and the lad opened his eyes.

Vv. 18–35

Elisha calls for the woman, not her husband, when the son is restored.

And he called Gehazi and said, "Call this Shunammite." So he called her. And when she came in to him, he said, "Take up your son."

Then she went in and fell at his feet and bowed herself to the ground, and she took up her son and went out.

Vv. 36, 37

CALLED TO UNITY

If God has ordained that the man be in charge, why did Elisha interact mainly with the woman? Why did the woman take charge of the situation and act on it? Why was she blessed for her behavior?

Judged Too Harshly?

One wife in the Bible has consistently been cast in a bad light. Bible teachers quickly draw firm conclusions about this woman, but the simplistic view of her behavior evades the complex nature of human response. That woman was married to Job. After Job had suffered enormously from losing his wealth, his children, and his health, her famous two-liner is: "Do you still hold fast your integrity? Curse God and die!" (Job 2:9).

I would be the last one to suggest that this recommendation is a good one. It isn't. Yet consider the strain Job's wife was under. First, all her wealth was destroyed. Then she learned that all her children had been killed.

Imagine her distress! Bereft of her fortune and her sons and daughters, she must now face the potentially fatal disease of her husband. Out of her grief came a bitter retort, "Curse God and die." Yet Job's response to her suggests that perhaps this was not her normal behavior, but an exception. For he responds, "You speak as one of the foolish women speaks. Shall we indeed accept good from God and not accept adversity?" (v. 10). Job rebukes his wife, not by stating that she is a fool, but by stating that she is speaking as a foolish woman might speak, perhaps implying that this was not her character to do so. Job wisely points out that she has misjudged God, then goes on to question God angrily, despair of living, and curse the day he was born (Job 3). Many people want to be fair in their treatment of women and do not knowingly apply a double standard; yet to denounce Job's wife and applaud the virtues of Job is harsh, stereotypical, and unfair.

In sharing this insight into Job's wife I am attempting to view people as individuals, assessing their behavior in light of the whole human experience rather than fixed and rigid role expectations. The harsh judgment cast upon Job's wife reminds me of a comment I overheard about a wonderful woman whose husband was an alcoholic. "She must be hard to live with," the speaker surmised. "Otherwise, why does he drink so much?" It was assumed that the wife was to blame. Husbands often receive the same unjust judgments, and this sort of judging comes largely from our contemporary "boxed" teaching which fails to see life in totality. The Christian community needs to get back to "relationship" teaching emphasizing the complexities involved with two individuals working out life together.

Commonsense Thinking

In short, we need to get back to commonsense thinking, as the story of Abigail and Nabal illustrates (1 Samuel 25).

In verse 3 Abigail is described as being intelligent (literally "of good understanding"—common sense). In contrast, the word *Nabal* means "fool," and he was well named. David, who has been anointed king, is in flight for his life from Saul. Yet he and his band of men who follow him have acted honorably to the sons of Israel. David and his men have protected and aided Nabal's servants, and David now asks only for their due, for help to celebrate a holiday. But Nabal does not understand *reciprocity*, that is, the importance of recognizing somebody else's generosity and responding to it.

When David's young men came, they spoke to Nabal according to all these words in David's name; then they waited. But Nabal answered David's servants, and said, "Who is David? And who is the son of Jesse? There are many servants today who are each breaking away from his master. Shall I then take my bread and my water and my meat that I have slaughtered for my shearers and give it to men whose origin I do not know?" So David's young men retraced their way and went back; and they came and told him according to all these words. And David said to his men, "Each of you gird on his sword."

So each man girded on his sword. And David also girded on his sword, and about four hundred men went up behind David while two hundred stayed with the baggage.

Vv. 9–13

Did Nabal really not know who David was? Everyone knew of David, who had killed the great Goliath, who had slain his ten thousand. And Nabal must have heard from his servants of David's band of men—more than six hundred—who were in his area.

But Nabal refused to reciprocate for David's protection of Nabal's possessions. As a result, his entire household was about to be destroyed. Yet his wife was not a fool, and the servants knew it.

But one of the young men told Abigail, Nabal's wife, saying, "Behold, David sent messengers from the wilderness to greet our master, and he scorned them. Yet the men were very good to us, and we were not insulted, nor did we miss anything as long as we went about with them, while we were in the fields. They were a wall to us both by night and by day, all the time we were with them tending the sheep. Now therefore know and consider what you should do, for evil is plotted against our master and against all his household; and he is such a worthless man [literally, "son of Satan"] that no one can speak to him."

Vv. 14–17

Answer a Fool According to His Folly

And what was Abigail's response? How did she respond to the situation? Did she immediately employ a one-rule-fits-all thinking? No. Did she go to Nabal the fool? No. She did not play games with herself, pretending that Nabal was really a fine husband. She did not think, *Well, Nabal is the authority of this house. What he says goes. And since his will is the same as God's will in my life, I know that God will protect me.* Abigail neither denied nor dismissed what Nabal really was, and she acted accordingly, in light of that understanding.

Then Abigail hurried and took two hundred loaves of bread and two jugs of wine and five sheep already prepared and five measures of roasted grain and a hundred clusters of raisins and two hundred cakes of figs, and loaded them on donkeys. And she said to her young men, "Go on before me; behold, I am coming after you." But she did not tell her husband Nabal. And it came about as she was riding on her donkey and coming down by the hidden part of the mountain, that behold, David and his men were coming down toward her; so she met them. Now David had said, "Surely in vain I have guarded all that this man has in the wilderness, so that nothing was missed of all that belonged to him; and he has returned me evil for good. May God do so to the enemies of David, and more also, if by morning I leave as much as one male of any who belong to him."

Vv. 18–22

As the story continues note Abigail's appropriate attitude and communication. Her term "my lord" does not refer to her husband, but to David.

When Abigail saw David, she hurried and dismounted from her donkey, and fell on her face before David, and bowed herself to the ground. And she fell at his feet and said, "On me alone, my lord, be the blame. And please let your maidservant speak to you, and listen to the words of your maidservant. Please do not let my lord pay attention to this worthless man, Nabal, for as his name is, so is he. Nabal is his name and folly is with him; but I your maidservant did not see the young men of my lord whom you sent. Now therefore, my lord, as the Lord lives, and as your soul lives, since the Lord has restrained you from shedding blood, and from avenging yourself by your own hand, now then let your enemies, and those who seek evil against my lord, be as Nabal. And now let this gift which our maidservant has brought to my lord be given to the young men who accompany my lord. Please forgive the transgression of your maidservant; for the Lord will certainly make for my lord an enduring house, because my lord is fighting the battles of the Lord, and evil shall not be found in you all your days. And should anyone rise up to pursue you and to seek your life, then

CALLED TO UNITY

the life of my lord shall be bound in the bundle of the living with the Lord your God; but the lives of your enemies He will sling out as from the hollow of a sling. And it shall come about when the Lord shall do for my lord according to all the good that He has spoken concerning you, and shall appoint you ruler over Israel, that this will not cause grief or a troubled heart to my lord, both by having shed blood without cause and by my lord having avenged himself. When the Lord shall deal well with my lord, then remember your maidservant."

Vv. 23-31

Like a skilled defense lawyer, Abigail states her case, first taking the blame for the offense and then asking forgiveness. Then she reminds David of his impending reign over Israel and pleads for him not to do anything hastily that will mar that victory. And what is David's response?

Then David said to Abigail, "Blessed be the Lord God of Israel, who sent you this day to meet me, and blessed be your discernment, and blessed be you who have kept me this day from bloodshed, and from avenging myself by my own hand. . . ." So David received from her hand what she had brought him, and he said to her, "Go up to your house in peace. See, I have listened to you and granted your request."

Vv. 32, 33, 35

Abigail was a woman of faith, and the proof of her faith was her action of intervention to prevent the future king of Israel from murder to satisfy his wrath. She risked misunderstanding and divorce from Nabal to save Israel from shame and disgrace.

Frankly, many husbands and wives bear the penalty of their dependence on simplistic rules and structures of relating rather than having a broad knowledge of the Word of God and ardently seeking the leading of the Holy Spirit for appropriate application. But sadder still is that many condemn those who have less structured marital unions. They simply don't know what they are missing.

Incidentally, a well-known seminar leader says that Abigail was sinning by coming to David, yet David declares that *God* sent her.

The story continues:

> Then Abigail came to Nabal, and behold, he was holding a feast in his house, like the feast of a king. And Nabal's heart was merry within him, for he was very drunk; so she did not tell him anything at all until the morning light. But it came about in the morning, when the wine had gone out of Nabal, that his wife told him these things, and his heart died within him so that he became as a stone. And about ten days later, it happened that the Lord struck Nabal, and he died.
>
> Vv. 36–38

Abigail did not do what her husband commanded or what he wished. She did what was appropriate. Some might suggest that Abigail should have followed her husband's dictates and trusted God to intervene. But where is the Old Testament teaching that a woman must arbitrarily carry out her husband's wishes? Such reasoning also misses the point that God *did* intervene. He intervened *through Abigail.* At least David felt that way and praised her for her discernment and courage. Later *God* took Nabal's life. Now, the conclusion!

David now credits God for the way He used Abigail.

> When David heard that Nabal was dead, he said, "Blessed be the Lord, who has pleaded the cause of my reproach from the hand of Nabal, and has kept back His servant from evil. The Lord has returned the evildoing of Nabal on his own head." Then David sent a proposal to Abigail, to take her as his wife.
>
> V. 39

She accepted. I love happy endings!

New Testament Examples

There are only a few Christian marriages mentioned specifically in the New Testament, but none of those—Mary and Joseph (Luke 1:26–56; 2:1–51); Elizabeth and Zacharias (Luke 1:5–25, 57–80); Priscilla and Aquila (Acts 18:2, 3, 18, 26; Romans 16:3; 1 Corinthians 16:19; 2 Timothy 4:19); Ananias and Sapphira (Acts 5:1–11); Peter and his wife as well as other apostles and brothers of the Lord and their wives (1 Corinthians 9:5)—suggests hierarchy in any sense of the word.

But all would agree that obeying the Holy Spirit was essential. This was true of Zacharias, who prophesied by the Holy Spirit; Mary, who conceived by the Holy Spirit; and Ananias and Sapphira, who lost their lives because they lied to the Holy Spirit. And they would agree that love is important to a Christian union as well.

ELEVEN

Love
Covers
a Multitude
of Sins

"He who loves . . . has fulfilled the law" (Romans 13:8).
". . . But the greatest of these is love" (1 Corinthians 13:13;
see also Matthew 22:36–38).

Before marriage, I feared that I might someday lose the love
of my potential mate. The basis for working out this fear lay in
recognizing the kind of relationship that my husband had with
God. His commitment to God and His principles is the foundation for his commitment to me.

When a person loves, many rules are not necessary. Fear is
overcome. Faith blossoms. Full men and women of stature
emerge. In fact, the love of a husband can enable a woman to
perform at maximum.

If the thinking presented in this book is new to you, may I
suggest that you evaluate your marriage and ministry in light
of Christian love? Is your marriage producing two Spirit-led

132   CALLED TO UNITY

believers who are exercising their gifts and abilities fully in the kingdom? Does your marriage give you enough room for personal growth and fulfillment? Do you function as a full person, as opposed to a child or an assistant?

If the answer is yes, then thank God that your unique marriage is producing a maximum man or woman for the kingdom of God. However, if you as a woman are discontent in your marriage or in your ministry, you may want to consider Jenny's story:

> Soon after I married, I encountered this "I am in charge" attitude in my husband. I was enraged, and as the months passed, I became more and more upset. My anger spilled over at work and affected my relationship with others and with God. Finally I made an appointment to talk with the woman who had first opened my eyes to the idea of teamwork in Christian marriage.
>
> I laid out my discouragement, and she said, "Jenny, you have done well to see this scriptural position on marriage. But in the process you have lost your scriptural position on other subjects, such as loving each other, trusting God to meet your needs, having a forgiving heart, and being willing to see others as more important than yourself.
>
> "You see, there is a difference between what you know to be truth and how the Holy Spirit may lead you to act in light of that truth. You must stay close to the Spirit of God. He can wisely tell you when it is appropriate to speak up or when it's best to shut up."

The woman suggested several practical ways for Jenny—or anyone—to deal with a spouse—or anyone else—who does not give proper respect to men or women as full persons.

> "First, realize that reeducation is basic to change. Suggest that your spouse read one of the several books available on the subject of team marriage or team ministry. Later, discuss the perspective at a quiet moment.
>
> "Second, you might suggest a Bible study centering around the theme of marriage.
>
> "Third, if you sense that the issue is primarily emotional in

nature, you might ask some pertinent questions such as, 'Do you feel a need to control what I do?' 'Are you somehow threatened by me? If so, why do you feel that way?' Good questions deserve responses. And a question asked in honesty often receives some sort of reply that may offer you insight as to how you should proceed.

"Be willing to give your spouse time to rethink his positions. The male-leadership teaching has been strongly advocated the last twenty years, and change in thinking doesn't come easily. Give every opportunity for consideration of your view.

"Finally, be sensitive. Other issues, such as unity in prayer or ministry, are sometimes more important than your proving the rightness of your case. However, if you find you're being constantly bullied or maneuvered, you may need to speak up, regardless. Inevitably, if two people aren't living in harmony in marriage and ministry, evangelism, prayer, and other Christian involvement will suffer accordingly."

Lynda, another Christian woman, adds:

I finally challenged the hierarchical system in my home. My husband was not at all sympathetic with my viewpoint and refused to read any of the books I suggested. He also refused to talk with our pastor, who had begun to teach the importance of team marriage.

Every time I brought the subject up, my husband would say that I was disturbing the harmony of our home. Then he lectured me, saying that my new viewpoint was causing the children to wonder about our relationship and causing some of our Christian friends to question my commitment to Christ.

For a while, I went along with his thinking, continuing to pray that he would be willing to consider a different point of view. But I finally told my husband that our marriage could not continue as it was. Though I certainly would not recommend this approach to all women, it was the catalyst needed to get my husband to look seriously into the matter. Frankly, I don't believe my husband would have ever gotten the point if I hadn't put my foot down and insisted on a change. I think that each woman must know her own situation and proceed accordingly. Had my husband not changed, that needn't have kept me from changing. After all, a person can't lead without a

CALLED TO UNITY

follower. And I would be amiss if my husband blocked my walk with God, who was my real leader.

A positive or receptive response will not always occur in a marriage. For that reason men and women should carefully think through their views before they make a life commitment.

I want to stress that I am not recommending that women destroy their marriages in an attempt to get their husbands to "see the light." I am suggesting that women know the Scriptures on God's perspective of full personhood and maximum utilization of gifts, then trust God to lead them to the fulfillment of these objectives or trust and honor Him in spite of the lack of fulfillment. God's ways are not always our ways. He may have a better plan in mind for you, one that takes time, calls for patience, and molds a deeper maturity.

On the other hand, you may be a marriage partner who seeks to control your husband. If so, you need to "see the light." Relinquishing control can be a scary business that may require professional help, but is well worth the effort. A controlling woman is not an inwardly happy one.

Also avoid the "do your own thing" philosophy. This road dead-ends in emptiness and lack of fulfillment, and it is not God's way. As Dr. Donald Bloesch, professor of theology at the University of Dubuque Theological Seminary writes, "The truly liberated man and woman are those who have been set free not to realize a vain ambition but to serve the advancement of the kingdom of God."[1]

And watch where you assess blame. Some women don't become what they are designed to be because they have not done their homework. Are you acting out a part that someone else has designed? If you are manipulated by others (Christian or non-Christian), why do you allow it to continue? Women and men both have the Scriptures. The pattern of the New Testament saints of Berea should be our pattern, ". . . examining the Scriptures daily, to see whether these things were so" (Acts 17:11).

Other women don't become all they were meant to be because they have not laid their lives down before the Lord and set their hearts to worship and serve *Him* whatever the cost. Thus they do not have the aid of His power and authority.

Still other women are held back because of their dishonesty. Some women who *lack faith* say they are "being intimidated." Some who *have fear* say they are "being threatened." Some who *lack courage* say they're "being held back." I know from personal experience that God is greater than any obstacle, and that includes biases, incorrect doctrine, and spouses.

For many years I felt intimidated by people. I was tossed to and fro by the many differing opinions within the Christian community. One day I faced what the problem really was: My intimidation was *my* fault. I was a victim because *I* didn't know my Bible well enough to direct my own life with confidence. I made up my mind finally to know God and the Scriptures so well that God, rather than circumstances or other people, would run my life.

How did I go about this? I have recorded part of my journey in *Staying on Top When Things Go Wrong.* But in addition, I clung close to God. "God," I would say, "So-and-so says one thing and So-and-so says something else. I've got to know. What is true? Teach me, God. You said if I am in Your Word I will know Your truth, and the truth shall set me free. I want freedom, Lord. And confidence. Teach me. Teach me."

If you think I prayed this prayer just once or twice, you are mistaken. I prayed it daily, even hourly, for years. I determined not to suffer because of ignorance or lack of the power of God in my life.

Learning is a personal responsibility. We are only tossed to and fro when we do not have a great enough grasp of the whole of Scripture to be able to weigh what we are being taught.

If you want to win, make sure you know God's perspective. If you are under His leadership, He will teach you what is appropriate, so your life can be all it is meant to be.

A Word to the Men

I have asked Rusty to make a few comments on this subject, out of his own experiences, and the rest of this chapter is written by him.

One of the great hindrances to Christian maturity is becoming comfortable in a certain mode of thinking or a certain lifestyle. One popular teaching suggests that an evidence that the man should be in charge is that being in charge comes "naturally" to men. It is in fact a *comfortable* doctrine. Actually, I believe that the very comfort involved in "being in charge" may be an indicator that "being in charge" may *not* be from God, as God's ways often run counter to the natural, the comfortable.

I believe that submission comes hard to some men because they feel comfortable "being in charge" and justify that feeling as God given. Hence they do not put up the appropriate fight to bring this inclination under God's control. But let's be honest about it. We all tend to want our own way. Yet God's way is humility for both men and women, and I see no exceptions to that in marriage.

To maintain a system where the man is in charge, one must clearly justify this position as God's intent and design in Scripture. Emotions, background, or preconceived ideas are not a basis upon which to decide this issue. We must shy away from assuming that the comfortable and natural are evidence that God has planned things this way.

Some men with whom I am acquainted have a further problem of equating "being in charge" with manliness. The two become so inseparable in their personalities that to deny them leadership or final authority in the home is to deny them their manhood. This is a grave error in thinking, for Jesus made it clear that servanthood was the key in the kingdom of God. Chauvinism and machismo have no place in the home or the church. As Jesus said, ". . . Let him who is the greatest among you become as the youngest, and the leader as the servant" (Luke 22:26).

From where then is manhood derived? Christian manhood is founded in *dependence* on the Lord. Christian manhood is based on unconditional, *sacrificial love*. Christian manhood is based on *denying oneself* for the sake of others. How is it that we preach these truths as the essence of the Christian life, yet turn around and assert that the man should and must have the final word in marriage? The two are incongruous. Gentleness and deference should be consistent with Christian living, in and out of the home. Personally, I feel that this is where many men fail as Christians.

Are you intimidated by the thought of a woman being right and you being wrong? This may indicate that you have bought into the world system. Don't get caught in the trap of believing that the fact that you are intimidated by a woman means that she is out of line. If you are intimidated by a woman, *you* have a problem. It is possible that the woman is simply stating her position. You may be the one who is threatened by her maturity and capabilities. Let's not mince words here. Face your insecurity as sin and cry out to God to make you someone who rejoices in the success of others (men and women), rather than one who is intimidated by their successes. This is a mark of a Christian.

Get to know God. Let Him become the ultimate source of your strength, identity, security, fulfillment, and gentleness.

Early in marriage, I had to come to grips with a pattern in my life. Probably from as far back as grade school, I had learned that when I was verbally attacked I could skillfully maneuver the conversation to make it look as if the other guy were really at fault. I brought this pattern into my marriage. But Linda had developed an uncanny ability to look below the surface and figure out my core thinking pattern. Ultimately I had to face the fact that sometimes maneuvering the conversation was my way of not dealing with my insecurity and my way of ensuring that I got what I wanted.

At the root of my problem in those situations was this: I did not practically acknowledge God as my source. I did day by day, and even moment by moment, determine to draw on His resources of love for Linda and me. But sometimes, especially in pressure situations, there were momentary lapses on my part. If Linda questioned my thinking, and I felt insecure, I needed to ask God to help me turn to the Scriptures for assistance in rebuilding my thinking and response patterns.

As I became secure, and only as I remain secure in the Lord, do I find myself able to love Linda unconditionally. That is, regardless of what I perceive coming from her, I can still respond in a way that is loving as well as glorifying to the Lord Jesus Christ. To lower myself and respond out of fear, resentment, or insecurity is not the Christian way, and frankly, when I have not acknowledged my problem squarely it has caused many marriage hassles.

I still have a lot to learn. One of the biggest challenges to our marriage is my busy schedule. I have found that I have difficulty loving Linda and being steady and Spirit filled as a person when I have too much on my mind. At the point where my schedule goes from orderly to harried, I begin to view Linda not as a woman I love but as an interruption to my busy plans. (Busyness is often not zealous Christianity as much as it is Americanism.) Building a pattern of getting hold of my schedule and planning times of rest and relaxation has perhaps been the second most important ingredient to a happy marriage, the first being my walk with God.

I find that maintaining my consistency as a Christian involves a minimum of an hour a day with the Lord. Now, some may do it for less, but the busier I am, the more I need that concentrated time with God, in dialogue with Him and in studying His Word. I highly recommend this.

Viewing Linda as a teammate, who, as part of her Christian function, is to love me, teach me, and challenge me (as I am to do for her) keeps the unexpected from happening. If I have set myself up as unteachable and unchallengeable by my wife, I will react defensively, should she have something to say to me. However, if I view her as a fellow heir, Spirit filled, with direct access to the throne of God, I can accept her wisdom as a needed word in my life. How you set up the system in the first place affects how you will respond. That is why it is so important to understand how God made women in general and the woman you live with in particular. Linda is not my child. She is not my assistant. She does not exist to center her life around me.

Instead, she is a child of God, led by God, serving God. And only my fallen ego (a result of the Fall) would demand that I be "in charge" of her. A surrendered life demands that God be in charge of both of us. Believe me, marriage can work far better this way.

A really secure man will go beyond accepting women as heirs of God and joint heirs of Christ. He will "help the weak." That is, should a secure man find himself in a marriage with a woman who lacks confidence, he will do what he can to aid her in her maturity. Included in that aiding may be teaching her to confront him or another person, teaching her to stand up for biblical convictions, and helping her to articulate her needs so that they can be filled. Of course, the same would apply to a woman helping a Christian man who lacks confidence.

Finally, I learned something recently when told of two different team concepts. One team concept stipulates that only one can win. That is, if one person wins a race, the other necessarily loses the race. However the Christian team concept is that when one of us wins we both win. Husbands and Christian men will do themselves a favor if they help the women win. Then our victory will be even greater. And together we can reach the world with the good news of Jesus Christ.

PART II

CALLED
TO
SERVICE

TWELVE

Glorifying God Together

A Christian friend and her husband had been receiving marriage counseling for two years. Some breakthroughs had occurred, but they still needed more.

"Why are you going for marriage counseling?" I asked her.

"To make our marriage better, of course," she said.

"Why do you want your marriage better?"

Puzzled, my friend replied, "Why do you ask?"

"Is getting your marriage together an end in itself?"

"I never thought about it," the thirty-seven-year-old woman said soberly. "What are you getting at?"

"What's the most important thing in your life, patching up your marriage or glorifying God in all you do?"

She thought a moment. "Well, if I'm honest, most all of my thinking and goals are centered on my marriage problems."

"You're more honest than most people," I replied. "Of course I am not opposed to your getting counsel for your marriage. But you and your husband may have unresolved problems because your focus is centered on marriage as an end in itself rather than a vehicle for glorifying God in all you do."

There is more to life than a fulfilling marriage. *When the higher charges of becoming what God has designed us to be become our preoccupation, a good marriage falls into line,* as one couple so wisely illustrate: "We are one of the fortunate couples," remark Bill and Jean. "We set out to honor God in all we did early in our marriage."

Bill continues, "Together we have sought first the kingdom of God. Yes, we have problems, but we can determine their solutions in light of the greater task of serving God. For example, last year we were considering where we should take a vacation—I had three weeks coming to me. Jean and I subtly had picked up the world's concept of vacation. 'You deserve a break today.' But then we were stopped in our tracks one morning when we read God's Word: 'Whatever you do in word or deed, do all to the glory of God.' For the first time it dawned on us that this included our vacation.

"For two-and-one-half weeks we had parties for children, quiet dinners with needy neighbors, and evangelized on the beach, with our kids, whom we had taught to witness. Thirteen lives were brought into the kingdom as a result of our efforts. And I believe we were more refreshed after those few weeks of helping others than we would have been, had we spent the time solely on ourselves."

The Chief End of Men and Women

"The chief end of man is to glorify God," says the Westminster Catechism. Pleasing and glorifying Him in the everyday details of our lives is bound to result in marriages that are happier, more meaningful, and productive. The reason? A person whose priorities start with pleasing God will be more likely to develop the proper character and attitude necessary to love and please his or her spouse.

Consider this. When *one* partner seeks to honor God and reflect His love, a positive dimension is added to a marriage. But when *both* teammates seek to honor God in their lives, the odds definitely increase for success. In addition their common bond and common goal can add to unity and understanding in marriage.

An interesting thing happens to a couple who take on a cause greater than themselves. In the wake of something that demands their all, petty differences are seen for what they really are. Compromise becomes essential in light of a higher good. Sacrifices can be seen in a positive light, when put in proper perspective to the whole.

As an example, many Christian organizations support the idea that *both* husband and wife should be called to their particular ministry. Why? They recognize that marital and work problems are decreased significantly if both spouses share the same desire to serve Christ.

Paul recognized this also when he wrote, "Do not be bound together with unbelievers; for what partnership have righteousness and lawlessness, or what fellowship has light with darkness?" (2 Corinthians 6:14). Paul's teaching can be applied to Christian living as well, for the individual who is not living under the leading of the Holy Spirit is walking in darkness "as the unbeliever" (*see* 1 Corinthians 3:3).

And what is that exciting adventure to which God has called Christians? Helping every individual understand the "good news"—that the love of God has been given in Christ and the free gift of forgiveness and eternal life is available to all. Consider some information:

United Nations statistics predict that by the year 2000, the earth's population will increase by one million every 4–5 days. The numbers of new arrivals *each year* will be greater than the entire population of the world in 1900.[1]

Though approximately 78,000 people become Christians every day at present, there are still today 2.3 billion who have not heard the message of Christ (73% of all non-Christians) who won't hear the gospel unless someone from outside their culture brings it to them.[2]

Every day more than 150,000 people die. What happens to them? Are heaven and hell realities? Was Jesus telling the truth when He said, "No one comes to the Father, but through me" (John 14:6)? Was Paul correctly informed when he said, ". . . How shall they hear without a preacher?" (Romans 10:14).

In light of the needs of the world, our Christian dedication to spread the Gospel is waning. In fact, in this decade, 55,000 missionaries will return to North America. If recruitment continues at its present rate (the rate of growth of the last decade), only 15,000 will replace them from our shores.

A booming population! The need for Christ! A decreasing missionary force! What are you and your spouse doing about it?

"Go Ye" Means You

What better way to enhance marriage than to glorify God *together*, not only in developing a Spirit-filled character, but in being available to God to be His instruments in reaching the world for Christ?

Yet in the midst of a world desperate for the message of Christ—where there are too few laborers to reach the more than 4.7 billion people with the Gospel, where qualified personnel are sought but not found—a controversy rages in the American Christian community over whether or not one-half of the adults (women) can teach, preach, lead, or pioneer missions to the lost.

One Christian worker expressed the confusion, "Men and women on both sides believe different things about the role of men and women in ministry. I respect many of them, yet I don't know what to believe."

A woman said, "I just don't think God meant the issue of women in ministry to be black and white. Some Scripture seems to lean in one direction, and other Scripture seems to contradict it."

CALLED TO SERVICE

Historical Disagreement

Several years ago, *Christianity Today* made a public statement of its support for women in leadership in Christian ministry.[3] This editorial view included the ordination of women to the pastorate. In the following issue, the magazine printed a letter to the editor that said in effect: If what you say is true about women, how could the church have missed it all these years? The implication was that if God intended for women to be pastors, leaders, and teachers, the American church would have come to grips with the Scripture on the issue long before now.

Yet consider the many other issues on which the church, as a whole, has differences: predestination, eternal security, water baptism, tongues, the role of government, social action, faith healing, baptism of the Spirit, divorce, observance of the Sabbath, friendship versus aggressive evangelism, and so forth.

These issues are important and demand careful study, using solid, biblical exegesis. Throughout the centuries the church has not been one-sided on the issue of women in the church. That is, since Pentecost, the restrictions placed upon women in ministry have not been consistently understood and applied. In fact, few restrictions were placed upon women before the third and fourth centuries. Around the time of Constantine, when Christianity was deemed a state religion, minimizing a personal relationship with God, many church doctrines, including women in major ministry, went astray.

Enlightened saints have seen the error of such a position and, led by the Spirit of God, have, if necessary, braved criticisms to live and act biblically rather than just culturally or traditionally. Stories of the team ministries of the Goforths of China, Catherine and William Booth, Ann and J. Hudson Taylor, and others are refreshing to read. In a letter to the Bohemian Brethren concerning the problems in the papal system, Martin Luther wrote that the "royal priesthood" in 1 Peter 2:9 applied to men, women, and children. Therefore women should be allowed to conduct baptisms and communion services. In 1739 John Wesley appointed women as class leaders and by 1787 wrote, "We give the right hand of fellowship to Sarah Nallet, and have no objection to her being a preacher in our connexion." With the great renewal under Charles G. Finney, women preaching "became widespread and developed into the full ordination of women," according to Donald and Lucille Dayton, in their article "Women as Preachers: Evangelical Precedents."[4] One of D. L. Moody's commissioned missionaries, Fredrik Franson, wrote "Prophesying Daughters," encouraging the church to use women for the evangelization of the world.[5] Hudson Taylor sent out woman missionaries by the score. William Carey begged for women missionaries to come help him in India. In 1900, the Women's Foreign Missionary Committee was formed, utilizing some seven hundred women in a major missionary outreach. Jessie Penn-Lewis was writing on the full use of women in the church in the early 1900s, long before the current investigation. (Her writing remains some of the best on the subject.)[6] Many evangelical denominations have had, since their founding, complete acceptance of women and their gifts. In fact, most denominations today ordain women to the pastorate.

But the main consideration is not who did what, but what does the Bible teach concerning all Christians—all of us, men and women, as full, mature believers? That is the purpose of our investigation.

Exegetical Tools

In any study a careful theologian first lays a thorough foundation, from Genesis to Revelation. Later, he or she examines the unclear passages and teaching more closely in light of the clear teaching and overview. We plan to take a look at the overview of women in ministry throughout the Bible. When we come to the difficult passages, they may then be seen in a clearer light.

Recently I listened to a tape by a well-known pastor and

writer on the biblical view on the role of women. He began, "If you want to know what God says about women in ministry there are several passages you should study." Then he cited only the controversial passages: 1 Timothy 2:8-15; 1 Corinthians 11:1-15; and 1 Corinthians 14:34-36. Why, I wondered, did he immediately cite controversial passages on the issue? Why didn't he give a biblical overview on the subject before he tackled the difficult passages? If asked to give the biblical position on salvation, you would rightly take me to an overview of God's plan, humanity's problem, and the message of the cross. You wouldn't begin with Hebrews 6:4, 6, ". . . Those who . . . have fallen away, it is impossible to renew . . . again to repentance . . ."; or James 2:17, ". . . faith, if it has no works, is dead . . ."; or Matthew 24:13, "But the one who endures to the end, it is he who shall be saved." (Most skilled theologians will immediately realize that these are tricky passages requiring a good study of the context, word study, and cultural implications to determine their meaning.)

Any investigative study takes time, effort, and an open mind.

Don't assume that a contemporary view on women in ministry is true because it is held by many American Christians. (America's viewpoint on women in ministry and marriage is not the view in much of the rest of the world.)

Respected Christians differ on what the Bible teaches concerning men, women, gifts, and the church, but the real questions are "Whom did God design to carry out ministry?" and "Has He set any biblical limits?" They are the issues I will attempt to answer in the following chapters.

THIRTEEN

Men and Women:
Prophets
and Priests
With
the Holy Spirit

Cecelia was attending her first Christian conference. During the main sessions she heard lectures on being led by the Holy Spirit, developing her gifts, developing good decision-making skills, leading others to Christ, and becoming an effective communicator. During the afternoon seminars, when sessions were divided between men and women, she heard lectures on being led by your husband and pastor and on the proper submissive demeanor of women.

"It was schizophrenic," she says. "They would teach verses in the general session as if they applied to all of us, then turn right around and tell us that those verses were forfeited by or severely limited when used by women. I wonder if they've ever seriously thought through the discrepancies in their teaching."

Cecelia is not the only one who senses some ambiguities in

CALLED TO SERVICE

the teaching of some Christians on women. The practices in many churches suggest a great deal of uncertainty and even hypocrisy on the subject, even though they're usually carried out with the best of motives.

Consider some rules that surround women teaching, preaching, and leading in many churches:

A woman may speak to the congregation on Wednesday night, but not on a Sunday.

A woman may teach men and women through books and music, but not through speaking or preaching.

A woman may teach men and women on video, but not in person.

A woman may teach in another culture or on the mission field, but not in America.

A woman celebrity, such as Corrie ten Boom, may teach, but not an "ordinary" woman.

A woman may teach in a Sunday-school class, but not during the church service.

An older woman may teach, but not a younger woman.

A woman may "share," but not teach.

A woman may teach, but not preach.

A woman may speak with her husband's permission.

A woman may speak if she does not stand in the pulpit.

A woman may give her testimony, but not teach through it.

A woman may prepare communion, but not serve it.

Two of the most common practices are that women can teach vulnerable children and "easily deceived" women, but not men. But if women are not qualified teachers, why expose to them those who are supposedly most vulnerable to misunderstanding? If they are qualified, why restrain them from teaching anyone who might benefit from their insight?

Why do some churches have these rules? Most of these pastors and biblical teachers desire to instruct their congregations in truth. Many believe that what they are teaching is biblical. Others are not so sure, yet go along with this view, thinking it is the way to honor God even though it confuses them.

Male dominance is another reason for ambiguity on the role

of women in the church. Hierarchical thinking in the church (men over women) stems basically from controversial scriptural passages, but is fed by other factors: the teaching that men are the final authority in the home, the suggestion that women aren't as capable as men (a difficult assertion to maintain in light of many successful women today), statements by other women against women in leadership (usually the women making such statements are not gifted in leadership and can't appreciate why a gifted woman would desire to use leadership gifts in the fullest possible way), an inability by insensitive leaders to appreciate the feelings and convictions of gifted men and women who are not able to find their place of greatest productivity in the kingdom of God, and by inconsistency (one leading Christian woman boldly states that women must be under the authority of men in the church, yet she herself speaks, teaches, preaches, and writes to both men and women on a worldwide scale).

But the biggest reason the system prevails is a lack of the "big picture." Who did God make *each* of us to be, and what did He call *all* of us to do? As Cecelia noted in the opening illustration, some of the particulars of teaching we present to women are inconsistent with teaching God has given all of us. Men and women of common sense recognize the dilemma. When they encounter an especially gifted woman, they can't deny the hand of God upon her. They therefore are prepared to "bend the rules" to benefit from her skills. But maybe we don't need to bend the rules. Maybe we need to take another look at foundational teaching on ministry presented to all of us—both men and women—and then examine the controversial passages in light of it.

What does that overview of Scripture show us about women in the church?

Back to the Beginning

Let's begin with some research we've covered earlier. Both man and woman are created in the image of God, in the likeness of each other, given the same responsibility, provision, and approval by God. We have already observed that no distinction is given in the creation account of a difference in personhood between the man and woman in marriage.

Neither is any distinction presented in ministry. How did God choose to minister in the Old Testament? Was it through men only or both men and women? Were there distinctions proclaimed by God that limited some areas to only one sex?

I have heard teaching that suggests Adam was given a special position in charge of evangelizing the world. This was then followed by other male patriarchs, who were commissioned to disseminate the Word. Where is biblical support for such a statement? Does the Old Testament say that men are to teach, preach, and lead, but women are not? No. Old Testament women and men were learning, worshiping leading, teaching, and ministering. God commanded the entire nation of Israel to be His witness (Isaiah 49:3, 6).

Men and women shared in the reading of the law (Deuteronomy 31:9–13); in sharing the Sabbath (Exodus 20:8); in offering sacrifices (Leviticus 12:6; 15:29; Judges 13:19; 1 Samuel 1:24); in equipping the tabernacle (Exodus 35:22); in participating in feasts (Deuteronomy 12:12, 18; 16:11, 14); in praying (Genesis 25:21, 22; 30:6, 22; 1 Samuel 1:10); in making vows, including the Nazirite vow (Numbers 6:2–20); in ministering at the door of the tent (Exodus 38:8); in singing (Ezra 2:65; Exodus 15:21; Judges 5:1); in dancing (Exodus 15:20; 1 Samuel 18:6; Psalms 30:11); in proclaiming good tidings (Psalms 68:11); in diplomacy (2 Samuel 14:1–20); and in holding major offices in Israel's society: in judging (Judges 4), prophesying (2 Kings 22:14), ruling a nation (2 Kings 11:3), and being a military leader (Judges 4).

After that brief overview, let's consider God's means of basic ministry in the Old and New Testaments.

The Prophet

God's primary means of communication—instruction (1 Samuel 28:15), rebuke (Jeremiah 26:12), and prophecy (2 Kings 21:10–15)—in the Old Testament was through the prophet. The office of prophet was an honored one and required great allegiance to God. There were true prophets and false prophets, faithful prophets and unfaithful prophets. And yes, there were men prophets and women prophets: Deborah (Judges 4), Anna (Luke 2:36–38), Huldah (2 Kings 22:14; 2 Chronicles 34:22), Isaiah's wife (Isaiah 8:3—could this have been a team ministry?), and Miriam (Exodus 15:20). Was this an accident, women acting as prophets?

In Numbers 11:29 Moses says, " ' . . . Would that all the Lord's people were prophets, that the Lord would put His Spirit upon them!' " He could have used a male noun, not a generic word for "people."

Let's take a look at a few of the women prophets.

> Now Deborah, a prophetess, the wife of Lappidoth, was judge in Israel at that time. And she used to sit under the palm tree of Deborah between Ramah and Bethel in the hill country of Ephraim; *and the sons of Israel came up to her for judgment.*
>
> Judges 4:4, 5, *italics added*

Some people argue that since Eve was deceived, all women are. (We'll take a look at 1 Timothy 2 shortly.) If God declared that all women are easily deceived, what is Deborah doing giving judgments to the sons of Israel? And why did *God* raise her up? (Judges 2:16–18). Deborah was greatly respected as a leader and prophet, for look what happened when trouble came:

> Now she sent and summoned Barak the son of Abinoam from Kedesh-naphtali, and said to him, "Behold, the Lord, the God of Israel, has commanded, 'Go and march to Mount Tabor, and take with you ten thousand men from the sons of Naphtali and from the sons of Zebulun. And I will draw out to you Sisera, the commander of Jabin's army, with his chariots and his many troops to the river Kishon; and I will give him into your hand.' "
>
> Judges 4:6, 7

God gave this message directly to her, and she related it to Barak, who then relies on her presence:

CALLED TO SERVICE

Then Barak said to her, "If you will go with me, then I will go; but if you will not go with me, I will not go." And she said, "I will surely go with you; nevertheless, the honor shall not be yours on the journey that you are about to take, for the Lord will sell Sisera into the hands of a woman."

Judges 4:8, 9

I don't know how many times I have seen a woman apologize all over the place for being a teacher or leader of mixed groups. Deborah made no apology for her office, her judgments, or her prophecy. She didn't feel it un-Godlike to be given credit for what she had done (Romans 13:7). In fact, God had decreed that a woman, Jael, would prevail (Judges 4:9, 10).

The victory over Sisera secured (Judges 4:11–24), Deborah and Barak sing a song, recorded in Judges 5 which concludes with, "And the land was undisturbed for forty years" (v. 31).

Huldah was another prophetess, and her story is told in 2 Chronicles 34 and 2 Kings 22.

Then the king commanded Hilkiah, Ahikam the son of Shaphan, Abdon the son of Micah, Shaphan the scribe, and Asaiah the king's servant, saying, "Go, inquire of the Lord for me and for those who are left in Israel and in Judah, concerning the words of the book which has been found; for great is the wrath of the Lord which is poured out on us because our fathers have not observed the word of the Lord, to do according to all that is written in this book."
So Hilkiah and those whom the king had told went to Huldah, the prophetess . . . and they spoke to her regarding this. And she said to them, "Thus says the Lord, the God of Israel, 'Tell the man who sent you to Me, thus says the Lord, "Behold I am bringing evil on this place and on its inhabitants. . . ."'"

2 Chronicles 34:20–24

One seminary professor maintains that God uses a woman only when a man is not available. But Huldah spoke God's words during the ministries of both Jeremiah and Zephaniah.

There were male prophets alive during the time of Anna, who spoke to Mary and Joseph when they took Jesus to the temple (Luke 2:36-38).

Instructing, rebuking, speaking for the Lord . . . these are the characteristics of a prophet and prophetess. *Nebiah* is the feminine form of the word *prophet* (*nabi*); no distinction between the two forms is presented in word usage, context, or function.

"Nevertheless," one man said to me, "women in leadership in the Old Testament were the exception, not the rule."

To say there are more men recorded as ministering is correct, but to say that women are an exception to a rule is greatly misleading. There is no *rule* that only men are to lead.

Some people feel that women, "being more easily deceived," are susceptible to becoming false prophets. But let's take a look at some of the cults and false religions and their deceptive founders:

Jehovah's Witness: Charles Taze Russell
Mormonism: Joseph Smith
Church of Scientology: L. Ron Hubbard
Unification Church: Sun Myung Moon
Buddhism: Buddha
Islam: Muhammad
Hare Krishna: A. C. Bhaktivedanta Swami
People's Temple: Jim Jones
Confucianism: Confucius
Christian Science: Mary Baker Eddy
Rajneeshee: Bhagwan Shree Rajneesh; at one time a woman was his chief implementer.

On the other hand let's take a look at leaders of some major Christian outreaches:

Gospel Light Publishers–Forest Home Christian Conference Center: Henrietta Mears
China Inland Mission: J. Hudson Taylor
Salvation Army: William and Catherine Booth
Women's Bible Study Fellowship and Men's Bible Study Fellowship: Wetherall Johnson

Children's orphanage and ministries: George Mueller, Amy Carmichael
Child Evangelism Fellowship: Frances Bennett
Important catalyst for antislavery movement: Harriet Beecher Stowe
Gospel recordings: Joy Ridderhof
Active in Girl Scouts of Europe: Corrie ten Boom
Campus Crusade for Christ: Bill and Vonette Bright

Many women led ministries in the face of cultural opposition. Evidently God's hand was so clearly on many of these women that many people who denied that women should lead, teach, and preach could not deny them their ministry. In fact, they even participated with them.

Women Are Now Priests

In the Old Testament, the prophets and prophetesses served to instruct, rebuke, and prophesy. The service of these men and women was invaluable. But there was another person who served as a spiritual instructor, even a spiritual mediator to Israel. The function of the priest was to care for personal forgiveness and expressions of thanksgiving and to minister for the Lord in the temple.

Some believe that God's original intention was to establish a nation of priests. That is, that all Israelites would serve as their own priests. But because of sin, this original plan was thwarted and the priesthood was relegated to the tribe of Levi (see Exodus 32:25–29). In the Old Testament only adult male Levites held this office, although female Levites served in other functions within the temple. (Note: males who were not Levites could not be priests either. Further, some of the tasks of the priests—killing and sacrificing animals—required great physical strength.)

Regardless of who was a priest in the Old Testament, the human office of high priest was clearly abolished when Jesus Christ became our great High Priest. A human priest was no longer needed, since Jesus' sacrifice on the cross was once and for all. Our access to God is now direct.

Since then we have a great high priest who has passed through the heavens, Jesus the Son of God, let us hold fast our confession. For we do not have a high priest who cannot sympathize with our weaknesses, but one who has been tempted in all things as we are, yet without sin. Let us therefore draw near with confidence to the throne of grace, that we may receive mercy and may find grace to help in time of need.

Hebrews 4:14–16

Each member of the body of Christ becomes his or her own priest. And: "But you are a chosen race, a royal priesthood, a holy nation, a people for God's own possession, that you may proclaim the excellencies of Him who has called you out of darkness into His marvelous light" (1 Peter 2:9; *see also* 1 Peter 2:4, 5).

In this church age, each believer (man and woman, husband and wife) has complete access to the throne of God. No human mediator is necessary. Note that the husband is not the priest, nor does the wife go to God through him. The pastor is not the priest. The men or women in the congregation do not go to God through him, nor do men in the church provide women's access to God. A male or female Christian has power, authority, high standing, direct linkage with the heavenlies, and the right to act in the name of the Father.

We've seen that the office of prophet in the Old Testament and the priesthood in the New Testament are available to men and women alike.

But what was Jesus' view of women?

FOURTEEN

Jesus
and
Women

When the Apollo spacecraft first landed on the moon, President Richard Nixon announced that this was the greatest event since the creation of the world. Billy Graham received national attention when he openly contradicted the president by saying, "The greatest event in the history of the world was the resurrection of Jesus Christ." I agree—and that miracle was first and deliberately revealed to a woman.

Did Jesus Christ view men and women differently? In His judgment were women restricted from ministry?

To appreciate His perspective, first let's take a look at the condition of women before Christ came. Throughout history the value of women in society had been grossly underestimated. In the areas of politics, marriage, economics, education, and religion, woman had often been denied her freedom. In politics she was without vote. In marriage most women abdicated their interests to those of their husbands. Except for a few privileged ones who educated themselves, most women who lived before the time of Christ had little or no education. Economically speaking, a woman was not allowed to own property; indeed she sometimes was property. Religion was monopolized by men, except in Judaism (until 500 B.C.) and in a few isolated cultures where, at the other extreme, women were worshiped as goddesses. Double standards prevailed throughout; what was allowed a man was denied a woman; what was excused in a man was condemned in a woman. Indeed, the Fall, the results of sin entering the world, had truly run its course.

Shortly before Christ, Socrates, one of the foremost Greek thinkers of his era, remarked, "Whom do you talk to less than your wife?" Demosthenes, another Greek thinker, wrote, "We have *heluerue* (courtesans) for the pleasures of the spirit, concubines for sensual pleasures, and wives to give us sons." Plato recommended that women be held in common by men.

In contrast, Jesus viewed women as full persons. Unlike most males of His day, Jesus was concerned that women find fulfillment, surmount difficulties, and make the most of their lives.

What did the coming of Jesus Christ do for women? The same thing it did for men. It released them from bondage to sin and opened the door to freedom in personal relationships with God and one another. But let's look a little more specifically at Jesus' influence on women.

Jesus' Associations

What were Jesus' *associations* with women? Alexander Whyte, a Scottish theologian, has noted that after Jesus' twelfth year, Joseph is not mentioned again. It is entirely possible, reports Whyte, that Jesus postponed His public ministry until age thirty in order to care for His family. Because Jesus was part of a fairly large family—with at least three sisters—He knew something of family situations: teenage romances, women's problems, financial concerns, and a mother's responsibilities.[1] Perhaps this accounts for the tender love He held for His mother. While on the cross, one of Christ's seven last recorded sayings concerned the care of His mother (John 19:26, 27).

A Jewish woman was never to be instructed openly, yet Jesus taught women publicly. He braved criticism, unabashedly teaching women in homes and in the streets of the cities. He did not confine Himself to "feminine" subjects by telling the women how to bake, sew, and clean. Rather He talked with them about eternal life, daily living, and relationships. At the same time, to help them understand, He used teaching objects with which women were familiar: a wedding feast, corn grinding, bread leavening, and children. There was no question that His teaching was for both genders (John 3:16). And He referred to a Jewish woman as a "daughter of Abraham" (Luke 13:16) when "son of Abraham" was the common term. It appears that Jesus deliberately used the title denoting the woman's worth, in contrast to cultural preference.

Jesus touched women (Luke 13:10–13), but not in a sensual way. His was the touch of love, healing, and assurance. This was unheard of by the Jews. A Jewish merchant would not even count money back into the hand of a woman, lest he touch her and become contaminated. In touching women for the purpose of healing them, Jesus ignored injunctions against incurring legal or ritual impurity (Matthew 9:18–26; Mark 5:25–34).

And women touched Jesus (Matthew 26:6–13). One day a young woman came and poured oil on Jesus' feet, washing them with her hair. When rebuked by His disciples for such an extravagant waste of money, Jesus rose to her defense.

As a result of the love and respect given them by Jesus Christ, women eagerly turned to Him and found lives of meaning and purpose. They followed Him from town to town, as did the male disciples (Luke 8:1–3; 23:27, 49, 55, 56). In gratitude they supported Him out of their own means (Luke 8:3). They opened their homes to Him and His disciples (Luke

10:38). At the cross, when most of the male disciples had fled for their lives, the women stayed until the end (Luke 23:27, 28; Mark 15:40, 41; Mark 14:50).

"Incidentally," a friend asked upon reading this, "why did Jesus choose twelve men for His disciples?"

"Why did He choose twelve Jews?" I smiled and asked in return. "Or why didn't He choose a handicapped person, a sick person, a barbarian, or a slave? There seem to be practical reasons for His choices. It would not have been proper to have the women sleep by His side on the hills, and they may not have been able to keep up with some of the exhausting road trips. Intimacy was a key factor during these three years, and the intimacy Jesus was able to experience with the twelve (all-night vigils, travel, and so forth) would not have been proper with the women.

"Or it could be that a man had a better opportunity to be heard than a woman. After all, in the Jewish culture, women received little, if any, respect. Their message may not have been heard in the critical first thrust of the church."

On several occasions Jesus revealed major truths when He was speaking only to women. To the woman at the well it is recorded that He declared He was the Messiah (John 4:25, 26). To Martha He declared, "I am the resurrection and the life . . ." (John 11:25). His resurrection, upon which Christianity is based, was first revealed to a woman (John 20:11–18); and it was no accident. Jesus deliberately waited until the men had left the tomb before He appeared to Mary. If being a witness to the resurrected Christ was qualification for being an apostle (Acts 1:22), surely Mary could have been one. Jesus had instructed her to relate this truth to the others. In Mark 16:14, Jesus rebukes the apostles "and He reproached them for their unbelief and hardness of heart, because they had not believed those who had seen Him after He had risen." Evidently Jesus held the apostles accountable for the message He had given them through men and women.

On one occasion some religious leaders brought an adulterous woman to Jesus and asked Him what His judgment was on

CALLED TO SERVICE

her (John 8:1-11). (It was their policy to stone an adulteress immediately.) Jesus said, "He who is without sin among you, let him be the first to throw a stone at her." Within minutes, every one of the woman's accusers had left.

"Neither do I condemn you," assured Jesus. "Go your way; from now on sin no more." His love and forgiveness present a picture of Jesus' attitude toward women and men. (See also Hosea 4:14; God has no double standard.)

We find yet another illustration when Jesus journeyed through Samaria (John 4:1-42). In the heat of the day, Jesus stopped to rest by a well and a woman came to draw water. Jesus said to her, "If you would only ask Me, I would give you water so you would never thirst again."

"Sir," she said, "You do not have anything to draw water with and the well is deep. From where would you get living water?"

Jesus returned, "Whoever drinks of this water shall thirst again, but whoever drinks of the water that I shall give him shall never thirst . . ." (see vv. 10-12). Later, "The disciples marveled that He was speaking with a woman" (see John 4:27).

This woman was immoral. Yet through her encounter with Jesus, she found something that brought a radical change to her way of living. Jesus crossed social and cultural barriers to make Himself known to a woman who had critical needs.

Jesus challenged traditional Jewish values about women, including the preeminence of their caretaking and childbearing roles.

Jesus visited the house of Mary, Martha, and Lazarus (Luke 10:38-42). Martha was in the kitchen, preparing food. She became upset that Mary, her sister, was seated at Jesus' feet, drinking in His teaching. Jesus tactfully said, "Martha, you are concerned with trivial things. Mary has chosen the best" (see v. 41). Martha's tasks were trivial in comparison to eternal values. Jesus did not shoo Mary back into the kitchen, but commended her for recognizing the need and rightness of preparing her soul and developing her person. (This is not intended to make light of necessary work, however.)

Shortly following this event, a woman shouted at Jesus from among the crowd, "Blessed is the mother who gave you birth and nursed you." Jesus returned, "Blessed rather are those who hear the Word of God and obey it" (*see* Luke 11:27, 28). Here Jesus challenges what had come to be seen as woman's dominant role—raising children. Jesus again checks priorities, pointing us back to our highest calling—hearing the whole Word and obeying it.

In another encounter, Jesus honored the faith of a woman. A Greek woman came to Jesus, imploring Him to heal her daughter, although it was socially improper for her to do so. He responded, "O woman, your faith is great; be it done for you as you wish" (Matthew 15:21–28; Mark 7:24–30. *See also* Mark 14:3–9; 12:41–44; Luke 7:36–50; 18:1–8). When Jesus discussed the importance of persistence in prayer, He used a woman to illustrate the importance of assertively requesting one's needs from the Lord.

Dorothy Sayers sums up Jesus well in her book, *Are Women Human?*:

Perhaps it is no wonder that the women were first at the cradle and last at the cross. They had never known a man like this Man—there has never been such another. A prophet and teacher who never nagged at them, never flattered or coaxed or patronized; who never made arch jokes about them, never treated them as, "The woman, God help us!" or "The ladies, God bless them!"; who rebuked without querulousness and praised without condescension; who took their questions and arguments seriously; who never mapped out their sphere for them, never urged them to be feminine or jeered at them for being female; who had no axe to grind and no uneasy male dignity to defend; who took them as he found them and was completely unselfconscious. There is no act, no sermon, no parable in the whole Gospel that borrows its pungency from female perversity; nobody could possibly guess from the words and deeds of Jesus that there was anything "funny" about woman's nature.[2]

CALLED TO SERVICE

Jesus' Assertions

Consider now the assertions of Jesus. First, Jesus stood on the Old Testament position that both men and women were made in the image of God. He quoted, "For this cause a man shall leave his father and mother . . . and the two shall become one flesh" (Matthew 19:5) and many other Old Testament passages indicating His acceptance of Old Testament Scripture.

We observe Jesus exhibiting both male and female characteristics of God. For example, the Book of Isaiah states that God labored over Israel as a mother about to give birth (42:14), and in Matthew 23:37, Jesus reveals how He wept for Jerusalem and longed to gather the Jewish people under His wing as a mother hen does her chicks (see also Psalms 131:2, 3; Deuteronomy 32:18; Isaiah 49:14, 15; 66:9–13; Job 38:27, 28; Isaiah 63:15; Jeremiah 31:20).

We also see that when the New Testament writers chose a word for God becoming man they chose anthropos, which commonly means "human," instead of aner, which commonly means "male" (Philippians 2:7; Romans 5:12, 15). Jesus Christ was God's representative on earth. The emphasis was not on His maleness, but on His humanity.

What are just a few of the assertions Jesus made to all?

SALVATION: "God so loved the world, that He gave His only begotten Son, that whoever believes in Him should not perish, but have eternal life" (John 3:16).

ABUNDANT LIVING: "I came that they [all] might have life, and might have it abundantly" (John 10:10).

ANSWERED PRAYER: "If you abide in Me, and My words abide in you, ask whatever you wish, and it shall be done for you" (John 15:7).

REST: "Take My yoke upon you, and learn from Me, for I am gentle and humble in heart; and you shall find rest for your souls. For My yoke is easy, and My load is light" (Matthew 11:29, 30).

PROMISE OF THE HOLY SPIRIT: "But when He, the Spirit of truth, comes, He will guide you into all the truth . . ." (John 16:13).

The message of Christ was for all—not limited in any respect to the men. Jesus asserted clearly that any person could establish a relationship with the Creator and participate in all He taught.

Jesus' Accomplishments

What were the accomplishments Christ brought about for women? Theodor Mommsen and Edward Gibbon, two well-known historians, extensively studied the Roman Empire and concluded that the second century A.D. was one of the most prosperous and peaceful times in all history. One of nine areas manifested in the success of this period is the unusually high status of women.[3]

This successful era paralleled the spread of the Good News of Christ to the ends of the earth.

If Jesus had been only a social changer, politician, or preacher, His life or messages would have lost much of their influence after a century. Social changes come and go. But history shows that where the true message of Christ has gone, women as well as men have responded with life-changing results. The unique thing about Jesus Christ was that He brought about changes on the inside of men and women, as well as on the outside.

According to the biblical perspective, God first created human beings to experience fellowship with other humans and with God. After creation both women and men were enjoying these relationships, but then Adam and Eve disobeyed God, and they died spiritually (Genesis 2:17). This spiritual death would eventually lead to physical death.

Paul later explains what happened. He said, "Therefore just as through one man sin entered into the world, and death [spiritual death] through sin, so death spread to all people . . ." (*see* Romans 5:12). Therefore, every boy or girl who is now born into the world is born physically alive but spiritually dead; that is, we have the ability to have fellowship with other humans, but not with God.

CALLED TO SERVICE

Often people know about Jesus Christ and have heard that He died for us, but they find it hard to understand what that means on a personal level. *How could His death on the cross, nearly two thousand years ago, have anything to do with our lives today?* Here is an illustration that may help clarify the issue.

Imagine that you are a traffic judge and also a parent. Let's say your son is caught speeding and is brought before you for trial. You try him, find him guilty, and sentence him to a $100 fine or thirty days in jail. Suppose he is broke and can't pay the fine. As a loving parent you might not want him to go to jail, but as a just judge you would have to send him to jail. What would you do?

There would be an alternative. You could pay the fine for him. You wouldn't have to, but you could if you wanted to. That is a picture of what God did when He sent Christ to die for us. He loved us but saw that we were separated from Him. Some psychologists call this separation alienation. The Bible simply calls it sin, meaning a condition of separation from God.

Because of sin, our access to God is blocked (Romans 6:23). If the plug of a lamp is pulled from the wall socket, contact with the electric current is broken and the light goes out. This is similar to our condition. Initially we all exist as "unplugged" from God.

The apostle Paul said that everyone has sinned and fallen short of God's perfect standard (Romans 3:23). (That's not too hard to believe. If university students tell me they've never sinned, I just ask their roommates! In a marriage, I ask the mate.) Unless something had been done for us, we would have had to spend time and eternity in this "unplugged," unfulfilled state.

The Solution

Christ came to solve the problem. When He died physically on the cross, He made the *total payment* for our sins. He died spiritually as well, so that we could be forgiven. Just as you, the traffic judge, could choose to pay the fine for your guilty son, so God chose to pay the fine for us. "He Himself bore our sins in His body on the cross . . ." (1 Peter 2:24). He took the rap for us. In other words, God took the sinless Christ and poured our sins upon Him. ". . . Then, in exchange, He poured God's goodness into us!" (2 Corinthians 5:21 TLB).

Spiritual Death

On the cross, Jesus cried out, ". . . My God, my God, why hast Thou forsaken me?" (Matthew 27:46). This was a rhetorical question to which He knew the answer. Christ had died spiritually and was separated from the Father. Then He cried out, "It is finished" (John 19:30). Sin was paid for. Now all men and women could establish fellowship with their Creator again.

This explains what Christ said to Nicodemus, a religious leader. Jesus told him, "You must be born again" (see John 3:3). The first birth makes our soul come alive. The second birth takes place when we accept Jesus Christ's forgiveness by faith, when we receive unto ourselves His work on the cross for us. Then our spirits are supernaturally reactivated and we reestablish relationship with God.

In the traffic-court illustration, your son could refuse your $100 payment of his fine and choose to go to jail. It's the same with Christ. God loves us. He offers us complete, total forgiveness of all our sins—past, present, and future (Colossians 1:14; 2:13, 14). There are no strings attached. We don't have to promise anything. All we have to do is to believe that Christ died for us and to accept His forgiveness as a free gift.

Jesus explained how a person can enter into a relationship with Him by faith. The Bible explains, "But as many as received Him, to them He gave the right to become children of God, even to those who believe in His name" (John 1:12). Christ stands at your life's door, seeking entrance. If someone were knocking at the door of your room, you could do one of three things: ignore him and hope he'd go away, tell him to go

CALLED TO SERVICE

away, or open the door and invite him in. It's the same with Christ; you can ignore Him, tell Him to get lost, or invite Him in.

Receiving Christ involves simply believing that He died for you, accepting the forgiveness He offers, and inviting the living Christ into your life. It's saying in faith, "Jesus Christ, I need You. Thanks for dying for me. I open the door of my life and receive You as my Savior [that is, the One who died for my sins]. Thank You for forgiving me. Give me the fulfilling life You promised."

The Christian life is lived by faith in God's trustworthiness and in His promises, not by feelings. Feelings come and go. Sometimes they are a result of believing God by faith. At other times they reflect more the complexities of human personality than the work of God in one's life. The important thing to remember is that Jesus will never leave you once He has entered your life. He said, ". . . I will never desert you, nor will I ever forsake you" (Hebrews 13:5) and "I am with you always" (Matthew 28:20). He gives you eternal life the moment you receive Him (1 John 5:11–13).

To summarize Jesus' perspective of woman: She is loved by God, honored for her faith, and applauded for her courage. Because of the contribution of Jesus Christ, a woman who teams up with God can have the strength and opportunity she needs to excel and triumph in life.

Does Jesus Christ still have the same impact on women today?

Kay was a self-assertive woman. After her divorce, her fear of being victimized compelled her to live on the offensive. Although she became successful in her career, she had little personal success. Fear and resentment controlled her. But where was an alternative? She probably wouldn't have found one, except for Mary entering her life.

"For a number of years," relates Mary, "I had asked God to expand my ministry to others. I told Him I was open to any challenge. Little did I know what was ahead."

Mary met Kay at a luncheon and felt the Spirit of God prompt her to take an interest in Kay. "Never would I have sought out Kay on my own," shares Mary. "But God's leading was so definite that I was compelled to obey."

For three years Mary prayerfully and carefully befriended Kay and, little by little, shared with her the change Christ could make in her life.

"I was a tough person to get to know," says Kay. "I had built so many defenses in my life that no one was able to penetrate them—except Mary. Her love and care for me were so steadfast that I finally began to let her into my heart.

"But I wasn't ready to let Jesus in. To me, the church was the superior oppressor of women. I hated the church. I believe I hated Christ, though I knew very little about Him. Yet Mary was persistent in suggesting I check Him out for myself. Am I glad I did!"

The night that Kay acknowledged Christ to be her own personal Savior is one she will never forget. "I sat on my bed for hours. It had been several years since I first heard of Christ, and the more I got to know about Him, the more I began to let down my defenses. Part of me was desperate for the love I felt He offered. But I had told myself I would never let anyone I wasn't completely sure of be involved in my life again. To me, that was a sure way to wind up a victim.

"Finally, I could no longer resist His love. Inviting Jesus Christ to forgive me and come into my life has challenged my fear and resentment. But most of all I have let go of most of my impenetrable shell, for Jesus surrounds and protects me. Men are no longer a threat to me. I can see good in men, not just their faults. This makes a successful man-woman relationship a new possibility. The greatest promises I have found in the Bible are the 'I am with you' promises. I am no longer in bondage. And I am no longer isolated and alone. Praise God!"

Does all this make sense to you? Have you received Christ yourself? Do you know He lives in your life? You *can* know. He said, "If you open the door, I *will* come in." Jesus Christ is no liar. You can take Him at His word and believe that if you

CALLED TO SERVICE

ask Him to forgive you and enter your life, He will do just that. I'm not talking about becoming a member of a church, joining an organization, or promising God that you'll live a perfect life. I'm talking about accepting a free gift and inviting the living Christ to live in your life.

Many who have desired to receive Christ have expressed their faith through prayer. Prayer is simply talking with God. You can talk to Him in the quiet of your own heart. He is much more concerned about your attitude than your specific words. Below is a short prayer that many people have used in receiving Christ:

> Lord Jesus, I need You. Thanks for dying for me. I want You to use Your death on the cross as the means of my forgiveness. I open the door of my life and receive You as my Savior [the One who died for my sins]. Thank You for forgiving me.

Does that express the desire of your heart? If so, I encourage you to pray it (or something similar in your own words) right now, wherever you are, and Christ will come into your life as He promised.[4]

FIFTEEN

Commissioned

Evelyn Christiansen and Kay Arthur are two ministers of the teachings of Jesus Christ. They are popular speakers and teachers of men and women throughout the United States and in other parts of the world. These women have terrific husbands who have recognized that God has specially gifted their wives for public ministry. Each man has wisely decided he can effectively serve Christ by teaming up with his wife as her business manager and/or support system.

In like manner, Ruth Graham and Evelyn Roberts have felt that one of the best ways they could promote the Gospel is to provide a solid home base for Billy and Oral, though each woman participates in other ministries as well.

Maturity in Action

What does the example of the first two couples tell us? The second two? What can we learn from them? That God called *all* of us to the work of evangelism and discipleship and that God uniquely gifted each member of the body of Christ to fulfill this call. Each marriage team must discern how to make the most of the gifts of the husband and the wife. Bill Bright has stated, "The responsibility of the husband is to help see that the wife is able to use her gifts fully." Likewise, that is a proper goal for every wife. The two teams mentioned in the opening paragraph have realized that the woman may have the more public gifts. They have used common sense and the leading of the Holy Spirit in their lives to maximize each other's gifts. Hurray for their maturity! Hurray for each other's good sense! And also for the good sense of wives who choose to aid more publicly gifted husbands!

Just think of the non-Christians and needy Christians who would not be ministered to should such men and women have no understanding of or obedience to what God has *called* and *gifted* them to do.

Commissioned to Spread the Word

But were women preaching, teaching, prophesying, and leading in the early church? Before Jesus left Earth, He gave us (all believers) the Great Commission. Technically the commission was given to the apostles, but it is understood to be for all believers, as the disciples were instructed to teach others *all* that Jesus had taught them. That command would include teaching the Great Commission to all believers.

Let's take a look at this command.

And Jesus came up and spoke to them, saying "All authority has been given to Me in heaven and on earth. Go therefore and make disciples of all nations, baptizing them in the name of the Father and the Son and the Holy Spirit; teaching them to observe all that I commanded you; and lo, I am with you always, even to the end of the age."

Matthew 28:18–20

Read this command in the Book of Mark: "And He said to them 'Go into all the world and preach the gospel to all creation' " (16:15).

In this first and foremost overview of God's plan for evangelism and discipleship in the New Testament, the command is for *all*. Women would be among those who are *made disciples, baptized, preached* to, and *taught*—and among those who would, in turn, *make disciples, baptize, preach,* and *teach*.

Consider Acts 8:1–4:

> . . . And on that day a great persecution arose against the church in Jerusalem; and they were all scattered throughout the regions of Judea and Samaria, except the apostles. And some devout men buried Stephen, and made loud lamentations over him. But Saul began ravaging the church, entering house after house; and dragging off men and women, he would put them in prison.
>
> Therefore those who had been scattered went about preaching the word.

Apparently men and women were preaching the word, and no restrictions are presented as to whom they addressed (*see also* Acts 9:1, 2).

Perhaps preaching was what Paul commended two women, Tryphaena and Tryphosa, for when he saluted them as "workers in the Lord" (*kopiosas*: Romans 16:12). Mary and Persis are equally commended in Romans 16 for their work (*polla ekopiasen*).

Recently a friend challenged me on this: "Wherever it mentioned evangelism—preaching or teaching Scriptures—it doesn't say women were involved."

"What do you mean?"

"Well, if women were active in preaching, as you suggest, why doesn't it say so more specifically?" I tried to clarify what

I was hearing him saying, "If the word *women* isn't in a passage, the women couldn't have been involved? Is that what you're saying?"

He thought for a moment. "Well, not exactly." He went on to explain. "For example, why doesn't the Scripture say that Lydia preached?" (Acts 16:13–15).

"Well, in essence, it does. The church at Philippi probably met in her home, where Paul was staying, and the early church was actively involved in preaching the word. The women in Philippi were not exempt from participating, with the rest of the church, in preaching and evangelizing. In fact, the church at Philippi was an excellent Spirit-filled church. Two women and two men are commended at the end of Philippians."

He wasn't convinced. "Well, for me to believe what you're saying, I need more Scripture that says specifically that women were involved."

"In other words, the Scripture always refers to men only, unless women are mentioned specifically?"

My friend was trying to shift the burden of proof onto me. Instead of reasoning that the church naturally included men and women, unless shown otherwise (in applying the Great Commission and other teaching), he reasoned that it excluded women, unless shown otherwise.

This reminded me of the dilemma of a friend of mine.

Beverly, an attractive middle-aged woman, was asked by her husband, Dave, to talk to his Sunday-school class of young marrieds on the biblical handling of finances in the home. Beverly was an experienced Bible teacher, and she carefully presented to the class the scriptural principles she had employed in her home.

A week later the board of elders received a complaint from one of the church members, and Beverly was asked to refrain from any further teaching of men.

> Did Beverly not possess a gift of teaching? (Was she incapable of communicating clearly?)
> Was Beverly scripturally wrong in what she taught?

Was Beverly's Christian character such that she was unqualified to serve as a church model?

Was the end result of her talk harmful or destructive to the church?

The answer to all of the above is no. Dave and Beverly wanted to know why such a decision was made and they were told that Scripture clearly says a woman should not teach men.

But does it?

Did women teach in the early church?

Besides Jesus' commissioning all of us to teach, Paul apparently thought teaching was appropriate for all. For in 2 Timothy 2:2 he writes, "And the things which you have heard from me in the presence of many witnesses, these entrust to faithful men, who will be able to teach others also."

As translated, this verse could appear misleading. The word *men* is actually *anthropos* in the Greek, which commonly means "humans" or "mankind," not "males." The word *other* is *heterous*, also a generic term for humans. The context in no way limits this verse to men. Clearly Paul wrote that the message was to be given to faithful Christians, who, in turn, are to teach others. The verse rightfully reads, "And the things which you have heard from me in the presence of many witnesses, these entrust to faithful people who will be able to teach others also."

Acts 18:24–26 gives a more specific example:

> Now a certain Jew named Apollos, an Alexandrian by birth, an eloquent man, came to Ephesus; and he was mighty in the Scripture. This man had been instructed in the way of the Lord; and being fervent in spirit, he was speaking and teaching accurately the things concerning Jesus, being acquainted only with the baptism of John; and he began to speak out boldly in the synagogue. But when Priscilla and Aquila heard him, they took him aside and explained to him the way of God more accurately.

Greek ordering of names suggests preeminence to the first person mentioned. Therefore Priscilla's name being men-

CALLED TO SERVICE

tioned first indicates that Priscilla was the primary teacher of an adult Christian man. (Priscilla and her husband are mentioned six times in the Bible. Four times Priscilla's name comes first.)

Men and Women Prophesy

What about prophesying?

Peter must have understood that both men and women would continue prophesying in the church age, for in Acts 2, at the very launching of the church, he announced that the prophecy of Joel 2:28, 29 was being fulfilled.

After the crowd had mistaken the outpouring of the Spirit for drunkenness, Peter said:

> "These men [applying to both sexes] are not drunk, as you suppose, for it is only the third hour of the day; but this is what was spoken of through the prophet Joel: 'And it shall be in the last days,' God says, 'That I will pour forth of My Spirit upon all mankind; And your sons and your daughters shall prophesy, And your young men shall see visions, And your old men shall dream dreams; Even upon My bondslaves, both men and women, I will in those days pour forth My Spirit And they shall prophesy.' "
>
> Acts 2:15–18

There are some who believe that all this passage from Joel is still not fulfilled, but Peter clearly states this is referring to the men and women who were standing in front of him, prophesying. (The second part of this prophecy (2:19–21) indicates fulfillment before the day of the Lord [perhaps in the future]. There are other prophecies that speak of two different times [see Isaiah 9:6, 7], and I mention this only to point out that it is possible to have one prophecy speak to two or more time frames.)

Did women continue to prophesy in the early church? Luke writes in Acts 21:8, 9: "... Entering the house of Philip the

COMMISSIONED 177

evangelist, who was one of the seven, we stayed with him. Now this man had four virgin daughters who were prophetesses." (*See also* 1 Corinthians 11.)

What do we mean by prophesying? In 1 Corinthians 14, the details of what prophesying includes (or results in) are listed: upbuilding, encouragement, edification (vv. 3, 4), evangelism (vv. 22–25), careful evaluation (v. 29), and teaching (v. 31).

"But," argued a friend, "you only have two or three references saying that women were prophesying."

"How many references do you need," I responded, "to establish a precedent?" After all, the command to observe the Lord's Supper is mentioned only twice (Luke 22:17–22; 1 Corinthians 11:23–29). Yet we take it seriously.

Do women and men still prophesy today? According to the definition cited in 1 Corinthians 14, they do. One needs only to look around at the numbers of women today involved in these tasks: Fay Angus, Gladys Hunt, Karen Mains, Florence Littauer, Ann Kiemel Anderson, Amy Grant, Sandi Patti, Joni Earickson Tada, Becky Pippert, Dale Evans Rogers, and many others.

But the gift of prophecy is not limited to a large visible or public role. I think of women I am surrounded by who minister to me and others. One woman, Kathleen, is an effective Christian counselor to men and women; another, Dorothy, works with handicapped men and women and has developed a curriculum she teaches to pastors, on church relations with the handicapped. Barbara, serving on a citywide church board, was chairman of citywide evangelism in Atlanta. During her tenure in the position, many came to Christ under her direction. Joyce has probably led more filling-station attendants, repairmen, waiters and waitresses, and car salesmen to the Lord than almost anyone I know.

Men and Women Are Evangelists

Shortly before Jesus ascended into heaven, He addressed the eleven with a promise and a commandment. "But you shall receive power when the Holy Spirit has come upon you; and

CALLED TO SERVICE

you shall be My witnesses both in Jerusalem, and in all Judea and Samaria, and even to the remotest part of the earth" (Acts 1:8).

How often we set up Andrew, who brought his brother to Christ, as an example of evangelism, yet overlook the Samaritan woman who brought an *entire village* to hear Christ (John 4:27–42).

Catherine Booth, with her husband, William, and eight children, forsook all earthly goods, believing God had called them *both* to minister to the destitute. The result was the forming of the Salvation Army, an organization that encourages all women to full ministry, including evangelist, pastor-teacher, and Christian leadership. She wrote:

> There seems to be a great deal of unnecessary fear of women occupying any position which involves publicity, lest she would be rendered unfeminine by the indulgence of ambition or vanity; but why should woman any more than man be charged with ambition when impelled to use her talents for the good of her race?[1]

Eva Burrows currently directs this worldwide enterprise.

To this day Salvation Army women are preaching the Good News of salvation, as are many other committed and obedient women in all parts of the world.

In the summer of 1983, Rusty and I team taught a seminar at Amsterdam '83. This significant conference for 4,000 itinerant evangelists brought godly men and women from around the world. Among them was a couple from Singapore. One evening the beautiful and expressive wife said to me, "Often America leads the secular world and the Christian world as well. But when it comes to women ministering, you are far behind the rest of us." This woman traveled full-time with her husband, preaching, evangelizing, and teaching. From the joy they radiated, it was plain to see that together they were functioning fully and satisfyingly in the kingdom.

Lillian Dickson was a woman who left her mark on the Far East. Heading teams of men and women, she attended the sick and dying. Through the power of God, she raised up others to meet the needs in the Asian world. One would never suspect that for years she felt impeded from being what God had designed her to be. "The change came," she states, "when I realized that I was not just a missionary's wife. I was a missionary!" Would to God that all women and men would grasp who and what they are in Christ and fully use their gifts and abilities.

Gladys Aylward was not an ordinary missionary. A biography of her life was made into a movie, *The Inn of the Sixth Happiness*. This English servant girl ventured to China and turned a heathen population toward the true God in such a way that mule-pack drivers traveling among villages carried news of her ministry to much of China.

During the past ten years the Christian church of China has grown from 3 million to an estimated 50 million people—primarily through home Bible-study groups (house churches) so common in the New Testament. According to the head of a Christian radio station that broadcasts into China, most of the church's miraculous expansion has been led by *women* evangelists, teachers, and pastors. (This is not unlike the New Testament pattern, where churches are identified as meeting in homes of women more than men—Acts 12:12; 16:40; Colossians 4:15; 1 Corinthians 1:11; 16:19; Romans 16:3–5). The fact that people then met in a woman's home does not necessarily mean she was the group leader, but it is a good possibility. Second John is addressed to "the elect lady." Although there is a great deal of dispute over what this means, she may very well have been a house-church leader. She is warned to protect the flock against false teachers. The writer concludes with a greeting from the "the children of your elect sister" (perhaps the leader of another house church). Consider what might have happened in China if America's popular teaching on restricting the role of women in the church had saturated the Christian culture there. Women would have waited for the men to lead, and millions would not have heard the Gospel.

Thank God that many in America and the rest of the world see Jesus' command, Paul's admonition, and Peter's interpretation as applicable to us all.

SIXTEEN

Are the Gifts Segregated?

"All my life," shared a successful pastor, "I taught that women could not have or utilize certain gifts. Then, challenged by a visiting woman teacher, I researched the issue and changed my view. Up until this time, I was deemed a theologically sound conservative. But when I changed my view on this one subject, I was termed a *liberal* by some in my denomination. Without hearing my rationale, they categorized me. What fear must lurk in the hearts of those who arbitrarily isolate themselves from others who seriously study the issue for themselves."

If they were to take a look at Paul's teaching, those who quickly categorize and dismiss an individual because of his stance on the issue of women in ministry may find they are at odds with the apostle. Unsegregated application is basic in

Paul's teaching on the gifts, which are most thoroughly discussed in 1 Corinthians, a book addressed to *all the saints* in that city.

The purpose of the gifts is for the *common good* (12:7), and those exercising their gifts are using them to help *all* the body (12:6). To whom are the gifts given? Members of the body of Christ:

> For to one is given the word of wisdom through the Spirit, and to another the word of knowledge according to the same Spirit; to another faith by the same Spirit, and to another gifts of healing by the one Spirit, and to another the effecting of miracles, and to another prophecy, and to another the distinguishing of spirits, to another various kinds of tongues, and to another the interpretation of tongues. But one and the same Spirit works all these things, distributing to each one individually just as He wills.
>
> 12:8–11

God Distributes the Gifts

Note that the church's job is not to choose who has what gift, but to utilize those gifts God has uniquely given, as the passage continues: "For even as the body is one and yet has many members, and all the members of the body, though they are many, are one body, so also is Christ. For by one Spirit we were all baptized into one body, whether Jews or Greeks, whether slaves or free, and we were all made to drink of one Spirit" (12:12, 13). Note the parallel here with Galatians 3:28, where Paul says there is neither Jew nor Greek, slave nor free man, male nor female, but that we are "all one in Christ."

First Corinthians 12 goes on with a further discussion of gifts without any mention of sexual distinctions.

Certain Gifts Are Not Limited to Men

In the Book of Ephesians, where he is again addressing *all* the saints, Paul also mentions the gifts given to believers:

And He gave some apostles, and some as prophets, and some as evangelists, and some as pastors and teachers, for the equipping of the saints for the work of service, to the building up of the body of Christ; until we all attain to the unity of the faith, and of the knowledge of the Son of God, to a mature man [person], to the measure of the stature which belongs to the fullness of Christ.

4:11-13

The third place the gifts are listed is in Romans 12:4-8:

For just as we have many members in one body and all the members do not have the same function, so we, who are many, are one body in Christ, and individually members one of another. And since we have gifts that differ according to the grace given to us, let each exercise them accordingly; if prophecy, according to the proportion of his [or her] faith; if service, in his [or her] serving; or he [or she] who teaches, in his [or her] teaching; or he [or she] who exhorts, in his [or her] exhortation; he [or she] who gives, with liberality; he [or she] who leads, with diligence; he [or she] who shows mercy, with cheerfulness.

Here the emphasis is on the mature use of gifts, concentrating on the motivation and the attitude as they are exercised. But again, they are for the entire body to use for the sake of the entire body. This is the theme through each discussion of the gifts.

Senseless Waste of Gifts

There are many unmet needs in the body of Christ. How can we spread the Gospel to the far ends of the world unless all of us work at full capacity?

If God chose to limit the gifts of a woman (teacher, leader, pastor, preacher, and so forth), why did He gift her in the first place?

Women Can Be Pastor-Teachers

Even those who feel that women may lead often still feel that the gift of pastor-teacher is restricted to men.

What does the Bible say about women having this gift? First, remember that the gifts are not segregated.

Second, many believe the listing of gifts in two of the passages cited are listed in order of importance. They are listed, "Apostle, prophet, evangelist, and pastor-teacher...." Since there is good reason to believe that Junia (feminine in the Greek) acted as an apostle (Romans 16:7) and women clearly were prophesying within the church assembly (1 Corinthians 11:5; Acts 21:8, 9), there is no reason to assume that they weren't pastoring and teaching.

Third, in the Scripture, no one is referred to by the term *pastor* or *shepherd* except Jesus Christ. However, the term used for church leaders (*deacon, minister*) is used to describe Phoebe (a woman) in Romans 16:1, 2. Phoebe may have been a pastor-teacher. Certainly she was a church leader, as Paul instructed all the family of God to assist her.

Fourth, today a special ceremony called ordination is used to designate the gift of pastor-teacher. This ceremony sometimes has the effect of setting apart and elevating this gift above others, for which we do not have ordination ceremonies.

No such exercise of ordination is mentioned in the New Testament. Jesus ordained the disciples (John 15:16) and sent them out, but this particular ordination did not center around the gifts. Likewise, a practice called "laying on of hands" was used, but again this was not limited to singling out a particular gift. (*See* Acts 8:18; 9:17; 1 Timothy 4:14; 2 Timothy 1:6; Matthew 19:15.)

I mention this not only because of the lack of a scriptural precedent for isolating and elevating this pastor-teacher gift above the other gifts, but one wonders if the act of ordination hasn't needlessly placed still another barrier in front of women. From a completely different standpoint, many pastors of local churches today need some elevating. A great many pastors do not receive proper appreciation (and sometimes finances) in return for their dedicated ministering.

A person in the New Testament with the gift of pastor-teacher didn't need a ceremony or the approval of the church at large to exercise his or her gift. This gift was not elevated above the others nor was it limited to one sex.

Titles May Not Be Important

As a man or woman can have the gift of evangelism without a church recognizing or employing it in a local setting, so the gift of pastor-teacher can exist without it being strictly employed by leading a church congregation or acknowledged through an ordination ceremony. In fact, Rusty and I know a number of men and women with the gift of pastor-teacher who use their gifts not in the structured church, but in neighborhood fellowships, in Christian organizations, or in children's work.

These men and women instruct, lead, and shepherd. Many of their charges flourish just as well as those of a local "ordained" pastor. This indicates that God appoints the gifts and blesses the one who uses them under His direction, whatever the setting may be.

Can a woman be an effective pastor today? Many believe that Henrietta Mears exercised that gift in the fullest sense of the word. Though her title was Christian education director, her function was shepherding, teaching, and leading men and women of all ages. Men such as Bill Bright, Billy Graham, Louis Evans, Jr., and Dick Halverson credit her with much personal shepherding and teaching in their own lives.

Years later, Billy Graham was asked on *Meet the Press* about his views on women pastors. After stating that he left the doctrinal position to the church theologians, he added that during a recent trip to India he observed many fine women pastors.

The world's largest Christian church, in Seoul, Korea (boasting more than 500,000 members), is built upon small cell groups of men and women that are shepherded and taught largely by women.

Whatever title you want to give many fine men and women around the world, they are doing an exceptional job of shepherding and teaching the flock of God.

Hats off to them!

The Faithful

The Holy Spirit distributes gifts in an unsegregated way, but the full utilization of those gifts depends on the person's dependence on God. The man or woman who walks with God will excel in being used by God with or without other Christians' approval. What a blessing not to have to exalt oneself. For God promotes whom He wills, when He wills!

In the early church, women were told to preach, and they did; they were told to teach, and they did. "Women will prophesy," said Joel and Peter. So they did. Women evangelized and conceivably pastored. At least we have no indication to suggest otherwise. And God saw that women as well as men were gifted to carry out His desire.

But did women *lead* in the early church?

SEVENTEEN

Leaders
of the
Church

Words. They begin with a distinct meaning. As they are tossed about they become pregnant with suggestion. Finally, they can develop a life of their own, distinct from their original meaning.

I took an informal survey and asked a number of individuals the following question: "Do men, women, or both come to your mind when you hear these words: *brethren, disciples, men, apostles, elders,* and *deacons?*"

Without hesitation, most people answered, "Men."

The word *brethren* is used as a general term for the body of Christ, though it is also used to refer to males. This double meaning (in the Greek as well as English) can give one the feeling of male dominance or majority. Yet Paul's references do not seem to carry such implications. Although his epistles to the Romans (1:13; 7:1; 8:12, and so forth), Galatians (1:11; 5:13), Ephesians (6:23), Philippians (1:12; 3:13); Colossians (1:2), and Thessalonians (1 Thessalonians 1:4; 2 Thessalonians 1:3) are clearly for the church, he uses the word *brethren* to address the whole body.

Recently I attended an evening service where communion was served. After singing, which was led by a man, came a time of sharing, led by another man. Then we heard a brief talk about communion, given by a man, and the service concluded with communion, served by the same man.

When I asked if women ever participated in any of these leadership roles, I was told no, and I was deeply grieved for the wives who could not participate on equal footing with their husbands.

Another person commented that I shouldn't be bothered by seeing that women aren't exercising certain gifts. "Every gift is important to God, so it doesn't matter whether she is preparing the communion or serving it."

She was right, of course, that every gift is important, but I don't view that as the issue involved. I answered, "It is not a question of importance, but whether or not men and women are free to function with their own particular gifts."

"But women don't want to lead," a woman told a pastor friend of mine. "They prefer other jobs that fit them better."

He knew that was often the case, but he went on to explain why. "I've seen that when women can visualize themselves in a position, they begin to aspire to it. Both men and women need to visualize themselves serving Christ to their greatest capacity."

One woman who visualized herself in a greater capacity was Kathryn. For many years she had loved the Lord and faithfully attended church. Her kitchen constantly smelled of baked goods, which she offered to all. Yet Kathryn had a desire to be involved more directly in evangelism, discipleship, and leadership roles. She reasoned that feeding stomachs that were already full wasn't as important as feeding hungry souls. Kathryn's church encouraged her and suggested she take classes on evangelism and discipleship.

CALLED TO SERVICE

One week Kathryn knocked on the door of every home on her block. She asked each person who answered about his or her spiritual condition. Warmly and wisely she befriended her neighbors as they answered her well-put questions. After the survey, Kathryn invited the families to her home to hear about an important message that had changed her life.

The evening of the get-together, Kathryn's home smelled of freshly baked goods. But she was ready to feed their spirits as well as their bodies. On her knees Kathryn had asked God to use her greatly. When the guests arrived, Kathryn told them how Christ had changed her life and what He could also do for them.

That night twelve neighbors invited Christ into their lives. Within three years all but one person on Kathryn's block was a Christian.

If Kathryn had been limited by someone teaching her that she could not lead other men and women, another block might have been lost to Christ. But she was not. That which she visualized, she aspired to—just as you can, with God's help.

As Paul stated, "If *anyone* aspire to the office of overseer . . ." (*see* 1 Timothy 3:1).

Were women leaders in the early church? There is evidence that points to an affirmative answer. But first let's have a brief history on church leadership. Unlike worldly leadership, church leadership was viewed as an avenue of service. The leader was not someone who was above the rest of the congregation. Instead leaders were to see themselves as servants to others (Luke 22:24–27). Although members of the church are asked to submit or subject themselves to leaders, nowhere are leaders told to subject others under them.

In many aspects the church is involved in corporate leading. When the apostles wrote the letters to various churches, they addressed them to entire congregations, not just to select leaders. It was the responsibility of the entire congregation to see that the letters were followed, and the entire church was admonished to "stimulate one another to love and good deeds" (Hebrews 10:24). *All* the congregation assumes responsibility for evangelism and discipleship, prophesying, teaching, rebuking, and comforting. Note that specific leadership, vested in elders, deacons, bishops, and so forth, does not take away from the individual leadership incorporated in each believer and in the church as a whole. In short, New Testament church leaders tended to be less structured than many of us believe.

In fact, from congregation to congregation, leadership varied, just as the number of women in leadership varied. Rome, where a good number of women are listed as leaders, would have been more culturally accepting of that idea than some other cities. Appropriateness is always a consideration as we determine how our own local body of believers will function.

Apostles

There's no question that the word *apostle* causes most of us to visualize men, and twelve men at that. Yet Paul considered himself an apostle (2 Timothy 1:11) and, in 1 Corinthians 4:6–9, Paul seems to indicate that both he and Apollos are apostles. Then he states in 2 Corinthians 11 that some are false apostles, "deceitful workers, disguising themselves" (v. 13). If it were well known that only the twelve were apostles, why would Paul admonish the Corinthians to beware of false apostles? As John records in Revelation 2:2, ". . . Test those who call themselves apostles. . . ." If names and identification were enough to confirm twelve apostles, why would he have required the test?

We have no idea how many leaders of the early church were called apostles, but several more are named. Paul wrote, "Greet Andronicus and Junia, my kinsmen and my fellow prisoners, who are outstanding among the apostles who also were in Christ before me" (*see* Romans 16:7). Junia is indisputably a woman apostle.

In the fourth century A.D., Saint John Chrysostom recorded, "Indeed to be an Apostle at all is a great thing; but to even be one amongst those of note; just consider what a great encomium that is. . . . Oh how great is the devotion of their women, that she should be counted worthy the appelation of Apostle."[1] How fortunate that we have this early comment about

CALLED TO SERVICE

Junia, as many modern interpreters choose to question the validity of the feminine ending on her name.

Elders and Deacons

Aside from the apostles, there are five New Testament terms used to denote church leadership: *elder* ("older"), *deacon* ("servant" or "minister"), *overseer, bishop,* and *spiritual leader.* These terms are used somewhat interchangeably. For example, the term *spiritual leader* is used in the Book of Hebrews, whereas elsewhere the terms *elder* and *overseer* seem to refer to a similar function.

How leadership is chosen varies. In Titus 1:5, Paul tells Titus to appoint elders in every city. In Acts 20:28, Paul, in speaking to the elders at Ephesus, remarks, ". . . The Holy Spirit has made you overseers [*episkopos*] . . . ," indicating a more natural rise to leadership.

We are not given many specifics concerning the duties of the leader, elder, deacon, overseer, or bishop. But the requirements of those serving in this capacity are given clear attention. There are two lists of character requirements given (1 Timothy 3:1–13; Titus 1:5–9). To analyze *overseer* ("elder") and *deacon,* we will be using the 1 Timothy 3 passage: ". . . If any man aspires to the office of overseer, it is a fine work he desires to do" (v. 1).

The first thing to note is that the "if any man" is really "if anyone" (*tis* in the Greek). Neither is the word *he* in the original text. The Greek language was written in such a way that, unlike the English language, there is an exact word for almost every thought. If a biblical writer meant to refer to the male gender, as opposed to people more generally, he did. The English Bible liberally uses *men* as opposed to *humans, mankind, anyone, all,* and so on, and often causes confusion. Let's continue:

> An overseer, then, must be above reproach, the husband of
> one wife, temperate, prudent, respectable, hospitable, able to

teach, not addicted to wine or pugnacious, but gentle, uncontentious, free from the love of money.

Vv. 2, 3

Paul's statement "the husband of one wife" may be limiting, but we'll come back to that shortly.

He must be one who manages his own house well, keeping his children under control with all dignity (but if a man does not know how to manage his own household, how will he take care of the church of God?)

Vv. 4, 5

Let's follow this part in a literal translation of the Greek:

The own household well managing, children having in control with all gravity (but if anyone the own household to manage not knows, how a church of God will [he, she, it] care for?).

Note again that the translators have added the masculine pronouns. We continue:

And not a new convert, lest he become conceited and fall into the condemnation incurred by the devil. And he must have a good reputation with those outside the church, so that he may not fall into reproach and the snare of the devil. Deacons likewise must be men of dignity [the words *he* and *men* are not in the Greek] not double-tongued, or addicted to much wine or fond of sordid gain, but holding to the mystery of the faith with a clear conscience. And let these also first be tested; then let them serve as deacons if they are beyond reproach.

Vv. 6-10

At this point, Paul speaks specifically of women: "Women must likewise be dignified, not malicious gossips, but temperate, faithful in all things" (v. 11).

What was Paul talking about when he brought up women? First let's establish that the word is *woman*, not *wives*, as some translations indicate. The word for woman is *gune*, which

CALLED TO SERVICE

comes from the Greek root word *ginomai,* meaning "to come into being." If the word meant *wives,* one would have expected the modifying word *their.*

Second, *likewise* is an important word that refers back to something already said. In context, it refers back to the discussion of overseers and deacons.

Some people assume that women can only be deacons because they are mentioned right after that reference. However, the entire discussion is on overseers (elders) and deacons, and nothing is specifically said to indicate that "likewise women" refers only to deacons.

If the passage, addressed to "anyone," specifically lists qualifications for men, followed by qualifications for women, as yet other people assume, then the "likewise women" would also refer to overseers, as well as deacons.

Let's now finish the passage and then address some other questions often raised.

> Let deacons be husbands of only one wife and good managers of their children and their own households. For those who have served well as deacons obtain for themselves a high standing and great confidence in the faith that is in Christ Jesus.
> Vv. 12, 13

This last sentence does not refer just to deacons, but to those ministering (in context, probably overseers [elders] and deacons), as the words *as deacons* are not in the original.

Now let's address some specific questions. What implication does "husband of one wife" have in reference to elders (v. 2) and to deacons (v. 12)? Many theologians agree that "husband of one wife" means "only one at a time," but there are at least six prevalent interpretations of what the phrase means. If the verse did mean "only one wife at a time," then only men needed this admonition. A woman never had more than one husband, though polygamy occasionally still occurred.

Second, the statement "husband of one wife" and what follows in no way insists that an elder must be a man anymore than it insists he must be married or have children. If we understand this phrase to mean an elder must be a man, then we *must* understand he has to be married and has to have children.

Recently someone challenged me on this passage, "Surely, the fact that the word *husband* is mentioned, and not *wife*, indicates that elders are to be men only."

"Not necessarily," I responded. "Many places in Scripture a general principle is followed by specific information for one group, but the general principle is applicable to all."

"Where do you find such teaching?"

"For example, the verse 'Fathers, . . . bring [your children] up in the discipline and instruction of the Lord' does not mean that women are excluded from the task. Elsewhere the command to teach and discipline children is given to both parents. 'Wives submit to your husbands' does not mean that husbands are not to submit to their wives. Elsewhere they are both told to submit to each other. 'Husband of one wife' does not exclude the wives themselves. Previously Paul addressed the passage to 'anyone who aspires.' If one is going to exclude women from being elders, he must base his statement on a clearer statement than that saying a man must have only one wife, found in 1 Timothy 3 or Titus 1."

Are there other passages dealing with elders that indicate both men and women?

Yes. *Presbyteria*, the feminine of *presbyter* (*elder*) appears in 1 Timothy 5:2, while the masculine form occurs in the preceding verse. If Timothy 5:1 refers to an elder who is to be entreated as a father (as is indicated in some versions), then verse 2 probably refers to a woman elder who is to be entreated as a mother. Some scholars believe that Titus 2:3, *presbytidas*, speaks of woman elders.

Is there any indication of a woman being a deacon or elder in the New Testament?

Yes. "I commend to you our sister Phoebe, who is a servant of the church which is at Cenchrea; that you receive her in the Lord in a manner worthy of the saints, and that you may help her in whatever matter she may have need of you; for she herself has also been a helper of many, and of myself as well" (Romans 16:1, 2).

The word translated "servant" is *diakonos*. It appears twenty times in Paul's epistles, and this is the only place it is not translated *deacon* or *minister*. There is little question that Phoebe was a deacon.

Next, the word translated "helper" is *prostatis*, the feminine form of *prostates*, which means "leader, chief, ruler, administrator, president, presiding officer, patron, guardian, benefactor." But the real meaning of this word is found when you examine the Greek verb, *proistemi*, which stands behind the noun. It means to "stand before, rule, manage, conduct, be concerned about, give aid." The verb combines the meanings of caring and ruling and is used in 1 Timothy 5:17, where Paul talks about "ruling elders." This word is also used in Romans 12:8 and 1 Thessalonians 5:12, ". . . who have charge over you in the Lord." Hence there is evidence that Phoebe was an elder in the church at Cenchrea.

Note the last phrase in Romans 16:2. Concerning Phoebe, ". . . for she herself has also been a *prostatis* of many, and *of myself as well*" (*italics added*). Whatever the word *prostatis* means, we can be sure that Phoebe had a spiritual ministry in Paul's life.

It is conceivable that Priscilla (Romans 16:3, 4), Euodia and Syntyche (Philippians 4:2, 3), and Tryphaena and Tryphosa (Romans 16:12) were elders as well, for Paul mentions them as "fellow laborers," using the same Greek word as the one he used for the work of Timothy, Barnabas, and others. Further, Paul admonishes the saints at Corinth to *be in subjection to such individuals* (1 Corinthians 16:16).

Is there any early church history that supports women elders, deacons, or bishops?

Yes. Pliny the Younger, writing about A.D. 104, refers to two women deacons or ministers.

The walls of the catacombs are etched with authoritative-looking women with arms upraised, like leaders or bishops. Stone coffins also show etchings of women teachers and leaders. And one of the oldest churches in Rome has a mosaic of Bishop Theodora.

Around A.D. 200 Tertullian wrote that there were four

orders of female church officers: deacons, widows, elders, and presiding officers. The word *deaconess* first appeared about A.D. 100.

Dionysius of Alexandria described one martyr as "the most holy elder Mercuria" and another as a most remarkable virgin elder, Appollonia (A.D. 250–251).

As we attempt to draw conclusions concerning women as elders, deacons, overseers, and spiritual leaders, two points stand out. There is no clear command that women cannot hold these offices. If such conclusions are reached they are *assumed*, rather than clearly stated. In addition, there is no evidence in the New Testament that a woman was forbidden from church leadership, and there is reason to believe that women or men held major leadership roles.

EIGHTEEN

Culture
or
Commandment?

A Christian woman was asked to teach a new convert who
had previously been an astrologer; a practitioner of Scientology, the I-Ching, and EST; a user of tarot cards; a prostitute;
and a heroin addict. She had also had five abortions, two children, and had begged money on the streets, for a living. She
had spent months in mental institutions, state-run homes,
even jails.

Does this read like exaggerated fiction? It isn't; in fact it describes the life-styles of many Americans. In contrast, most
American Christians do not relate to such a background and
therefore are ill-prepared to lead these people to Christ and
disciple them. But helping these converts emerge from their
pasts is one of the challenges we face.

In this particular case, another church member intercepted
some communication between the mature Christian and the

new one. The third party was appalled and immediately passed on the information to his friends, saying, "This woman is telling the new Christian not to worry about having abortions, that her involvement in astrology will be an aid in helping others, that God will take care of her son without her participation in his life."

Suspicion surrounded the teacher until one Christian lovingly approached her for clarification: She had been talking about the woman's past abortions; a previous knowledge of astrology might allow someone to be effective in winning other astrologers to Christ; if the woman's son had been given to another, and he was out of her sphere of control, God was her refuge.

This example points out what we are often up against when we interpret the Bible. The direct recipients of the New Testament letters understood what Paul was saying, just as the new convert understood the context of what she was being taught. Although we are the indirect recipients of the epistles, we can be the direct recipients by application, through the Spirit of God, if we understand the situation that was being addressed. Otherwise, like the suspicious individual in the above story, we may wrongly interpret the meaning of certain teaching.

This problem of correct interpretation, particularly of old letters that deal with cultures vastly different from ours, is difficult. Cultural differences must be taken into consideration, yet we cannot use the cultural issue to disregard parts of the Bible with which we don't want to deal. Ask the most traditional interpreter of 1 Timothy 2:9, 10 why he or she doesn't enforce Paul's clear commands against women wearing braids, gold, or pearls, and he or she will reply, "Oh, that's cultural!" That interpreter will recognize that some things in the Bible were not meant for all Christians, in all places, at all times.

We should also be aware of translation errors and personal biases in previous interpretations. All in all, when we look at these passages, we are up against serious difficulties—ones that require diligent study, open-mindedness, and the Spirit of God.

As we take a look at several difficult passages regarding a woman's freedom in her church life, we must see them in the light of the rest of Scripture, which we've already studied.

Dr. Walter Kaiser, academic dean of Trinity Evangelical Divinity School, writes in *Worldwide Challenge*, September 1976:

> The daily controversy over what the Bible really says about God's purpose for women has brought forth two dangerous positions. The first is an evangelical backlash mentality against libertine statements on women and society, and the second is an easy capitulation to whatever current fad holds sway over society, with very little authoritative biblical basis for the latest change. These views are dangerous for opposite reasons: The first espouses a low view of women, and the second takes a low view of Scripture!

Fortunately, it is possible to keep a high view of Scripture (that is, that Scripture is our final word on any subject) and see women and men with a high view as well.

The three controversial passages on women that we have not yet investigated are 1 Corinthians 11:1–16; 1 Corinthians 14:34–36; and 1 Timothy 2:8–15. As Dr. Walter Kaiser points out, these are "sensitive" texts, difficult to understand and ones that require that the reader keep an open mind.

Let's look first at 1 Corinthians 11:1–16. Please read that text thoroughly before proceeding.

In addressing the 1 Corinthians 11 text, I've primarily relied on the work of Berkeley and Alvera Mickelsen,[1] adding my own insight and research.

The Mickelsens openly express their belief in the absolute authority of God's Word; they have spent years studying it and using their communication skills to make the Word "real and vital to other people." They agree that 1 Corinthians 11:1–16 has been "misused" to support male dominance, and they rely on sound principles of biblical interpretation to determine Paul's meaning.

First, they looked to determine what the passage would have said to the Corinthian readers. Paul had apparently received

CULTURE OR COMMANDMENT?   199 reports of problems in this new church, and he wrote this letter out of concern. In 3:3–9 Paul indicated that believers were arguing. Chapter 5 starts out saying that Paul had heard of a case of incest in the church. Chapter 6 tackles the problem of lawsuits. Toward the end of chapter 11, Paul mentions their misuse of the Lord's Supper. The worship services seemed disorderly, with many people talking at the same time, and Paul was writing to instruct the church on proper conduct.

A Question of Hair Length

The passage in question, 11:1–16, discusses public prayer and prophecy. Paul would have known the Joel prophecy that Peter had said was fulfilled at Pentecost: ". . . Your sons and your daughters shall prophesy . . ." (Acts 2:17). But he would have been equally aware that many Greeks and Jews thought it disgraceful for a woman to speak publicly. These two conflicting views would have made the issue of orderly worship especially pertinent.

Also, this passage seems to be developing the principle laid out in chapter 10, concerning appropriateness: "All things are lawful, but not all things are profitable . . ." (v. 23). Other clues, such as reference to tradition (11:2), custom or practice (11:16), and nature (11:14), might lead one to believe that this is an argument for appropriateness rather than doctrine.

You'll note that this passage includes complicated discussions about hair length and head coverings, but the Mickelsens point out:

> . . . Although most translations speak about veils, there is no word for *veil* or *unveiled* in the Greek text.
> The literal translation is "having it down from the head." This could refer to veils, as most translators assumed, but the passage makes better sense if we see this as referring to hair styles rather than veils. For example, why should Paul say it was a disgrace for a man to pray with his head covered, when men in Jewish services always had (and still have) some covering on their heads?

Other scholars, including Jerome Murphy-O'Connor of École Biblique in Jerusalem, agree with this hair-style interpretation.[2]

Immorality and homosexuality were rampant in Corinth, a Greek city in which goddess cults abounded. In that culture, long, ornately fixed hair on men could signify sexual ambiguity. Often a woman wearing very short hair indicated she was a lesbian.

These insights into the first-century Greek culture shed light on Paul's hair-length discussion. Concerned lest the differences between the sexes become obscured, Paul makes a point to say that when anyone prays or prophesies, he or she should do so in a way that does not hide his or her sexual identity. The word *head* used in verses 4, 5 (one's head being disgraced) probably refers to one's "whole person."

The Mickelsens say, "Paul's point is the distinction between the sexes—not the dominance of one over the other."

Authority or Source?

Chapter 6 and the Appendix thoroughly discuss the meaning of the word *head*, used in 1 Corinthians 11:3, ". . . Christ is the head of every man, and the man is the head of a woman, and God is the head of Christ."

The Greek word, *kephale*, did not imply authority, but often origin or source. This meaning of the word seems to be reinforced, as Paul, in verse 8, refers to creation: "Man does not originate from woman, but woman from man," and in verse 12, "As the woman originates from the man, so also the man has his birth through the woman; and all things originate from God."

In 1 Corinthians 8:6, Paul refers to Christ being the origin of man, and in Galatians 4:4 he says, "God sent forth His Son, born of a woman," indicating that God was the source of Christ.

Although this idea of *head* meaning "source" may seem farfetched to twentieth-century readers, it would have been quite logical, even obvious, to a Corinthian.

The Mickelsens say:

> Those who believe that 1 Corinthians 11:3 teaches some "chain of command" (the very idea opposes the oft-repeated teachings of Christ regarding leadership as servanthood) must rearrange the verse. If Paul had been thinking of a "chain of command," he surely would have used a less ambiguous word than the Greek word for *head* and also would have arranged it in proper order—God, Christ, Man, Woman. Instead it is arranged Man-Christ, Woman-Man, Christ-God.

Actually this passage shows the wonderful interdependence and equality of women and men—Eve coming from Adam's rib, but man being born of woman, and both sexes originating from God (vv. 11, 12). That is, in spite of the fact that woman was first made for the sake of man (man realizing his loneliness and incompleteness without woman [v. 9]), the Lord so arranged things that woman was first taken from man and brought back to him; now man is taken from woman and given back to man.

Verse 10 has caused some confusion: "The woman ought to have a symbol of authority on her head, because of the angels." The Mickelsens say, "Authority to do what? To pray and prophesy in the public gathering of the church, of course. That's what this long discussion is all about!"

Several modern versions, including *The Living Bible, Good News for Modern Man,* and *Phillips' New Testament in Modern English,* make reference to woman being under *man's* authority, but the Greek doesn't mention men, husbands, veils, or head coverings. Once again, one can see how preconceived ideas have a way of influencing a translator's work.

Why was the woman's own authority mentioned? Again it may be in reference to the need for the believers to judge for themselves (v. 13). If a woman is to act in an appropriate manner, to do all "to the glory of God" (10:31), then she must decide based on the local traditions, customs, nature, and so forth. Judging from Paul's lack of *clear* command in the passage, this may be his approach in dealing with this conflict concerning public worship.

CALLED TO SERVICE

Dr. Walter Leifeld, professor of New Testament, Trinity Evangelical Divinity School, writes: "In the larger context of this passage, we find *exousia* used five times in 9:1–12 in the sense of 'right.' Chapters 8–14 pertain in part to the limiting of rights and freedom that the believer possesses for the sake of winning others to the gospel and not stumbling the 'weak.' Paul thus is affirming that women do have a God-given right to pray and prophesy (cf. Acts 2:17 f.), but that they can exercise that right only if they do so without causing social offense by bringing shame to their husbands through uncovered heads."[3]

Prayer and Prophecy

Verses 13 and 14 return to the earlier topic—that women and men should not confuse their sexual identities, then verse 15 closes with: ". . . For her hair is given to her for a covering"—*covering* meaning "a mantle" in the same sense that the Old Testament prophets had mantles.

I especially love Paul's closing statement on the matter: "But if one is inclined to be contentious, we have no other [such] practice, nor have the churches of God."

If we keep in mind the nondogmatic approach, then "such" is probably the better translation for "other." Indeed, there is no evidence of this practice being taught at other New Testament churches. The message: "Think carefully and appropriately, but choose for yourself" still seems predominant.

In her excellent book *Women in the Bible* Mary Evans concludes: "Paul in this chapter is supporting the equality of women in worship and their full participation in prayer and prophecy. He points out that this equality does not imply a necessity for a false identity between the sexes, and that there is no reason therefore to overthrow any conventions of dress that emphasize their distinction."[4]

Ian Pitt-Wilson, professor of preaching at Fuller Theological Seminary, recently commented that in the last few years the best preachers in his classes have been women. When he heard these students preach, he heard a perspective on the Gospel that had been missing when proclaimed only by men.

Another man put it this way, "I hear another dimension of the Gospel when I hear it taught or preached by women."

What is the benefit of women praying, prophesying, preaching, and contributing to public worship? We are all the poorer if the Gospel is filtered through only half the human race—and likewise the richer to have the insights of all.

And what if the Gospel had not come through Mrs. Phoebe Palmer? It can be documented that at least 25,000 people were won to Christ in the 1800s as a direct result of her public ministry.

Regardless of whether her hair was short or long, she publicly prayed, prophesied, and related the Gospel to the glory of God. Paul would have been pleased!

First Corinthians 14:34-38

Or would he? Some say Paul did not allow a woman to speak at all in public worship. The text they base this on is the next text we will consider: 1 Corinthians 14:34-38.

> Let the women keep silent in the churches; for they are not permitted to speak, but let them subject themselves just as the Law also says. And if they desire to learn anything, let them ask their own husbands at home; for it is improper for a woman to speak in church. Was it from you that the word of God first went forth? Or has it come to you only? If anyone thinks he is a prophet or spiritual, let him recognize that the things which I write to you are the Lord's commandment. But if any one does not recognize this, he is not recognized.

The Book of 1 Corinthians is a letter that was written at one time and was meant to be read in entirety. Why would Paul speak of women praying and prophesying in public earlier (chapter 11) only to announce later in the same letter that women cannot even speak or ask a question in public?

Schooled theologians believe there are two possible meanings to this passage. The first is that Paul may be admonishing the wives to stop interrupting the services by asking their husbands what everything means. The second is that Paul may be quoting the false teachings of the Judaizers, who wanted women to be silent in the church, as had been required in the synagogues; then he may be refuting that teaching.

Let's look at the first possibility. Women are the third group in this chapter that are told to "be silent" (*see* verses 28 and 30). Some see that this third "problem group" being admonished is specifically women who have Christian husbands. If so, then the nature of the problem can be cleared up by the solution Paul prescribes.

Already he has stressed the importance of order during worship, in verse 26 (". . . Let all things be done for edification") and in verse 33, preceding the admonition to women ("For God is not a God of confusion but of peace, as in all the churches of the saints"). Now he suggests that instead of interrupting the spontaneity and order of the worship, wives should refrain from asking questions until they are home.

This rendering may be credible for several reasons. Most of the women coming into this church would have been uneducated, whereas their husbands would have had some book learning, which might have aided their understanding of Christian doctrine. It is also possible (in light of 1 Corinthians 14:22–25 and 7:12–16) that some wives were not yet Christians. At any rate, in view of the background of the Corinthians and the exciting freedom they were experiencing in the Christian assemblies, it is not difficult to imagine that many women were filled with comments and questions that they felt free to express in the church setting.

In general, the Book of 1 Corinthians is an attempt to establish order in that church, and chapter 14 specifically addresses the issue. In church assembly it seems everyone was trying to talk at once. Chapter 11 addresses women as well as men on this issue. For example, in verses 26, 30, 31 Paul states, ". . . When you assemble, each one has a psalm, has a teaching, has a revelation, has a tongue, has an interpretation. Let all things be done for edification. . . . If a revelation is made to another who is seated, let the first keep silent. For you can all prophesy one by one, so that all may learn and all may be exhorted. . . ."

"*All* may prophesy" and "*all* may learn" in public worship are major themes in chapters 14 and 11; it hardly seems conceivable that verses 34, 35 should contradict what Paul has just stated.

Let's look now at another possible meaning of 1 Corinthians 14:34–38.

It is entirely possible that Paul was quoting what the Judaizers taught. He may have been stating their teaching in verses 34 and 35 and then rebuking the Corinthians for holding this view in verses 36–38. Paul had a practice of quoting from letters sent to him and then responding. (This is seen elsewhere in 1 Corinthians.) Keep in mind that there were no quotation marks in the Greek manuscripts that were handed down. Punctuation and capitalization were inserted by the translators.

Since verses 34 and 35 are not quoting the Old or New Testament (as is easily verified), we can assume that the Corinthians and Paul are referring to some other law with the words "just as the Law says," and that by all rights *law* should not be capitalized. Most probably this refers to human laws in existence in the Greek culture at the time. Some believe this is a law of the Judaizers, as the man-made Jewish law states "a woman may speak to no man other than her husband" (M. Ket. 7:6). (Also the phrase "for they are not permitted" is part of the technical vocabulary of Judaism.)

This rendering of the passage would also make sense of the verses following 34 and 35, "Was it from you that the word of God first went forth? Or has it come to you only? If anyone thinks he is a prophet or spiritual, let him recognize that the things which I write to you are the Lord's commandment. But if anyone does not recognize this, he is not recognized." These words are clearly a rebuke to the Corinthians. When Paul says "Was it from you that the word of God first went forth? Or has it come to you only?" he most likely is referring to the arrogant attitude of the men who want to exclude women from speaking or teaching the Scriptures. If so, this rebuke is a

CALLED TO SERVICE

harsh one. The word of God came to *all* and for *all*. As Paul stated in verse 31, "All should prophesy . . . that *all* may learn."

But Paul told Timothy not to let a woman teach a man. Or did he? Next, let's consider Paul's admonition to the church at Ephesus.

NINETEEN

Women in Leadership

One of the flaws of human nature is that we're prone to assume responsibility before we are ready. It is presumptuous to elevate oneself prematurely, but it is also presumptuous to set up others in a position above his or her understanding and maturity. This error can be seen when foreigners abruptly pull out of countries they have led, leaving unprepared nationals to assume leadership. It can be seen when a teenager becomes an unwed mother, when a young radical is given too much political power, and, yes, when an unseasoned Christian assumes major leadership in a church.

But the Bible teaches us to be prepared (2 Timothy 2:15), ready for responsibility (1 Peter 3:15) and leadership (1 Timothy 3). Paul admonishes Timothy, "Do not lay hands upon anyone too hastily [placing them in leadership] and thus share responsibility for the sins of others ..." (1 Timothy 5:22). James warns, "Let not many of you become teachers, my brethren, knowing that as such we shall incur a stricter judgment" (3:1).

We observe a clear thread in the Scripture: Be mature before you assume responsibility. Learn before you teach.

Before you proceed any further, read 1 Timothy in your own Bible.

First Timothy is a personal letter to Paul's friend who was a "pastor" in Ephesus, a godless city much like Corinth. This is one of Paul's last letters, and in it he offers Timothy advice on how to deal with pressing problems, primarily false teaching.

After Paul's salutation, he writes about certain persons who were teaching various doctrines. Then, in verses 12–19, Paul thanks God that he has been delivered from his former life and urges Timothy to maintain his faith with a good conscience. Again in verse 20 Paul mentions two false teachers by name.

I'd like to begin 1 Timothy 2 now by citing research by Richard and Catherine Kroeger.

The Kroegers are theologically conservative and strong on the position of biblical inerrancy. Two of their papers have been presented at annual conventions of the Society for Biblical Literature. Together they have taught university courses on the role and status of women in the Bible and early church. In the next few pages I will summarize material they prepared for congregations that struggle with the question of women and men in ministry.[1]

Most scholars agree that a lot of questions come to light when they consider 1 Timothy 2:9–15, because it seems to contradict other passages. Deuteronomy 24:16 and Ezekiel 18:14–20 say that children do not carry guilt for their parents' sins. Romans 5:12–19 and 1 Corinthians 15:22 blame Adam rather than Eve for the Fall. If women are saved by bearing children, what about childless women? And aren't we all saved through the atonement of Jesus Christ? Why did Priscilla teach Apollos in Ephesus, where Timothy was when he received this letter from Paul?

Paul and the Gnostics

Like Galatians; Jude; 1, 2, 3 John; 2 Peter; and Colossians, 1 Timothy addresses doctrinal and moral problems. The Acts of the Apostles 19, 20 and Ephesians 4, 5 indicate that heresy was a problem in the Ephesian church, where Timothy was ministering; 1 Timothy 4:7; 5:11-15 and 2 Timothy 3:5-7 indicate that women were involved in this church's heresy.

First Timothy 2:5 is the familiar "For there is one God and one mediator. . . ." Verse 7 says that Paul was "appointed a preacher" to proclaim this truth. Verse 8, beginning with "therefore," shows that what follows is based upon this mission of Paul. The Kroegers say:

> Greek religion was heavily committed to many mediators, and Paul is saying here that both men and women must learn new ways in worship. Men were to pray for themselves, lifting their own hands in prayer, not relying on formal rites conducted by a cult official. In their former non-Christian rites, certain religions required only that the men arrive at the right time and attend the ceremony in the right place without any demand of personal faith or commitment. According to Paul, all men, not just the priest, should pray everywhere. . . . For the women, the mediatorship of Jesus presented other problems, since many of them had heretofore served in Ephesus as sacred prostitutes, mediators of the goddess Artemis or of Aphrodite the Harlot.
>
> Beyond this, there were many traditions of special revelations given to women and available to men only through women. The most famous example is that of the prophetess of Apollo at Delphi. It was she who pronounced the oracle to those who came to find out the will of the god. The priests interpreted the message, but a woman was always the mouthpiece.

Paul's Dress Code for Women

First Timothy 2:9 says in the Greek, "Likewise I want women to pray, adorning themselves with proper clothing, modestly and discreetly, not with braided hair and gold or pearls or costly garments." Women were not to dress like the promiscuous women of the day, when they prayed in public.

In verse 11 Paul changes noun form from *women* to *woman*, and he uses this form until the second half of verse 15. Paul may have been referring to a certain woman, as he does name other heretics (1 Timothy 1:20; 2 Timothy 2:17, 18; 4:14, 15) or refer to them indirectly (1 Timothy 1:3, 19; 5:15; 6:21). The Kroegers note that "Women or 'a woman' are to learn 'in silence and submission'—a phrase denoting receptivity. This in itself is unusual in a day and age when few respectable women were allowed an education."

Paul on Women Teaching and Bearing Rule

First Timothy begins with an instruction: Timothy is to instruct certain people not to teach false doctrine (vv. 3, 4). It is possible that 2:12, "I do not allow a woman to teach or exercise authority over a man . . ." may refer only to women heretics. In the pastoral epistles, the Greek word *didaskein*, translated "teach," usually means either "teach sound doctrine" or "teach error." This 2:12 reference appears to be speaking of women teaching error or heresy, as elsewhere Paul appears to applaud women who are known to teach truth (2 Timothy 1:5; 4:19). (*Note:* in the Greek, 1 Timothy 2:12 is not a command; the sentence would more accurately be translated, "I am not presently allowing a woman to teach. . . .")

Concerning this passage, Dr. David Scholer, dean of the seminary, and Julius R. Manley, professor of New Testament, at Northern Baptist Theological Seminary, write: "These statements are not to be understood as universal principles encoded in a suprasituational 'church order manual' that limit women in all times and all places. Rather the instructions of

2:11-12 are directed against women who having been touched or captivated by false teachings are abusing the normal opportunities women had within the church to teach and exercise authority."[3]

Authentein, the Greek verb used later in verse 12 and usually translated "to rule over" or "to dominate" occurs nowhere else in the Bible. Its usual meaning was "to be responsible for a misdeed," even murder. Priestesses of Artemis did sentence men to death. (Euripides' *Iphigenia in Tauris* mentions this.) Greek myths relate several murders of men by women. Up until the second century A.D. humans were sacrificed to Artemis.

The Kroegers continue:

> *Authentein* sometimes had a sexual connotation, and it may here refer to promiscuous rites by which women professed to teach men religious truths. . . . Perhaps we should translate, "I forbid a woman to instruct or initiate a man into fertility rites." Proverbs 5:3-5; 7:24-27 tells us that seduction by a woman was considered tantamount to murder, and Jewish tradition taught that it was Eve's seduction which brought death to humanity. In the New Testament, we also find the concept of seduction bringing death (Romans 7:11).
>
> Another translation is also possible if one understands the syntax as a double negative with a verb of prohibition: "I forbid a woman to teach that she is superior to a man." A woman who sets herself up as a mediator is obviously claiming an inside connection with God. The Quintillians, who honored Eve as the first to bring knowledge, claimed for their prophetesses "a something superior to Christ, the apostles, and the prophets." Now that's what we call heresy!

David Scholer writes: "If Paul were referring to the normal exercise of authority, his otherwise constant *exousia/exousiazō* ("authority/ to exercise authority") vocabulary would most likely have been used. The choice of such an unusual term indicates that Paul intended a different nuance of meaning."[4]

Adam, Then Eve

As we continue, again note what Paul is talking about—learning and teaching in light of false teaching in Ephesus.

In verse 13, the Greek verb *plasso* is often translated as "created": "For it was Adam who was first created, and then Eve." But why didn't Paul use the word "created" (*ktizo*), which would have clearly suggested Adam being made first? One possibility will be suggested.

Is creation-order teaching, "The man came first; therefore he is in charge" and/or "the man came first; therefore he is the teacher," supported in 1 Timothy 2? Consider what sense does this passage make to say that Adam was first created, therefore Eve was deceived? *Created* and *deceived* are not properly juxtaposed. Consider another alternative: that education is the theme of this passage and a proper juxtaposition to deception. The passage would then read: "Adam was educated; then Eve was educated; but Eve was deceived."

From the Greek word *plasso* ("shaped" or "molded") we get the word *plastic* or *plasticize*. In one recent Greek-English lexicon, the authors give several meanings for the word *plasso*. The second meaning is "mold, form, by education, training, etc." Another usage these scholars give is: "form an image of a thing in the mind, imagine."

They refer to Aristotle and other writers close to the time of the New Testament, who used *plasso* to mean "educated."[2] Paul, who was widely educated, most certainly had been schooled in the readings of many of those who used this form of *plasso*.

In Kittel's *Theological Dictionary of the New Testament*, Herbert Braun, a Greek scholar, writes concerning *plasso*, "In the Greek world and Philo, though hardly in the LXX and not at all in the New Testament, there is a series of figurative meanings in addition to the original one; 'to fashion by education and training' (Plato. Resp. II 377c) 'to invent,' 'devise' (Plato. Phaech. 246c) 'to invent in opposition to the truth' (Herodotus VIII, 80)."

Braun states that neither of the two New Testament uses of *plasso* should be translated "to form by education." This is clearly *his* opinion, based on his philosophy. Braun backs up his interpretation of 1 Timothy not by denying that *plasso* could mean "educated" but because he believes in creative order (the man came first, therefore is the teacher).[5]

Adam was educated by God. Eve was educated also, but we have no record of her direct instruction by God. It is probable that Adam taught her rather than God, for when confronted with the serpent, she had the story somewhat mixed up. (She said to the serpent, "God has said, 'You shall not eat from it or touch it, lest you die' "[Genesis 3:3], yet God had said only not to eat from it.) If this is a case of inadequate teaching by Adam, perhaps 1 Timothy 2:13, 14 suggests that man is not a good teacher.

Though scholars do not necessarily concur with my position here, and more research is needed, what do I believe Paul may be trying to say? In light of false teaching and probably much ignorance on the part of a newly converted and uneducated woman or women, "Let a woman learn quietly and with a teachable and submissive attitude. For I am not allowing women to teach and exercise willful or harmful authority over men. Women must first learn. For Adam learned first, then Eve, but she was deceived. Therefore learn properly so as not to be deceived and exercise harmful authority over another."

Women—or anyone who is ignorant or promoting false teaching—learn before you teach! A great message for the church today!

Childbearing ·

This passage presents yet another problem in verse 15: "salvation by childbearing." This verse may refute a Gnostic teaching that the Kroegers describe: "Women would be saved by becoming males and that Jesus had come to do away with the works of women, specifically childbearing." If this is what Paul was doing, he was stating that women are saved just as they are—as women and as child bearers.

CALLED TO SERVICE

Others believe it has to do with the birth of the Christ child, who was the salvation of us all.

Dr. Walter Kaiser, dean of Trinity Evangelical Divinity School, has spent hundreds of hours researching the role of women in the church. In *Worldwide Challenge* magazine he interrelated the three difficult passages we've discussed.[6] I'd like to share his summary with you.

> Several theses must be used to summarize the relevant texts [concerning women in ministry]. The first is that God encourages women to lead in public prayers of the church in an orderly and decorous manner. 1 Timothy 2:8, 9 says: "I desire therefore that men pray in every place, lifting up holy hands without wrath and doubting. In like manner that women adorn themselves in modest apparel with reverence and restraint."
>
> In the very passage most frequently used to urge women to absolute silence in the church, Paul encourages them to "Lift up their hands in every place" in prayer. The key word comes at the beginning of verse 9, "likewise" or "in like manner." But what is the "like manner" referred to in verse 9?
>
> Paul wants women to "*pray* in like manner" as men do in every place. Thus the missing main verb in verse 9 is the same verbal idea he has just given in verse 8. "Likewise (I desire that women pray in every place) adorning themselves. . . ." That is why women must be conscious of their apparel, for public prayer, unlike private prayer, puts one in the public view. But of Paul's desire there can be no doubt: He wants women to participate in public prayer.
>
> The similarity of this passage to 1 Corinthians 11:5, which contains instructions for ". . . every woman praying or prophesying . . . ," strengthens this interpretation. The reference here is also to public worship.
>
> As A. J. Gordon so tersely commented, "It is quite incredible, on the contrary, that the apostle should give himself the trouble to prune a custom which he desired to uproot, or that he should spend his breath condemning a forbidden method of doing a forbidden thing."[7]
>
> The second thesis is that God encourages women to lead the church in edification, yet with a quiet and submissive spirit.
>
> If women may lead in public prayer, what else may they do? 1 Timothy 2:11 advises: "Let a woman learn in silence [*he-*

suchia] in all subjection." Likewise, I Corinthians 14:34b, 35 reads: "Let the women keep silence [*sigatosan*] in the church: it is not permitted to them to speak; but let them be in subjection, as the law also says. And if they would learn anything, let them ask their own husbands at home; for it is shameful for a woman to speak in the church."

Isn't this a demand for "silence"? Does not Scripture tell women never to speak in church? The answer to this problem is twofold.

First, the Greek word of I Timothy 2:11—hesuchia—is better translated "quietness" or "quiet spirit." Many of the same translators properly rendered the same word in II Thessalonians 3:12, "That with quietness [*hesuchia*] they work and eat their own bread." Fortunately, no one has yet advocated on the basis of II Thessalonians 3:12 that men should refrain from ever speaking while they eat or work on the job!

The other half of the answer is to identify the "law" mentioned in I Corinthians 14:34. Since nowhere in the Old Testament is such an injunction given, the presumption is more than likely that Paul is referring to a type of legalistic bondage newly raised by the Jewish community. The Talmud, not the Old Testament, had said: "It is a shame for a woman to let her voice be heard among men," and again, "Out of respect to the congregation, a woman should not herself read in the law." Rabbi Eleazer asserted, "Let the words of the law be burned rather than committed to women."

This would also explain Paul's sharp rejoinder in verse 36: "What? Did the Word of God come out from you, or came it unto you [men] only [masculine]?"

We conclude that in verses 34b, 35 Paul is quoting from the letter sent to him by the Corinthians, just as he had done in I Corinthians 6:12 "all things are lawful for me," and in 8:8 and 10:23. Such quotations became headings for the new subjects Paul introduced.

We can be sure of the presence of a quotation, commented Sir William Ramsay, ". . . whenever Paul alludes to their knowledge, or when any statement stands in marked contrast either with the immediate context or with Paul's known views."[8]

The contrast is strongly apparent in verse 36, "what?" and verse 31, "*all* may prophesy." And Paul's views have already

CALLED TO SERVICE

been exposed in I Corinthians 11:5, "every woman who prays or prophesies." The allusion to the Corinthians' knowledge is also found in verses 37, 38: "If anyone thinks that he is a prophet or spiritual, he should acknowledge what I write to you is the Lord's command." Hence we can be sure Paul is quoting the Corinthians' letter and the argument on "silence" is corrected.

If Paul did not totally reduce women to silence in the church, what specifically did he allow them to do? He allowed them "to pray and prophesy" in I Corinthians 11:5. In I Corinthians 14:31 he is even more emphatic: "*All* may prophesy so that *all* may learn" and "*all* may be encouraged." And Paul's definition of prophecy is given in this same context—I Corinthians 14:4 says, "He who prophesies *edifies* the church." Furthermore, the same groups that can learn and be encouraged—"*all*" can compose the group from which the prophets may come—"*all!*" Given the large number of women in the early churches, this is an even more startling statement.

Paul knew, of course, as did the Corinthian church, about the Corinthian lady Priscilla, wife of Aquila, who taught men of such importance as Apollos (Acts 18:26). In Romans 16:3 Paul called her and Aquila his "*fellow-laborers* [*sunergoi*] in Christ Jesus"—a phrase he usually reserved for his companions in the work of the church (I Corinthians 3:5-9; Romans 16:21—referring to Timothy). . . . About this same time Paul also visited Philip the evangelist, who had "four unmarried daughters who prophesied" (Acts 21:9).

Add to both of these cases Phoebe, a deacon (sic), an official functionary, in the church at Cenchrea,[9] and Euodia and Syntyche, women who "labored side by side with me in the Gospel together with Clement and the rest of my fellow-laborers" (Philippians 4:2, 3, 8), and the evidence begins to definitely show a real active participation on the part of women in official positions ("deacon," "helper") and particular ministries (prayer and edification) in the church.

Next we find that God wants women to be taught the Scriptures.

I Timothy 2:11 commanded, "Let a woman learn"—a real bombshell for many in the society of that day.

But then Paul immediately added: "I do not allow a woman

to teach or control a man, rather she is to be in quietness, because Adam was shaped first, then Eve; and Adam was not beguiled but woman being thoroughly beguiled was in the
transgression. Yet she shall be saved through the childbearing
if she continues in faith. . . ."

This is a most difficult and sensitive text! It has as its background the historical context of the persecutions of Nero. In
light of the antichristian mood of the time, Paul insists and directs first of all that women must be allowed to learn. However,
since the teaching of women led in those days to persecution,
Paul urged that it be done in quietness, or with discretion and
submission.

The apostle further advised women not to teach or to control
a man (delete the article *"the"* [man] which is not in Greek).
The comma after "teach" in most versions is misleading and
should also be deleted. Paul advised that women should not
"teach or control a man" during these times. In this passage
Paul is expressing a personal preference (*epitrepo*)—a phrase reminding some interpreters of his advice in I Corinthians 7:7: "I
would that all men were even as I myself," i.e., unmarried.

Whether or not the two phrases are identical, we cannot say
for sure, but we are convinced of the fact that equally perilous
times in different historical contexts necessitated both statements. In a more relaxed day, Paul had thought Timothy most
fortunate that his mother and grandmother had instructed him
in the Scriptures (II Timothy 1:5). But now things have
changed, or so it would appear.

The reason Paul cautiously gave this advice is now stated in
verses 13 and 14. The man, like Adam, has had the advantage
of being "shaped, formed, molded" [*plasso*; not *ktizo*, "created"
(in doctrine and experience?)] first. Since women were at this
time only beginning to be taught, even as Eve had been shaped
by doctrine and teaching after Adam, so now men must assume
the entire responsibility for the church. Witness, also, how Eve
was the one who had suffered the full blow of Satan's crafti-
ness, while Adam, who presumably might have known better
given the same attack, simply sinned without any trickery on
anyone's part. Therefore, the situation called for men to take
the lead while the women learned.

Is this what Paul intended by such delicate use of words

written from the very citadel of the opposition (a Roman prison with the Praetorian guard surrounding him constantly)? Believers must proceed slowly in this text. Above all, we must continue to hold our finger on the text while we agree to disagree agreeably with each other. All of us, this writer included, are still coming to a full knowledge of the truth—none of us has arrived.

Finally, God has purposely given to woman a special sphere of authority.

I Corinthians 11:10 says, "That is why women ought to have *authority* or *power* [exousia] on her head because of the angels."

The almost universal mistranslation of this verse has been *veil*. . . . The Coptic word *authority* or *power* would be *ouershishi* while the word *veil* was *ouershoun*. . . .

God has specially given the woman an authority and a sphere of power totally her own to which, apparently, even the angels cannot attain. Every time Paul uses *exousia*, "authority, power" in I Corinthians, he uses it in an active, not passive sense (7:34; 8:9; 9:4, 5). Thus, she is a co-ruler with man over parts of the created order. Whether or not the sign of accepting this divine purpose is her hair style we shall leave to wiser men to finally decide.

But there is more. Men and women are not independent of one another (I Corinthians 11:12) for God has made woman "for [dia with the accusative] the man" while God has brought man "through [dia with the genitive] the woman." "And all things are of God." Such teaching is hardly cultural! It is high theology.

Women, then, do exercise separate spheres of authority given by God which outrank even powers given to angels. She is fully equal in dignity, worth and value to the man and functions not in his shadow, but in harmony, though at times separately, to the glory of God.

Far from being repressive, hostile or demeaning to women, the Scriptures have consistently elevated women and given to them places of honor and credit in the life of the community and church. Even in the divine provision of her hair, God saw to it that she was a co-worshiper equal to the man. In I Corinthians 11:15 we see that "her hair [was] given to her *in place of* [or instead of: Greek *anti*] a covering [a hat]." So all chapeau requirements, Paul went on to assert in verse 16, were not sanctioned by him or the churches at large.

No, "in the Lord" (I Corinthians 11:11) women are to be dealt with exactly in the same manner and on the same level with men. . . .

The church throughout the world would be robbed of significant teaching on prayer and Christian living if Evelyn Christiansen had been restricted from teaching men and women. (Some churches and conferences have asked their members not to attend her seminars. In fact, as an indication of how far a person can come in this area, before we were married, Rusty refused to attend her seminars because she was a woman. Some years later he attended one and thought it was outstanding.) Concerning men and women's use of gifts, Evelyn writes: "We have felt that both men and women are to be used fully by the Lord. Chris [her husband] and I have both studied diligently, prayed regularly, and been 'doers of the Word.' Our children have witnessed that God prepares both men and women for the task of reconciliation and we are responsible to meet that challenge."

Evelyn continues: "Occasionally someone asks me if I am teaching material that Chris researched and developed. I assure them that it is gleaned personally from the Lord. I do not depend on Chris for spiritual feeding nor he on me. We both answer directly to God how we use our lives."

Then, Evelyn offers a bit of insight into how her worldwide ministry came about, and how she and her husband (formerly a pastor and Bible teacher, currently an administrator at a Christian college) now practice team marriage and team ministry, "There was a time Chris was not aware that God had a plan for my life. In fact, he did not want me even to be a Sunday school teacher, feeling that would be unbiblical. But gradually he saw how God had given me a gift. And through personal Bible study, Chris came to see that God had a plan for my life also. Recently in an interview, Chris remarked that

220   CALLED TO SERVICE

as a Christian husband and father, he is the steward of the gifts of his wife and children. He now believes firmly that it is his job to see that his wife and his children become all that God meant them to be."[10]

TWENTY

Is
There
Hope?

Years ago, I met an exceptionally competent woman. At the age of thirty, she directed a ministry within a Christian organization. At a board meeting I attended, her presentations were superior. Within this organization, she supervised and motivated men and women successfully—with good results.

Then she attended a week-long seminar where she was taught that God had decreed men to be the leaders; women, the followers. Overnight, she changed. She thwarted her own effective manner of leading and began deferring to men. In the process, she gained forty pounds and lost much of her self-esteem.

It has taken this woman ten years to undo the effects of a viewpoint that denies the possibility of a side-by-side ministry of equals. She has paid a price, as has the Christian community, for this teaching. But why does it continue?

CALLED TO SERVICE

From years of working through practical biblical theology, I have come to one firm conclusion. Many people make choices in their lives based on built-in emotional needs and responses, rather than on careful study of the Bible. Why? Because emotional responses are so dominating. In fact, one of the most difficult challenges of our lives is overcoming our own personal emotional biases, with which we have grown comfortable.

Conditioned Response

An individual can be conditioned and programmed to accept *any* idea, but feeling comfortable with an issue should never be the determining factor in judging its rightness; feelings of ease may merely gauge how much something corresponds to a person's conditioning.

Many women and men are conditioned to think of men as the leaders and women as the followers. Teaching that solidifies this perspective "feels right" to them. Unfortunately, many interpret their conditioned acceptance as God's assurance that the teaching is biblical, when it isn't.

The familiar is always more comfortable than the unfamiliar. Going into new territory is always frightening, because there we cannot predict our own conditioned responses or those of others.

Let's look a little closer at the emotional obstacles that seem to block the church's progress toward team ministry.

Fear of New Relationships

Self-esteem, in both men and women, is a delicate mechanism. Feeling good about ourselves provides that comfortable threshold of living that we all desire. But how easily it is disturbed. The unknown causes discomfort and breeds fear. The truth is most men are unfamiliar with how to work with women as equals. In business, they may be accustomed to women as secretaries or assistants. At home, if a husband maintains a hierarchical marriage, his wife will not be seen as a capable equal either. A man's fear of not knowing how to respond properly (without betraying himself or his masculinity), may be a real obstacle that will have to be overcome.

Carolyn, a bright seminary graduate, was turned down for missionary service because she failed to meet the rigorous health requirements. Still eager to serve Christ, she took a job as church Christian education director.

"I'm not so sure all the problems the pastor and I experienced are due to the fact that I am a woman," began Carolyn. "After all, we both have sinful natures. Yet over a period of time I came to realize that I was never respected as a person with ideas or spiritual maturity. The pastor and I were about the same age and of a similar theological background, yet I was never free to initiate even the smallest effort on my own.

"The pastor, it turns out, had wanted a male assistant, but desperate for some immediate help, the board of elders overruled him. Whether he was troubled by my appointment or just insecure around women, I couldn't say for sure at the time. But he avoided me, sending most of his messages to me through his secretary or through short, curt notes, often overruling my plans.

"This ordeal went on for two years. I tried every way I knew to befriend the pastor. On one occasion, when I made an appointment with him and expressed that the problem between us was possibly my fault and one that I wanted to make right if I knew how, he clammed up and dismissed me.

"Finally the true problem came to light in an unusual way. I had been assigned to chair a benevolence committee. It was a job requiring few of my abilities. I could tell that the pastor had been under a lot of pressure, so at first I made no attempt to relate my feelings about the job. But after six months, I made an appointment with him and expressed my frustrations. When I finished my short discourse, he became very quiet.

" 'I just wanted to get you out of the way,' he admitted. Stunned, I continued to listen. Struggling with his emotions, he confided that he had not known what to do with me since

CALLED TO SERVICE

the day I came. He had never worked with a woman before. 'I have never had a woman for a friend in my life,' he continued, 'not even my wife.'

"That confession took place three years ago. Today he and I work as a team. I even got my title changed to assistant pastor. There is no more avoiding me and no hurting cuts meant to push me away. There have been a few bumps in the road as we have learned to respect each other, but it's been well worth the effort."

Fear of Loss of Control

Another common fear is that women will run the church. What does "running the church" mean? Because women are often more spiritually sensitive than men, churches tend to have more active female than male members. Women's eagerness to help is often seen in their willingness to volunteer for committees on which they express good ideas for expansion, evangelism, teaching, and so forth.

Those people who honestly believe women should be seen and not heard see any attempt to exercise a public or leadership gift to be "too much."

Others discourage women from church participation because they fear it discourages Christian men from taking active roles. In a sense, women have become convenient scapegoats; their activity is blamed for the inactivity of men, when in reality there is enough for all of us to do.

Still other people who fear women running the church do not trust God to lead through anyone but themselves. A pastor illustrates: "All through seminary I had developed a fear of letting God lead in other people's lives. I was sure that it was my job to protect people from misusing the Scriptures and God. Therefore, I took it upon myself to exercise strict control over my congregation. Especially women. I feared what they might do, given opportunity.

"Sure enough, I found women who resisted my leadership and even behind my back tried to get church policy changed.

How easy it was to label these women as rebellious—wanting to get out from under authority. I resisted them, remaining firm in the conviction that I was God's protector.

"Then God began to take me through personal trials. My marriage practically fell apart. I gradually saw that I had little faith in anything but my own ability to control a situation. I needed to learn to trust God in other people's lives. My job as pastor was to teach people how to honor God and His Word for themselves, not to try to limit them lest they fail or challenge my ideas and opinions. Ups and downs were to be expected in others as part of their growth. My job was to encourage them in their own growth and make opportunity for their gifts . . . and that included the gifts of women."

Stories abound concerning churches where a bossy, selfish woman tried to control the church membership. But how many churches have male bullies? We need not fear women in ministry, only carnal people of either sex, who set their hearts on their own plans, not on the plan of God. What the church needs is men and women who know how to be led by the Spirit of God and who know the Word of God for themselves. Then we needn't fear men or women in leadership.

Some men and women fear other women as leaders in the church. They may have a woman for a hairdresser, congressional representative, health-spa or child-care instructor, school principal, sales clerk, TV commentator, and the like, but the thought of a woman as pastor is intimidating—even though many may receive spiritual instruction from women, via books, tapes, videos, and home Bible teachers. One cannot help but think that such a fear of a woman as pastor is cultural, because they have not become accustomed to having women serve them in certain capacities.

"Why," asked a male friend, "wouldn't a woman appreciate seeing another woman excel in a Christian setting?"

"For the same reason that some men don't appreciate seeing other men excel," I suggested. "Jealousy, fear, insecurity."

A woman once chided me for believing that any avenue of service open to men was also open to women—that team ministry was possible.

After a lengthy discussion, she choked up and said, "I'm tired of feeling inferior to every woman I meet. The last thing I need is to feel I have to compete with some wonder woman in my church."

Matter of Semantics

On another occasion a curious man asked me, "Why do women put up with being treated as inferior in the church?"

I suggested that they put up with a lot because of the clever games that are played with words. Consider a few of the lines given:

"We're all equal in the sight of God, but women are restricted in leadership." (That's similar to saying, "Yes, the blacks are equal to the whites, except the blacks can't vote.")

"Women are not inferior. God has simply designed a different role for them." (The problem, of course, is that they are talking about a restricted role.)

One woman argued, "The men are the presidents; the women are the vice-presidents. This doesn't mean we have any less worth or privileges." I was puzzled by her reasoning and answered with a simple question, "Since when is the vice-president given the status, pay, responsibility, or privileges of the president?"

"But," another friend commented, "surely some women can see through such double-talk. Why don't they revolt?"

Sometimes their conditioning, the comfort they find in the familiar, is a fence so tall that they can't see over it; those women are satisfied to live with the double-talk. Other women just see no hope of any change and have given up even dreaming of anything better. But some women have "revolted." One friend of mine recently left her job at a Christian organization after being there eleven years. She returned to school for her master's degree and entered the secular workplace.

She told me why she made her major career change: "If you challenged someone calling you 'girl' or questioned that a man was promoted over you, even though you had the greater skills, you were considered 'unspiritual' and quickly put in your place with questions such as, 'Are you a feminist?' or 'Why make trouble over something so minor?' "

In the secular world she didn't find this subtle pressure, but respect for her person and gifts.

Still other women choose to fight for equality in ministry through less drastic means. One pastor told a woman parishioner, "As long as you stay in your place, we'll get along."

"What place is that?" she asked.

"Keeping silent," he said.

"Jesus never commended women for keeping silent," she answered. "He commended them for faith, spiritual assertiveness, persistence, courage. . . ."

"Well, regardless," he said, "in my church you'll keep silent."

This woman, however, was not to be silenced. She fought as believers are instructed to fight. She prayed, "Do something, God. Protect me and uplift me as You promised."

Although one never knows all the whys and wherefores of God's workings, that pastor had left the ministry within a year of the woman's prayer, and she now teaches evangelistic classes to hundreds in her church.

God does promise that if we are "faithful in small things," He will put us over much. He never asks that we seek the comfort of man-made rules, but that we seek His truth—the truth that sets all His people free.

Afterword

Florence Nightingale, who distinguished herself as a woman who unselfishly served God and man, nursing in hospitals and on the battlefields, wrote concerning Christian work, "Keep clear of all jargons about men's and women's work and go straight to God's work in simplicity of heart."[1]

In this paraphrased quote and other writings, Miss Nightingale was reminding us that defined roles could be a danger. She knew that the real issue was seeing the need and meeting it as God has equipped us. Ironically, a Christian magazine recently used this quote, but misrepresented it to mean, "Let's get back to defined roles for men and women." One shudders to think how easily her words were misconstrued.

Similarly, it would be easy to misinterpret a book such as this, which deals with complex and highly emotional issues.

To guard against this, I'd like to briefly summarize what I've said.

Christian marriage is the union of two Christians, who are indwelt by Jesus Christ, who have the empowering of the Holy Spirit, the authority of the Word of God, the gifts of the Spirit; their task is the Great Commission. How should such a Christian marriage, in its truest form, operate? Those two Christians should value the lordship of Christ in each other; respect and yield to the leadership of the Holy Spirit in each other; yield to the authority of the Word of God as discerned by each other; honor the gifts of each other, including the gift of administration, which may be possessed by either partner; seek to fulfill the Great Commission, using all God has made them to be.

How then does specific teaching on marriage come into play? What of Ephesians 5; 1 Corinthians 7; 1 Peter 3; and the like? How do they affect this relationship? Does it alter or change it? No, not if it is seen in context to the whole of Scripture and to specific passages.

Ephesians 5 presents the issue of "head." The issue is not whether or not the Bible states that man is the "head," but rather, what does *head* mean? In answering this, two issues are very important: word definition (*see* the Appendix) and how the context develops that word concept. In Ephesians 5, the context shows that the word *head* does not mean "authority" or "leader," but "enabler," or "completer." The context supports the usage by the usage given to the word in Ephesians 4:15; by the clarification phrase "He Himself being the Savior of the body"; and by illustration. The husband is told to "minister to," "die for," and "build up" his wife. In short, in this passage the husband enables or completes the wife; he does not rule over her.

Yes, the husband may be given more responsibility, but not authority, over his wife, except in 1 Corinthians 7:4, where both husband and wife are given authority over each other's body. This is the only place the word *authority* is used in reference to marriage.

How does this apply to decision making? Doctrinal teaching

on this subject is presented only in 1 Corinthians 7:5, where the husband and wife are told to come to "agreement." Why is this so? Because both husband and wife are to seek the Lord for the best answer. This causes growth and maturity in both partners and gives them greater preparation to stand for Christ in the world.

First Peter 3 illustrates the plight of non-Christian spouses and is not meant to be a standard for Christian marriage. Here both husband and wife are encouraged to have a submissive attitude: "be submissive to your own husbands" (3:1); and "grant her honor as a fellow-heir" (3:7). This attitude will, in Peter's mind, most facilitate the non-Christian partner coming to Christ.

And what of this word *submissive*? Does it mean "obey"? Does it suggest absolute adherence to the other partner? No, for no person is to ever take the place of God in our lives. Rather, it is an attitude of preference, which should be taken into consideration in the light of other teaching on obedience to Christ and the leadership of the Holy Spirit.

Is submission asked of just one partner or of both? Definitely both, as the Greek text explains in Ephesians 5. Both partners must remember what they are called to be as Christians and what their partner is called to be as a Christian.

What then is Christian ministry? Does it differ for men and women?

Again, we must go back to God's most basic purpose and design. What is God's purpose in the world? That every man, woman, and child may come to know Him through the death and resurrection of Jesus Christ, who Himself paid for our sins and opens the gift of eternal life to all that would receive it.

How does God make this message known? Clearly through any man, woman, or child who allows himself or herself to become an instrument of reconciliation. Are there any restrictions on one sex or another? Does God limit a man's or woman's participation in ministry?

The fact is that there are no clear statements to this effect. In contrast, there are pointedly inclusive statements for men and women: "You can all prophesy . . . so that all may learn . . ." (1 Corinthians 14:31); "Go into all the world and preach the gospel to all creation" (Mark 16:15); "These things teach . . ." (*see* 2 Timothy 2:2). The few texts that have been used to try to silence women from certain responsibilities do not stand up to the test of true exegesis. Rather, they become innuendo to the mind-set that has already precluded women from ministry.

The troublesome passages are: 1 Corinthians 11—a thesis on the interdependence of men and women; 1 Corinthians 14—a commentary on confusion; and 1 Timothy 2—an age-old principle, "learn before you teach." Concerning the appointment of church leadership, instructions to deacons and elders (1 Timothy 3 and Titus 1) should not exclude women on the basis of a phrase "husband of one wife." Such an effort to limit one-half of the mobilized force from leadership demands much more than a phrase that can be interpreted in a number of ways. One would expect a clear statement to the effect that women cannot lead, especially when the text itself lays out "If any *person* aspire to leadership"(1 Timothy 3:1 *italics added*) and when the Old and New Testament both illustrate that God called women to leadership.

But even more basically, one must remember that the Bible wasn't written to men, with a comment for women inserted every now and then. The Bible was written for men and women. All its commands and principles are for both, and any exceptions should be *clearly* spelled out.

More than anything else, I am trying to say that as Christians we have a monumental task ahead of us: sharing the Good News of Jesus Christ with every man, woman, and child on the face of the earth. If we're going to do this, we need every Christian working at full capacity. We need to be free of unbiblical restrictions, and we need to know how to interpret correctly and use cautions, directions, and the whole Word of God to maximize our efforts.

However, let's not lose sight of our highest command—to love one another. What does love do? Love reconciles. A general rule to remember is: Satan separates; God reconciles.

In the Garden, by one ploy, Satan was able to separate men and women from God, men and women from each other, and men and women from themselves.

The cross changed that. Some people may still believe that world reconciliation can take place while restricting women. Some people may still feel that a woman is led by God by being led by her husband. But consider this: If the perspective presented in this book is heeded, we have only served to lift all the body to maturity under God's leadings. Further, the world will have a better chance of being reached because a full, unrestricted force of Christians can operate at peak level.

If we continue in the old restrictive ways, then many women will not mature because they will not be encouraged to grow in all areas. Many men will not mature because they are not allowed to be challenged. The world that needs Christ will suffer from Christian immaturity as well as from restricted gifts.

If you were God and wanted to see the world reached with love and forgiveness, wouldn't you want to employ every available Christian to his or her fullest in the accomplishment of that goal?

If you were Satan and wanted to thwart the church from reaching the world for Christ, wouldn't you want to hinder the church from full participation? Isn't there one area to which you might give a great deal of attention—the doctrine of women in marriage and ministry in the church?

Why? Because if it can be made to appear biblical that a woman is to be under the leadership of men, rather than women and men both being directly and fully under the leadership of the Holy Spirit, the fulfillment of the Great Commission would be thwarted in the following ways:

1. Leadership gifts of women would not be utilized fully, seriously cutting back Christian productivity.
2. The church would not thoroughly benefit from the developed insights and spiritual perceptions of women, since they would often not be in a position to be heard.
3. Many women would become discouraged that they could

not function fully in the church and would use their gifts elsewhere; the church would thus lose valuable person-power to interests other than the Great Commission. As Florence Nightingale also commented, "I would have given the church my heart, my hand, my everything. She would not have them. She told me to go back and do crochet in my mother's drawing room."[2]

4. Non-Christian women, who value their persons and abilities, would see the restraints on women in Christianity and not desire a relationship with Christ. Women leaders who could have a great influence on reaching the world would not join our forces. Many men who value women operating as full persons would observe the Christian teaching on women in ministry (and marriage) and not want to become Christians either.

5. Christian women who are discouraged from functioning as mature decision makers in the home would be less prepared to make decisions of value in the church. Hence, many would continue to be seen as incapable of assuming leadership in the church.

6. Women who are not encouraged to be, first and foremost, bondslaves of Jesus Christ, but who are encouraged to look to men for direction, would not develop as full Christians. The church and the world would miss their mature input.

Genesis 3:15 notes that enmity exists between Satan and the woman. As he attempts to suppress her, let's make sure we're not taking his side.

My friends Steve and Judy have refused to let Satan defeat them. They exemplify the attitude presented in this book. They know that the key to a successful team marriage and team ministry is not just finding the "right person," but being the right person. Maybe that's why they have such a powerful impact for Jesus Christ . . . both of them!

In their single days, they made up their minds that nothing would come between them and the Lord. After dating for more than five years, they tied the knot. In so doing, they created a synergism.

"Our philosophy," shares Judy, "is that we're both accountable to God, and we're both accountable to each other."

For example, money is set aside for housekeeping help and occasional child care so that Judy can have time to minister. For the last seven years she has led a Christian wives' group in the area of spiritual growth. In addition, Judy writes for publication and spends a great deal of time in prayer for others.

Steve and Judy both teach married couples at their church. "We try to be strong on planning," says Steve. "We specifically ask God for direction is using our time, talent, and resources for His kingdom." Out of their own planning came a talk on "Maximizing Your Potential" which they have given many times in evangelistic outreach. "Each time we have given the talk together," continues Steve, "we have seen a high percentage of those present indicate that they wanted to know Christ."

"We make an effort to complement and contribute to each other's lives and ministry," shares Judy, "but that takes commitment. Often I use our home to entertain people with whom Steve works. Our children's needs can make this difficult. Sometimes Steve needs me to be a springboard for his latest idea at the most inconvenient times. Since most of those ideas affect people who need Christ, I'm eager to do it, though.

"I think you make up your mind about something," continues Judy, "and then pay a price as needed. You can't wait for things to happen and then evaluate at every point whether or not you want to continue. We've laid our lives at God's disposal, and we really think that makes a difference when it comes to rearranging our schedule, losing sleep, or forfeiting vacations to reach our goals. But it's worth it. Nothing can replace the deep satisfaction of knowing that you are in the will of God, even when it may be difficult."

One of the greatest contributions Steve makes in Judy's life is to help her organize her schedule. Judy's big challenge, "How can I manage the kids so I can have time for other ministries?" is cut down to size by Steve's ability to see a goal and determine steps to get there.

"He is also helpful in staying with the kids some evenings so that I can help a friend, speak at a conference, or share my testimony with others. Since we are in firm agreement about *no* television in our home, Steve and I are both kept on our toes entertaining and teaching our kids."

(Steve works with a Christian resource group that can provide valuable training in how an individual couple can evangelize and disciple.[3])

Evaluate Your Marriage and Ministry

How can you and your spouse help reach this world for Christ and participate in building up the rest of the body? Begin by asking yourself some questions.

> Does your marriage allow for the full growth of both partners?
>
> Does your family set an atmosphere where children can develop their Christian lives and ministry?
>
> Have you sat down together and planned how each member of the family can use his talents fully?

In carrying out the above, you may want to apply the following:

> List gifts or possible gifts of each family member.
> List obvious areas of need in your community.
> Correlate needs with gifts.
> Consider entering Christian work on a full-time basis.
> Consider taking your faith to another culture.

Most important, ask God to search your heart, to help you know the truth, and to seek to find where you can make the greatest impact for our Lord Jesus Christ.

Let's look at another couple who also practice the teaching set forth in this book.

Hugo and Kathleen met while students at the University of California at Berkeley. They soon married and sought to honor the Lord in all they did.

Their family gradually grew to seven, and together Hugo and Kathleen began a neighborhood church.

"We basically believed that we should respect each other's opinion and gifts and leading by God," shares Hugo. "But occasionally we fell into roles that temporarily caused us to lose sight of each other's individuality and unique contribution to the marriage."

After eighteen years in business Hugo had the opportunity of ministering at a small Christian college. It meant losing a pension and financial security, uprooting the family, and starting a new life.

"We made this decision," shares Hugo, "the way we make most important decisions. Kathleen and I talked about the pros and cons. We sought counsel from Christian friends. We prayed and tuned our hearts to hear God's leading. Eventually we both felt it was God's will for us to make the move.

"Should one partner force a decision on another, there is bound to be resentment," continues Hugo. "Under the teaching that the men are God's instruments to make final decisions, undue pressure is forced upon the woman to carry the spiritual load of having to deal with resentment and to make most of the adjustment."

In terms of team marriage, Hugo and Kathleen shared the load of teaching, and later advising, their now grown children. "We have no rules," shares Kathleen, "as to who must always assume what role in regard to our children. Common sense largely dictates those decisions." Today Hugo is a pastor and Kathleen is a counselor.

In team ministry, Kathleen is Hugo's "best critic" on sermons. Kathleen discusses with Hugo how to counsel certain individuals or how to improve a speech she is writing. Together they open their home to a multitude of young people.

Clair and Richard have also made their life together a team ministry. Having married late in life, they opted for spiritual children rather than physical children. This decision left them free to pour all their energies into ministering to others: Richard is a Bible teacher's Bible teacher, spending much of his time gleaning deep truths from the Bible. His teaching inspires Christians to greater consecration.

Because Richard has health problems, Clair supports the family as a staff member of Christian Literature Outreach.

Their gift of hospitality ministers to the needs of many who come to their door.

"It's important," shares Richard, "that churches, Christian organizations, and seminaries see men and women as instruments of God. To deny the gifts of any individual is to deny the work God has for that person to do."

How do you determine what church, seminary, or Christian organization you want to attend, join, or support? You should feel free to ask any of the following questions to determine whether or not you're comfortable with their answers. (Of course there are many other questions that should be asked that do not relate to women, and many of these may, in fact, be more important.)

1. How many people serve on your board of directors? How many of those serving on the board are women?
2. In your organization, can women supervise men?
3. Is mutuality emphasized between men and women, or is a hierarchical structure practiced?
4. If you provide marriage counseling to your staff, is hierarchical marriage presented, or the concept of team marriage?
5. Are there any positions that are limited to either men or women on your staff? If so, which positions and why?
6. Do women teach all believers on your staff? What subjects?

Recently I talked with a woman at Wycliffe Bible Translators. She informed me that two members of their international board of directors were women. Women often teach at the Summer Institute of Linguistics. Their main area of service—translation—is open to both men and women. "The important consideration is how well we get the job done and who is available to do it," shared Wycliffe leaders. Women are not limited to directing other women, but in some instances supervise men. "We do not teach that either sex is the leader in marriage," I was told. "However, some within the organization may adhere to this idea. We try to emphasize that both men and women are to be led by God and work as a team."

Many Christian organizations are currently reevaluating their position on women in ministry. In light of the great need to reach the world, they are seeking to place women in leadership roles. As Bill Bright, president of Campus Crusade for Christ, commented recently, "We should see that many qualified women are placed in strategic leadership."

There are other alternatives. Why not look to examples set in the 1800s and begin a Women's Missionary Organization, placing thousands of dedicated Spirit-led women in strategic places around the world? What would be the requirements for service? A sound Christian character and devotion to the cause of Christ. Such an effort should not be seen as a move to "prove a point" about women's ability, but as a means of accomplishing the job that we are all called to do.

Bart and Jennifer are yet another couple who illustrate team marriage and team ministry. Bart was a carpenter, Jenny, a doctor, when they bowed their wills to the Lord Jesus Christ. "We had both been Christians since college," shares Bart, "but later, several years into marriage, we admitted that we were not our own. Our lives belonged to God to do whatever He desired. In submitting to His will, Jenny and I experienced a new peace and excitement. Even though we had a hectic work schedule plus three small children, Jenny and I would alternate child care and paid for a housekeeper and a sitter two nights of the week so we could study the Bible together."

Upon completing their correspondence course, Bart and Jenny applied to a Christian organization. After a year of training and eight months of raising support, they left for the Middle East. "We're happier than we've ever been," shares Jenny. "We don't wish we were doing more for Christ. We're doing it. Laying down our lives and giving our all is the most satisfying life you can imagine. We are needed here, and we love it."

How did Jenny and Bart know where they were needed?

"First," shares Bart, "we realized that there were plenty of carpenters and doctors in America. People were standing in line to take our jobs. But laborers for God's kingdom are in short supply. We were greatly needed to reach the world with the Gospel. We could find no overlap. We wanted our lives to fill a need no one else could fill."

"Second," continues Jenny, "we asked God to give us a vision for where the need was great and a visualization of how we could meet that need."

Third, Bart and Jenny wrote to Intercristo, a nondenominational ministry that gives career counseling for Christians and matches individuals with specific ministry needs worldwide.[4] They match skills in areas such as:

> Administration and office work
> Agriculture
> Camping and recreation
> Communications and arts
> Construction
> Data processing
> Education
> Food services and hospitality
> Health care and medicine
> Maintenance and repair
> Marketing and public relations
> Ministry
> Mission
> Music
> Science and technology
> Social science and services
> Teaching organizations
>> Social work
>> Counselors
>> Child care
>> Rehabilitation
> Translation and linguistics
> Transportation

The last time I heard from Bart and Jenny, they didn't even want to come home for furlough!

That's the attitude many Christians today have. Whatever comes, we're soldiers in the spiritual battle for the minds and souls of men and women. We work side by side in a team marriage and a team ministry for that end! Because we function as a cord of three strands—God, woman, and man—we have His uniting power, direction, and love. Praise God!

Appendix: The "Head" of the Epistles by Berkeley and Alvera Mickelsen

What did Apostle Paul mean when he wrote, "For the husband is the head of the wife as Christ is the head of the church, his body" (Eph. 5:23)? And, *"The head of every man is Christ and the head of the woman is man, and the head of Christ is God"* (I Cor. 11:3)?

Discussion about the biblical role for men in church society and home is based on these verses. The meaning of these verses rests largely on the meaning of the Greek word *"kephale,"* translated *"head"* in the New Testament.

One possible way the word "head" is used today means *leader, chief,* or *director.* We say, "He is the head of his company," or, "He is the department head." In husband-wife and male-female relations this idea popularly carries over to suggestions of authority. The husband is said to be the boss of the family. Before we accept that idea, we must ask what the

Greek word "kephale" (head) meant to Paul and to his readers.

To find the answer, we must first ask whether "head" in ancient Greek normally meant "superior to" or "one having authority." In the *first half* of this article we will introduce *three kinds of evidence:*

1. *Lexicographers* Liddell, Scott, Jones, and McKenzie (*A Greek-English Lexicon,* ninth edition, Clarendon Press, 1940, a really comprehensive Greek lexicon) *give no evidence of such a meaning.*
2. *The Septuagint translators took pains to use different words than "head" (kephale) when the Hebrew word for head implied "superior to" or "authority over."*
3. In his commonly used lexicon (*A Greek-English Lexicon of the New Testament and Early Christian Literature,* William Arndt and F. Wilbur Gingrich, eds., U. of Chicago Press, 1957/1979), Walter Bauer gives little or no salient support for such meaning outside of his personal interpretation of five Pauline passages in the New Testament.

In the second half of the article, we will answer the fundamental question: If "head" does not normally mean "superior to" or "authority over," what does it mean in those seven New Testament passages where Paul uses it figuratively?

First, what about the differences in the lexicons? One of the most complete Greek lexicons (covering Homeric, classic, and koine Greek) is the work by *Liddell, Scott, Jones, and McKenzie.* It is based on examination of thousands of Greek writings from the period of Homer (about 1000 B.C.) to about A.D. 600, which, of course, includes New Testament times. Significantly, for our purposes here, it does not include "final authority," "superior rank," or anything similar as meanings of kephale. Apparently ordinary readers of Greek literature would not think of such meaning when they read "head."

However, another commonly used lexicon is the koine Greek lexicon by Arndt and Gingrich (usually called Bauer's). *It does list "superior rank" as a possible meaning for kephale.* It lists five passages in the New Testament where the compiler thinks kephale has this meaning. As support for this meaning in New Testament times, the lexicon lists two passages from the Greek translation of the Old Testament, the Septuagint, where kephale implies leadership or authority.

Those who support Bauer's view that kephale meant "superior rank" point to these passages in the Greek translation of the Old Testament as evidence that this meaning of kephale was familiar to Greek-speaking people in New Testament times.

However, the facts do not support the argument. *About 180 times in the Old Testament, the Hebrew word ro'sh (head) is used with the idea of chief, leader, superior rank* (similar to the way English-speaking people use "head"). However, those who translated the Hebrew Old Testament into Greek (between 250 and 150 B.C.) rarely used kephale (head) when the Hebrew word for head carried this idea of leader, chief, or authority. *They usually used the Greek word archon, meaning leader, ruler, or commander.* They also used other words. In only 17 places (out of 180) did they use kephale, although that would have been the simplest way to translate it. Five of those 17 have variant readings, and another 4 involve a head-tail metaphor that would make no sense without the use of head in contrast to tail. *That leaves only 8 instances (out of 180 times) when the Septuagint translators clearly chose to use kephale for ro'sh when it had a "superior rank" meaning. Most are in relatively obscure places.*

Since kephale is so rarely used when ro'sh carried the idea of authority, most of the Greek translators apparently realized that kephale did not carry the same "leader" or "superior rank" meaning for "head" as did the Hebrew word ro'sh.

There are seven passages in the New Testament where Paul uses kephale in some figurative sense. The concept of a hierarchy, with men in a role of authority over women (at least over their wives) rests largely on two of these: *I Corinthians 11:3 and Ephesians 5:23. When Paul used kephale in these two passages, was he thinking of one of the usual Greek meanings of head, or a common figurative Hebrew meaning?*

Paul knew both Hebrew and Greek. Although he was a

Pharisee who knew Hebrew well, he grew up in Tarsus, a Greek-speaking city. Greek was his native tongue. *In all the passages where he used kephale, he was writing to Greek-speaking people in cities where most Christians were converts from Greek religions.* Their contact with the Old Testament would be limited to hearing parts of the Septuagint read in their services. They might go to church for years without ever hearing those eight relatively obscure places in the Greek Old Testament where kephale seemed to have a different meaning from the usual meanings in their own language.

Since Paul was a Greek-speaking Jew, he would likely write to Greek-speaking Christians using Greek words with Greek meanings they would easily understand.

If "head" in Greek did not normally mean "supreme over," or "authority over," what did it mean in those seven New Testament passages where Paul used it figuratively? *Careful examination of context shows that common Greek meanings not only make good sense, but present a more exalted Christ.*

1. Colossians 1:18 (context 1:14–20): kephale means *"exalted originator and completer."* "He [Christ] is the head of the body, the church; he is the beginning, the firstborn from the dead, that in everything he might be preeminent." Paul seems to be using *kephale with common Greek meanings—"source or beginning or completion" (Liddell, Scott, et al.)—* in a sense that Christ is the exalted originator and completer of the church. Bauer does not list this passage among those where kephale means "superior rank."

2. Colossians 2:19 (context 2:16–19): *kephale means "source of life."* Christ is the source of life who nourishes the church. Christians are told to hold fast to Christ, who is described as the "head," from whom the whole body, nourished and knit together through its joints and ligaments, grows with a growth that is from God." Bauer agrees that in this passage kephale does not mean "superior rank."

3. Ephesians 4:15 (context 4:11–16) is very similar to Colossians 2:19. It reads, "We are to grow up in every way into him who is the head, into Christ, from whom the whole body,

joined and knit together by every joint with which it is supplied, when each part is working properly, makes bodily growth and upbuilds itself in love." This passage stresses the unity of head and body, and presents Christ as the nourisher and source of growth. Bauer classifies kephale here as meaning "superior rank," although he does not see that meaning in the very similar Colossians 2:19.

4. *I Corinthians 11:3* (context 11:2–16): *kephale seems to carry the Greek concept of head as "source, base, or derivation." "Now I want you to realize that the head of every man is Christ, and the head of the woman is man, and the head of Christ is God"* (NIV). In this passage Paul is discussing how men and women should pray and prophesy in public church meetings. His instructions apparently relate to the customs, dress, and lifestyle in Corinth and the tendency of the Corinthian believers to be disorderly. Paul discusses women's and men's head covering and hair styles. (Veils are not mentioned in the Greek text.) Paul says, "man was not made for woman, but woman for man" (v.8): he also says, "woman was made from man" (v. 12). This suggests that Paul used "head" in verse 3 with the meaning of *"source or origin." Man was the "source or beginning" of woman in the sense that woman was made from the side of Adam.* Christ was the one through whom all creation came (I Cor. 8:6b). *God is the base of Christ (John 8:42: "I proceeded and came forth from God").*

When we recognize one Greek meaning of kephale as source or origin, as Paul explains in verses 8 and 12, then verse 3 does not seem to teach a chain of command. Paul's word order also shows he was not thinking of chain of command: Christ, head of man; man, head of woman; God, head of Christ. Those who make it a chain of command must rearrange Paul's words. In fact, *Paul seems to go out of his way to show that he was not imputing authority to males when he says, "For as woman was made from man, so man is now born of woman. And all things are from God"* (I Cor. 11:12).

5. *Ephesians 5:23* (context 5:18–23): *"head" is used in a head-body metaphor to show the unity of husband and wife and of Christ and the church.* "For the husband is the head of the wife as Christ is

the head of the church, his body." *Paul often used the head-body metaphor to stress the unity of Christ and the church.* In fact, this unity forms the context for this passage. *The head and body in nature are dependent on each other.*

This verse follows Paul's explanation of what it means to be filled with the Holy Spirit. His last instruction is, "Be subject to one another out of reverence for Christ" (v. 21). This is addressed to all Christians and obviously includes husbands and wives. Naturally, as part of this mutual submission of all Christians to each other, wives are to submit to their husbands.

The Greek word "submit" or "be subject to" does not appear in verse 22. It says only, "wives to your husbands." The verb supplied must therefore refer to the same kind of submission demanded of all Christians in verse 21.

To stress the oneness of husband and wife, Paul then returns to his favorite head-body metaphor: "For the husband is the head [kephale] of the wife as Christ is the head [kephale] of the church, His body."

Paul develops his head-body metaphor at length in I Corinthians 12:22–27. *If he thought of "head" as the part of the body that had authority over the rest of it, would not that meaning appear in this long passage?* We know that the brain controls the body. But Paul did not use that concept in his metaphor. He refers to the ears, eyes, and nose; the head as a whole is mentioned only in verse 21: "The eye cannot say to the hand, 'I have no need of you,' nor again the head to the feet, 'I have no need of you.' " Paul taught here the unity and mutual dependence of all parts on each other: "If one member suffers, all suffer together; if one member is honored, all rejoice together" (v. 26). There is no suggestion that the head has authority over other parts of the body.

Christ does have authority over the church (Matt. 16:18). But most of the passages that deal with Christ as the head of the church do not point to his authority over the church, but rather the oneness of Christ and the church. In Ephesians 5:18–33, this oneness is applied to husband and wife.

If we are to see a meaning in "head" in Ephesians 5:23

beyond the head-body metaphor of mutual dependence and unity, we must do so on the basis of the immediate context. Christ's headship of the church is described like this: "Christ loved the church and gave himself up for her" (v. 25). Christ gave himself up to enable the church to become all that it is meant to be—holy and without blemish.

As Christ is the enabler (the one who brings to completion) of the church, so the husband is to enable (bring to completion) all that his wife is meant to be. The husband is to nourish and cherish his wife as he does his own body, even as Christ nourishes and cherishes the church (v. 29).

The concept of sacrificial self-giving so that a spouse can achieve full potential has been the role that society has traditionally given to the wife. Here Paul gives it to the husband. Of course, giving oneself sacrificially for the other is an excellent example of the submission wives and husbands are to have toward each other (v. 21).

6. Ephesians 1:20–23 (context 1:13–23): kephale means "top or crown." Paul presents an exalted picture of Christ and his authority over everything in creation: ". . . when he raised him from the dead and made him sit at his right hand in the heavenly places, far above all rule and authority and power and dominion, and above every name that is named, not only in this age, but also in that which is to come: and he has put all things under his feet and has made him the head over all things for the church, which is his body, the fulness of him who fills all in all." The authority of Christ, established in verses 20–21, is extended to every extremity from crown (head) to feet—including the church which is his body.

7. *Colossians 2:10 (context 2:8–15): kephale again seems to have the Greek idea of life-source, as well as the idea of top or crown.* This verse emphasizes the church as the "fulness" of Christ. "For in him the whole fulness of deity dwells bodily, and you have come to fulness of life in him, who is the head of all rule and authority" (vv. 9–10).

Paul uses two metaphors here—the head-body metaphor, with the church coming to "fulness of life" in Christ (the life-source, nourisher, enabler) and also the concept of top or crown when he speaks of Christ as the head of all rule and authority. In these two passages, "top" or "crown" emphasizes Christ's position by virtue of the cross and resurrection. He is the victor, and is crowned with glory and honor (Heb. 2:9; Ps. 8:5).

These are the only passages in the New Testament where kephale is used figuratively. They include the five given by Bauer as examples of kephale meaning "superior rank," despite the fact that such a meaning for kephale does not appear in the secular Greek of New Testament times. *If Paul had been thinking about authority, or leader, there were easily understood Greek words he could have used, and which he did use in other places. He used exousia (authority) in Romans 13:1–2; and archon in Romans 13:3.*

The passages where Paul used kephale in a figurative way make better sense and present a more exalted, completed view of Christ when kephale is read with recognized Greek meanings that would have been familiar to his original readers. Among these meanings are *exalted originator and completor; source, base, derivation; enabler (one who brings to completion); source of life; top or crown.*

Can we legitimately read an English or Hebrew meaning into the word "head" in the New Testament when both context and secular Greek literature of New Testament times seem to indicate that "superior rank" or "authority over" were not meanings that Greeks associated with the word, and probably were not the meanings the apostle Paul had in mind? *Has our misunderstanding of some of these passages been used to support the concept of male dominance that has ruled most pagan and secular societies since the beginning of recorded history?* Has this misunderstanding also robbed us of the richer, more exalted picture of Christ that Paul was trying to give us?[1]

Concerning the use of *kephale* in secular sources the Mickelsens (drawing from references provided by Catherine Kroeger) write:

Richard Braxton Onians, professor of Latin at the University of London, wrote a volume entitled *The Origins of European Thought.*[2] He gives many illustrations to show that approximately from the time of Homer to the classical Greek period (Plato, etc.) the head was regarded as the *life* or the *seat of life,* and because of that was to be highly honored. "It was natural and logical to think that the 'life' issuing from a man must come from the 'life' in him, from his *head* therefore, and, helping that location, to see in the seed, which carries the new life and which must have seemed the very stuff of life, a portion of the cerebro-spinal substance in which was the life of the parent."[3] This explains why, when the god Zeus wished to have a child and dispense with a mother, he "gave birth" to it (Athene) "from his head."[4] The author of the Homeric Hymn to Pythian Apollo says that he "engendered it" "in his head." Later, it was generally believed by the Greeks that the seed (sperm) was stored in the head.[5]

This, of course, explains the Orphic line that appears in numerous places in Greek literature. In some instances *kephale* appears, and in other writings, *arche* (beginning) appears in the same places in the line describing Zeus. *Arche* (beginning) could hardly be considered a synonym for "ruler," but it surely could for *kephale* (source). One writer attempts to draw a great difference between the meaning of "source" and "beginning," but such a distinction is in most instances largely semantic. The headwaters of a river can be considered either the "source" or the "beginning."

In the Orphic references to Zeus, the contexts sometimes also use the terminology of *on aitios*, which means "cause"—an idea closely related to "source." Some of the references to Zeus where he is called *kephale* (head) include the following (Fragment 21ª[46]):

> Concerning the world: And as the Totality spoke being heavenly and that which sprang from the earth, giving the Totality's name (Zeus) to all nature and providence in reference to which things he (Zeus) is *cause* of all things. Wherefore also in the Orphic sayings it does not say wrongfully:
> Zeus became first; Zeus is last, ruling the thunder;
> Zeus, Source *(kephale)*; Zeus, Middle, and *from* Zeus all things are brought to completion. Zeus base both of earth and heaven arranged in constellation.

Another Orphic fragment, 168 (123, 43), reads:

Zeus became first; Zeus, the last, ruling the thunder;
Zeus, Source (*kephale*); Zeus, Middle, and *from* Zeus all
things have been produced. . . .
Zeus, King; He is the first *author, origin* of all things. . . .

In a third version of this Orphic saying, 21 (33), the term
arche (beginning) appears in place of *kephale* (head):

He says that God is plainly the creator in reference to the
Old Orphic saying which is this:
Zeus, beginning (*arche*); Zeus, Middle; and *from* Zeus all
things have been made. Zeus [made the] base (*puthmen*),
both of the earth and of the heaven arranged in constella-
tions.
And this one (Zeus) is beginning (*arche*) as creative cause (*poie-
tikon aition*); And he (Zeus) is end (*teleute*) as final causality
(*telikon*); And he is middle as equally present to all things;
and indeed since all things share him (Zeus) in a variety of
ways.

Note that in the saying above, Zeus is considered the "creative cause" and the "final causality."

Another Orphic line about Zeus[6] comes to the question
from another side. One writer addresses Zeus thus: "*All-gen-
erating* father, oh king, because of your head (*kephale*), the following things appeared: Rhea Gaia [a goddess], and sea
[personified son of goddess], and all things as many as heaven
works within." Can anyone seriously question the meaning of
"source" or "cause" for head (*kephale*) in this quotation?

Onians explains further that Alcmaeon of Croton wrote ex-
plicitly that the seed came from the brain. A later sect, called
the Templars, actually worshipped heads because the head
was considered the source of wealth.[7] This concept became
imbedded in European thought and is no doubt the reason we
still speak of a "head" of corn. (The source of seed.) In Greek
thought the head was also considered to be the source of
strength, and this lingered on in Roman thought.

The Greek writer Artemidorus yields numerous examples
of head (*kephale*) meaning "source." In Lib. I, Cap. 2, Paragraph
6, we read, "He [the father] was the cause (*aitos*) of the life and
of the light for the dreamer [the son] just as the head (*kephale*)

is the cause (*aitios*) of the life and the light of all the body." In another section (Cap. 35, Paragraph 36) Artemidorus writes, "Indeed, the head is to be likened to parents because the head is the cause [or source] of life."

In many instances, the preconceived idea of the translator will determine the meaning assigned, but these are clear instances of the meaning of source, cause, or beginning, as the meaning of head. All of these meanings—beginning, origin, head, author, creative cause, final cause—point to the wide range of meanings of which *kephale* (head) was a part.

The possible meanings of *kephale* (head) are important because this word in I Cor. 11:3 and in Eph. 5:23 has been consistently used as proof that since man is the "head" of the woman, he is in a God-ordained position of *authority* and leadership over her. If *kephale* (head) has other more probable meanings, these passages take on a quite different emphasis. In the Genesis narrative, man is the source, or base of the woman as mentioned in I Cor. 11:8, 12. In Ephesians 5:23, the husband has Christ as a model. As Christ enables the church and brings it to completion (effective cause or agent) by giving his life for the church, so the husband is to be an enabler (or effective cause or agent) for his wife. By his self-giving love, he helps her reach her full potential of all that God meant her to be.

Paul and other early Christians clearly knew that the characteristic of Christian ministry and leadership was *service* rather than authority. They had heard clearly the words of Jesus, "You know how the Gentiles . . . lord it over you . . . it shall not be so among you, but whoever would be first among you must be the servant. . . . "

In practice, *servanthood* has never been denied to women in the church! Women through the centuries have prayed, healed, helped the poor, taught young and old to follow Christ, carried the gospel around the world—all the marks of servant leadership. Perhaps when we all stand before the judgment seat of Christ, we will learn that in the eyes of our Lord, women through the centuries have been the real leaders of the church.

Notes

Introduction

1. Berkeley and Alvera Mickelsen, "Does Male Dominance Tarnish Our Translations?" *Christianity Today* (October 5, 1979): 25.
2. Ibid., editor's note.

Chapter 3 Created for What?

1. *See* Ludwig Kohler, *Hebrew Man* (Nashville, Tenn: Abingdon Press, 1956); *see also* the Book of Ruth, chapter 4 and note the elders (appointed judges) assembled at the gate.

Chapter 4 As God Created . . .

1. Francis Brown, S. R. Driver, and Charles A. Briggs, *A Hebrew and English Lexicon of the Old Testament* (Oxford: Clarendon Press, 1907), 617.

2. Dr. R. David Freedman, "Woman, a Power Equal to Man," *Biblical Archaeology Review*, 9:1 (January/February, 1983): 56–58.
3. Edith Schaeffer, *The Tapestry* (Waco, Tex.: Word Books, 1985), 184–185.
4. Ibid., 132.

Chapter 5 Overcoming

1. Dr. Katherine Bushnell, *God's Word to Women: One Hundred Bible Studies* (Ray B. Munsen, Box 52, N. Collins, N.Y., 1930).

Chapter 6 *Head* and *Submit*: Definitions, Please

1. Berkeley and Alvera Mickelsen, "The 'Head' of the Epistles," *Christianity Today* (February 20, 1981): 23.
2. Richard Braxton Onians, *The Origins of European Thought* (Cambridge: Cambridge Univ. Press, 1951), 117.
3. Linda Raney Wright, *Raising Children*, 3rd ed. (Wheaton, Ill.: Tyndale House, 1975), 138.

Chapter 7 For the Sake of the Gospel

1. J. Vernon McGee, *Esther: The Romance of Providence* (Nashville, Tenn.: Thos. Nelson, 1981).

Chapter 11 Love Covers a Multitude of Sins

1. Donald Bloesch, *Is the Bible Sexist?* (Westchonter, Ill.: Crossway Books, 1982), 105.

Chapter 12 Glorifying God Together

1. *U. S. Press* (June 1, 1984): 5.
2. C. Peter Wagner, "The Greatest Church Growth Is Beyond Our Shores," *Christianity Today* (May 18, 1984): 30–31.
3. *Christianity Today* (February 20, 1981): 10, 11.
4. Donald and Lucille Dayton, "Women as Preachers: Evangelical Precedents," *Christianity Today* (May 23, 1975): 4–7.
5. Fredrik Franson, "Prophesying Daughters," trans. Vernon Mortenson (Wheaton, Ill.: The Evangelical Alliance Mission), unpublished.
6. Jessie Penn-Lewis, *The Magna Charta of Women* (Minneapolis, Minn.: Bethany Fellowship, 1975).

Chapter 14 Jesus and Women

1. Edward Alexander Whyte, *Biblical Characters* (London: Oliphants, 1952).
2. Dorothy Sayers, *Are Women Human?* (Grand Rapids, Mich.: Eerdmans, 1971), 46.
3. Theodor Mommsen, *Provinces of the Roman Empire: The European Provinces* (Chicago: Univ. of Chicago Press, 1968); Edward Gibbon, *Decline and Fall of the Roman Empire* (New York: Harcourt, 1960).
4. If you have just received Christ, I would like to send you some materials (at no cost to you) that will help you begin to grow in your faith. If you will drop me a postcard at the address shown below, telling me you have made this decision, I will be happy to get this information to you: Linda Wright, Arrowhead Springs, San Bernardino, CA 92414.

Chapter 15 Commissioned

1. Catherine Booth, *Female Ministry* (New York: Salvation Army Prtg. & Pub., 1859), 5.

Chapter 17 Leaders of the Church

1. Saint John Chrysostom, *Commentary on Romans, Nicene and Postnicene Fathers*, vol. 11 (Grand Rapids, Mich.: Eerdmans, 1973), 555.

Chapter 18 Culture or Commandment

1. Berkeley and Alvera Mickelsen, "Sexual Ambiguity in Corinth," *The Standard* (March, 1984): 31. Berkeley is professor emeritus of New Testament interpretation at Bethel Theological Seminary, Saint Paul, Minnesota. Alvera was assistant professor of journalism at Bethel College. Berkeley has a Ph.D. in New Testament literature from the University of Chicago; Alvera has a master's degree in journalism from Northwestern University.

Dr. Berkeley Mickelsen has written several books, including *Interpreting the Bible*, a textbook in hermeneutics. Together he and Alvera have written *Understanding Scripture*, a layperson's guide to interpreting the Bible (Regal Books), and *The Family Bible Encyclopedia* (David C. Cook).
2. "Sex and Logic in 1 Corinthians 11:2–16," *Catholic Biblical Quarterly*, 42 (October, 1980), 482–500.
3. Walter L. Liefeld "Women, Submission and Ministry, in 1 Corinthians," *Women, Authority and the Bible*, ed. Alvera Mickelsen (Downers Grove, Ill.: Inter-Varsity Press, 1986), 146.

4. Mary Evans, *Women in the Bible* (Downers Grove, Ill.: Inter-Varsity Press, 1983), 94–95.

Chapter 19 Women in Leadership

1. Catherine Kroeger, "I Timothy 2:12—A Classicist's View," *Women, Authority and the Bible,* ed. Alvera Mickelsen (Downers Grove, Ill.: Inter-Varsity Press, 1986); Richard and Catherine Kroeger, *Women Elders: Sinners or Servants?* (New York: Presbyterian Pub. House), 1981.

Richard Kroeger is an ordained Presbyterian minister and Yale graduate. He has a master's of divinity from Fuller Theological Seminary and a master's of sacred theology from New York Theological Seminary. He pursued his doctoral program at the School of Religion, University of Iowa.

Catherine, a graduate of Bryn Mawr, has been a teaching associate in biblical Greek, at the University of Minnesota, where she did her graduate work. She is founder and has been cochairperson of the section on Women in the Biblical World of the Society for Biblical Literature.

2. H. D. Liddell, R. Scott, H. S. Jones, R. McKenzie, *A Greek-English Lexicon* (Oxford: Oxford Univ. Press, 1968), 1412.

3. David Scholer, "I Timothy 2:9–15 and the Place of Women in the Church's Ministry, *Women, Authority and the Bible* ed. Alvera Mickelsen (Downers Grove, Ill. Inter-Varsity Press, 1986), 203.

4. Ibid., 205.

5. Gerhard Kittel, *Theological Dictionary of the New Testament,* vol. 6, trans. Geoffrey W. Bromily (Grand Rapids, Mich.: 1968), 254–262.

6. Dr. Walter Kaiser, "Paul, Women, and the Church," *Worldwide Challenge* (September, 1976): 9–12.

7. A. J. Gordon, "The Ministry of Women," *Missionary Review of the World,* 7 (December 1894).

8. Sir William Ramsey, cited by Katherine C. Bushnell, *God's Word to Women: One Hundred Bible Studies,* 4th ed. (Ray B. Munsen, Box 52, N. Collins, N.Y., 1930), lesson 27, paragraph 205.

9. Ibid., lesson 34.

10. Linda Raney Wright, *Raising Children,* 3rd ed. (Wheaton, Ill.: Tyndale House, 1975), 137.

Afterword

1. Elmer C. and Foster Adams, Warren Dunham, *Heroines of Modern Progress* (New York: Macmillan, 1935), 146. According to the

Adams, the original quote read, "Surely woman should bring the best she has, whatever that is, to the work of God's world without attending to either of these cries. It does not make a thing good that it is remarkable that a woman should have been able to do it, neither does it make a thing bad, which would have been good had a man done it, that it has been done by a woman. O leave these jargons and go your way straight to God's work in simplicity and singleness of heart."

2. Russell C. Prohl, *Women in the Church* (Grand Rapids, Mich.: Eerdmans, 1957), 77.

3. For more information write to Christian Resource Center, Arrowhead Springs, San Bernardino, CA 92414.

4. For more information, write to: Intercristo, 19303 Fremont Avenue, North, Seattle, WA 98133.

Appendix

1. Berkeley and Alvera Mickelsen, "The 'Head' of the Epistles," *Christianity Today* (February 20, 1981), 23.

2. Richard Braxton Onians, *The Origins of European Thought* (Cambridge: Cambridge Univ. Press, 1951).

3. Ibid., 109. Onians refers this quotation to Aristotle on Page 111, n. 6.

4. Ibid., 111. Onians quotes Hesiod, *Theog,* 924.

5. Ibid., quoting Aesch. *Eum.* 658–666.

6. Ibid., 112. Fr. 21a, 2:21, 1; cf. 168, 2 Kern.

7. Ibid., 144.